WOMEN'S FICTION OF THE
SECOND WORLD WAR

121-3
139-

+W novels writ at time EL, K+HqT Trauta?
≠ poetry   gn Comps of the scene

WOMEN'S FICTION OF THE SECOND WORLD WAR

Gender, Power and Resistance

Gill Plain

EDINBURGH UNIVERSITY PRESS

For my parents, Prim and Arthur Plain

© Gill Plain, 1996

Edinburgh University Press
22 George Square, Edinburgh

Typeset in Linotype Bembo
by Hewer Text Composition Services, Edinburgh and
printed and bound in Great Britain

A CIP record for this book is available
from the British Library

ISBN 0 7486 0661 0

The more wars there are, I suppose, the more we shall learn how to be survivors.

Elizabeth Bowen, 'Mysterious Kôr'

Contents

Preface

Women are not inherently opposed to war, any more than they are congenitally inclined towards sentimentality, nurturance or the colour pink. Rather, they are set in opposition to conflict by the cultural codes and norms of twentieth-century society. Within this patriarchal framework, both women and men have been obliged to survive war – they have been called upon to withstand the imposition of mechanised warfare upon the society in which they live, and they have had to adapt as best they could to the radically altered conditions and terms of reference imposed by an economy of war. My analysis of gendered responses to the Second World War begins, then, not from a belief in the essential pacifism of women writers, but rather from an observation of the complex and contradictory frameworks within which women's wartime identities and roles are constructed.

The equation of women with peace and creativity is as old as the association of women with a domestic sphere detached from the politics of public life. Society has long constructed women in opposition to war. Woman has been appropriated as a symbol of peace and domesticity, a repository of the values that must be left at home in the heat of battle, and she has constituted the object of battle – a prized possession that must be protected – the struggle for which personalises war aims that are otherwise abstract and distant. In time of war, an abstract notion of woman symbolises the nation under threat. The nation is feminised as an indicator of its vulnerability and its need for protection, in contrast to which the corporeality of women is utilised as a more prosaic symbol of a sexual threat both to the soldier's integrity and to his rights. The female body is used in propaganda as a virginal territory upon which the brutality of the enemy may be inscribed, and in a remarkable paradox the same body is seen to threaten the soldier's destruction through disease or treachery. In the absence of war, men return to women and the home they represent, in the expectation of finding them fundamentally unchanged by the passage of time. This expectation of stasis is then reinscribed across the potentially liberating and disruptive record of women's wartime experience.

The complexity of women's symbolic appropriation during wartime and its aftermath cannot easily be summarised, but it seems crucial to emphasise that, irrespective of their personal feelings about conflict, women are constructed into a particular relation to war by their exclusion from government and the armed forces, and by the discourse of the family which remorselessly posits their position as carers and nurturers in opposition to the supposedly 'masculine' role of territorial defence.

In wartime, then, women exist in a contradictory space in which their symbolic representation is frequently at odds with the practical demands of the war economy. This book, however, is neither a history of women's involvement in the Second World War, nor a comprehensive survey of their literary contribution to the period 1939–45. Rather it aims to consider the impact of war's contradictions upon the texts of a diverse group of women writing in time of war. Through the work of five contrasting writers I have tried to conceptualise how war might be inscribed upon texts that otherwise seem to direct our attention away from the fact or prospect of conflict. The works explored might seem superficially to have little in common, crossing as they do the boundaries of 'highbrow' and 'popular' culture – but such divisions are arbitrary and unhelpful in relation to the moment of war. All these texts can be read as products of a wartime, or a pre-war economy, and considering them in conjunction throws light upon the unexpected connections that link women writers within a given historical moment. This is a process of recategorisation, or perhaps, *de*categorisation. These are women responding to war, rather than modernists, detective-story writers, or even, in the traditional understanding of the term, war writers. The blending of detective fiction with historical sagas and the late flowerings of the modernist aesthetic will also, I hope, serve to continue the process, begun so impressively by Alison Light (1991), of breaking down the boundaries between high and low culture that function only to limit and constrain our analysis of the period.

Women's Fiction of the Second World War is primarily a work of literary criticism that moves, to serve its purposes, through the fields of historical and cultural studies. It is also firmly rooted in a tradition of women's studies that challenges the gendered blindspots of critical orthodoxy. This book is driven by a dual purpose. A consideration of the multiple meanings of war will, I believe, illuminate the texts under consideration, while the study of the works should augment our understanding of both the theoretical scope and the practical reality of the term 'war'. The book is fundamentally concerned with the reality of war in all its complexity, but it cannot hope, and will not try, to duplicate the process of documentation already admirably performed by so many historians and memorialists of the conflict. Its focus is instead a tangential one, concerned less with defining the 'reality' of war than with exploring the response to those realities. To what extent can the Medusa's head of war be faced? And how are the contrasting strategies of engagement and avoidance encoded in the textual products of the period? Ultimately, my aim is to explore the textual conjunction of conflict and creativity with a view to asking a question seldom heard in any of the critical commentaries of the period: how did women think about, write about, and crucially, survive the cultural, emotional and physical dislocations of the Second World War?

Widespread thanks are due to the many people who have offered help, advice and support during the writing of this book. The project began its life at the University of Newcastle upon Tyne, and the thesis from which it grew could not have been written without the remarkable combination of constructive criticism and supportive friendship provided by my supervisor, Linda Anderson. A similarly vast debt of gratitude is due to my editor at Edinburgh University Press, Jackie Jones. I could not have asked for a better editor – her friendship, advice and enthusiasm made the process of writing an infinitely more pleasurable task. Many people have contributed their time and effort to reading and commenting on drafts of this book. Chief amongst these is Helen Boden, without whose incisive comments this would have been a far woollier work. I am indebted to Nick Lawson and Alison Smith for early directions, and to Jan Montefiore for her later encouragement and advice. All important moral support was provided by Gordon McMullan, Clare Tarplee, John Wells, Ben Winsworth, Pauline Young and the Women's Studies Network, where I found support and enthusiasm to offset the isolation of research. Thanks are also due to the University of Glamorgan UniR research fund which admirably supported the process of revision, and to colleagues and students in the School of Humanities and Social Sciences who nobly withstood my war obsession. Finally, and most especially, I am indebted to James McKinna, whose support set the whole thing in motion, and to Kaite O'Reilly whose friendship enabled me to bring it to a close.

Gill Plain
University of Glamorgan, 1996

1

Introduction

In September 1939, with the memories of the First World War only twenty years old, few in Britain could be said to have regained their appetite for conflict. The late 1930s are characterised by a remarkably tentative response to international events from both politicians and public. Organisations new and old adopted pacifism as their creed, and were rewarded by considerable support. The Peace Pledge Union, initiated in 1934, boasted 80,000 members after only one year; while the long-established Women's Co-operative Guild, an organisation of over 87,000 members, proclaimed its beliefs through the wearing of white 'peace' poppies on Armistice Day. The League of Nations, meanwhile, seemed to have adopted pacifism by default. After major setbacks over Manchuria and Abyssinia, its response to the Japanese invasion of China in 1937 was an offer of 'moral' support (Liddington, 1989: 152–71). This lack of enthusiasm for war which, in Britain, had seen Appeasement preserved long beyond its natural life was reflected in the literature of the early days of conflict.[1] 'Where are the war poets?' demanded leader writers to no avail (Calder, 1969: 517). To a certain extent, war poets were redundant. With the myths of heroism and glory long since exploded, the Second World War had no place for the simple certainties of Brooke or the irony and anger of Owen and Sassoon. Even the creative potential of social and political revolution had been effectively covered by the literary response to the Spanish Civil War. As Angus Calder bluntly states in his brief survey of the wartime literary output, 'In any case, whichever way you felt, Owen or Cornford had been there before you, and the war poems had already been written' (1969: 518). Calder's assertion is supported by the bemused voices of established writers. The Second World

War opened to the sound of silence, and the fragmented voices that later arose never achieved the cohesion of a single identifiable literary movement. Instead, 1939 saw a literary 'sealing off' that came in marked contrast to the eruption of verse in 1914 (Shires, 1985: 3). Louis MacNeice introduced his *Collected Poems 1925–40* (1979) with a comment that illustrates the literary establishment's sense of hopelessness and disorientation in the face of history's remorseless repetition:

> When a man collects his poems, people think him dead. I am collecting mine not because I am dead, but because my past life is. Like most other people in the British Isles I have little idea what will happen next – I shall go on writing, but my writing will presumably be different. (quoted in Shires, 1985: 4)

Two years later, Elizabeth Bowen attempted to define the indefinable something that made the Second World War seem to stifle creativity:

> there is at present evident in the reflective writer, not so much inhibition or dulling of his own feeling as an inability to obtain the focus necessary for art. One cannot reflect, or reflect on, what is not wholly in view. These years rebuff the imagination as much by being fragmentary as by being violent. (*New Statesman*, 23 May 1942; quoted in Shires, 1985: 5)

It was the end not just of an era, but of a whole way of life, and this transition is evident across the spectrum of literary activity. The war may not have curtailed the imagination of the crime writer Margery Allingham, but it is interesting to note that even in 1945, after six years of conflict, the sense of a lost world still pervades her fiction: 'The brilliant picture of the past faded into the dust and rubble of the present', 'for a moment they were all transported into that other world before the war' (1945/1987: 10, 23).

Thus the business of war writing underwent a fundamental change of emphasis. Paul Fussell describes the mindless dehumanising routine that characterises an army in waiting, and observes that some of the most significant fiction of the war came, not from combat, but from this grotesque war of attrition on the human spirit that he terms 'chickenshit'. Discussing Kingsley Amis's story 'I spy strangers', Fussell concludes:

> The story is not about damage to the body but damage to principles and to personal freedom and integrity. It is about the natural alliance between chickenshit and totalitarian conceptions of personality. (Fussell, 1989: 88)

The spiritual oppression depicted by Fussell was not the only inhibiting factor faced by the potential poets of the Second World War. Sebastian Knowles, in his study of seven male modernists writing during the war (1990), proposes censorship as another contributory factor towards the perceived 'lack' of combat poetry. Wartime censorship of the armed fores, he suggests, would have made it impossible for soldiers to express the levels of anger and hostility found in the letters and poetry of 1918. Within the propaganda war of 1939–45, argues Knowles, '[t]o write anything at all was subversive; to write poetry in the sardonic, lacerative spirit of the first war was next to impossible' (1990: xx).

To a considerable extent, then, war poetry was replaced by poetry written in wartime, and although Fussell's *Wartime* was an exclusively masculine affair, the distinction is equally applicable to women writers. Elizabeth Bowen makes this claim for her own writing in the remarkably lucid preface to the American edition of *The Demon Lover*:

> These are all wartime, none of them *war*, stories. There are no accounts of war action, even as I knew it – for instance, air raids . . . These are, more, studies of climate, war-climate, and of the strange growths it raised. I see war (or should I say feel war?) more as a territory than as a page of history: of its impersonal active historic side I have, I find, not written. (Bowen, 1950: 48; ellipsis mine)

While established women writers as diverse as Virginia Woolf and Vera Brittain turned their pens to war, their preoccupation was less with the outward destruction of war, than with a more introspective contemplation of the human condition under war.

This distinction is, of course, not universally applicable. The war gave rise to much documentary fiction and journalism, alongside a wealth of short stories and poems that chronicle the Blitz as accurately and effectively as ever Vera Brittain chronicled the demise of the 'lost generation' – albeit in a tone far removed from Brittain's almost apocalyptic grief.[2] As the most famous (and, to many, the only) woman writer of the First World War, the changing concerns of Brittain's writing are worth exploring. The 'lost generation' still haunt the pages of *England's Hour*, her 1941 religio-pacifist morale booster, and curiously the grief expressed in this text seems divorced from the trauma of the bombardment under which it was written. In *England's Hour* Brittain still mourns for the dead of the first war, and her observer's prose remains almost clinically detached from the mounting corpses of the second. Driving through the shocking destruction of blitzed London, Brittain's preoccupations are evident in the space she devotes to a catalogue of the city's demolished churches. Returning to Westminster, the by now familiar ghosts appear:

> What is it, I ask myself, of which this long journey through the devastated areas of my own city has reminded me? Suddenly my memory leaps

back over nineteen years, and I recollect driving, for many hours of an
autumn day, round the ruined villages of the Somme in 1921. (Brittain,
1941: 275)

An earlier outburst is more telling:

This second war, like the last, has wrecked – for how long? – my personal
life; it has taken my children away from me, sent my husband after them
to America, compelled me, like so many London dwellers, to abandon
my home. (Brittain, 1941: 226)

Behind the churlish anger of this cry there lies perhaps an inability to feel
again the pain of 1914–18.

   This strategy of detachment is utilised more consciously, and certainly more
effectively, in Inez Holden's powerful *Night Shift* (1941). The attitudes and
anxieties of Holden's assorted home front war workers catalogue not just the
physical but also the economic realities of war. Structurally, the novel obtains
much of its impact from the effacement of the narrative voice. The narrator's
comments are carefully rationed, and when they come, make their impact
either through the use of a brutal imagery of alienation or through abrupt
and powerful understatement. Early in the working week of the eponymous
'night shift', Holden describes the walk from the factory floor to the works
canteen:

We walked along, on either side of us there was the wire netting; it
gave the impression of a cinema set concentration camp. The light was
dim and in this underground passage the round metal cases looked like
heaped up skulls. (Holden, 1941: 25)

Multiple levels of reality are collapsed into the image of the 'cinema set
concentration camp'. The image suggests that for the British public, the
'knowledge' of Nazi atrocities had been made less, rather than more, real by its
cinematic representation; while at the same time suggesting an awful familiarity
and even comfort with the idea of such a camp. The skulls meanwhile evoke
not only the death camps, but also the factory's *raison d'être*. The shell cases will
carry death by bombing – a threat that ironically foreshadows the imminent
destruction of the factory and all those workers within it who, in economic
terms, are 'trapped' by the net of war production. Holden's documentary text
is vivid and evocative, and strives to do justice to its subjects – yet, following
the bombing of the factory, she concludes not with pleas or laments, but with
a shattering simplicity:

The names and faces of my workmates on the night shift ran through
my brain . . . and before fatigue fell across my mind like a final blanket

it was quite clear to me that each one of them had been worth a second
chance. (Holden, 1941: 126; ellipsis mine)

A similar vein of detachment is evident in women's poetry of the war years.
Margery Lea and Patricia Ledward are two of many who contemplate the
destruction around them with an ironic eye and a keen sense of the absurd.
Both poets use narrative verse to create dramatic and evocative pictures of the
war environment. Patricia Ledward's 'Air-raid casualties: Ashridge Hospital'
manages to be both poignant and unpleasant:

> On Sundays friends arrive with kindly words
> To peer at those whom war has crushed;
> > (Reilly, 1984: 77)

The sympathy of 'kindly words' and the power of 'those whom war has
crushed' are swiftly undermined by the voyeuristic fascination with others'
misfortune inherent in the word 'peer'. Margery Lea's poem 'Bomb story
(Manchester 1942)' celebrates the Blitz's 'business as usual' reincarnation of
trench camaraderie. The uncertain and unpredictable nature of life under siege
is evident in the erratic metre of her abrupt prosaic verse:

> Our neighbour's garden had a crater that would hold two buses.
> He said the rich soil thrown up was most productive,
> And round the perimeter he grew excellent lettuces
> The next spring of the war.
> > (Reilly, 1984: 75)

The prevalence of 'business as usual' is very revealing. Cartoons, headlines
and photographs all proclaimed that the 'bulldog breed' was 'smiling through'.
Artists portrayed old maids with shotguns sipping cocoa as they awaited
invasion, and the suburban home, described by Alison Light as the heart of
English life in the 1930s, undergoes the transition from 'Lilac Villa' to 'Lilac
Fort' (McCooey, 1989: 60, 41; Light, 1991: 7–8). None the less, the image of
the 'little man' survived unchanged. He might have been digging for victory
instead of pottering in his herbaceous borders, but he remained stubbornly
ordinary throughout. This very unmartial emphasis on survival and continuity
is typical of the wartime ideal of a national character. The national identity was
a composite picture. It drew extensively upon the imagery of an anachronistic
rural myth, which was combined with a reaffirmation of long-established
opinions upon the nature of the British character – the paradoxes of which
can be juxtaposed to create a truly conservative Everyman. Insular yet
tolerant, anti-intellectual but full of common sense, the British were a nation
of home-loving imperialists crowned above all by their irrepressible sense of
humour (Richards, 1988).[3] The Ministry of Information actively encouraged

film-makers to portray the approved national character (Richards, 1988: 43), and to support the cause of collective unity, a series of age-old generalisations were injected with new life. George Orwell captures the paradoxes inherent in the fictions and realities of nationality:

> Myths which are believed in tend to become true, because they set up a type or persona which the average person will do his best to resemble . . . [I]t is probable that the stolid behaviour of the British town populations under the bombing was partly due to the existence of the national 'persona' – that is, to their preconceived idea of themselves. Traditionally the Englishman is phlegmatic, unimaginative, not easily rattled, and since that is what he thinks he ought to be, that is what he tends to become. (quoted in Richards, 1988: 60)

The apparati of ideology formed and reformed the national character, and at its most successful the propaganda machine produced an image of British identity that was eagerly consumed and assumed for its value as a strategy for survival. 'Business as usual' became a collective strategy for coping with sudden violent change and the terrifying proximity of death. Short films made by the Ministry of Information exemplify the utilisation of this attitude. The following description of the GPO film unit's *Dover Front Line*, from the Mass-Observation survey of 1941,[4] draws on the same imagery as Margery Lea's 'Bomb story' and illustrates the development of a common language of plucky Britishness:

> Description of life in Dover with nobody worried by bombs and shells. The wardens and firemen. The balloon barrage men and the anti-aircraft batteries. The man and women in the streets taking shells near them calmly and complaining about the effect on their beans. (Richards and Sheridan, 1987: 431)

This is a very different Britain from the imperial nation of 1914, or indeed, from the shell-shocked victors of 1918. In exploring the literature of the two wars it seems that the personal cost of grief is the only continuity of conflict. Every war creates its own very flexible image, and the self-presentation chosen by the Second World War was undoubtedly that of the 'reluctant' war. In May 1940, Naomi Mitchison reported the change of mood within the Carradale Labour Party. 'Both Angus and Alec . . . had decided that this was after all a war for survival, not an Imperialist war, as they had thought at first' (Mitchison, 1986a: 61). A war for survival could appeal to the new ideal of Britishness in a way that the tainted claims of imperialism could not – and this was not simply a question of personal or individual survival, but the survival of an ideal. In their recent analysis of the ideological manoeuvrings of the Second World War, David Morgan and Mary Evans observe that:

> From the very beginning, the war against Hitler's Germany was presented to the British people as a fight against tyranny and the destruction of civilised ways of life. In that respect, the confrontation was as much ideological as territorial . . . Unlike the politically complicated alliances that drew Britain into the First World War, the reasons for engagement were readily understood: it was a 'just' war that would allow no compromise short of Hitler's unconditional surrender and the restoration throughout occupied Europe of democracy and civil rights. (Morgan and Evans, 1993: 15)

Thus, for all its territorial complexity, the Second World War presented an ideological façade of the utmost simplicity, presenting the public with a clearly defined and evil other on to which the weight of contemporary anxieties could be projected. In her examination of the psychological determinants of war, Jacqueline Rose has observed that '[i]f you produce the enemy, then you must fight him' (Rose, 1993: 28–9). Something similar can perhaps be said of the creature that is national identity. The act of defining a nation carries with it an obligation to defend as 'eternal' even the most recent of constructions.

In *Britain Can Take It: The British Cinema and the Second World War*, Anthony Aldgate and Jeffrey Richards describe the characteristic style of 'the two men who first come to mind as speaking for England in the darkest days of the war' (1986: 46). The first of these two is, predictably, Winston Churchill – 'patriotic, passionate, romantic, huge' (1986: 47) – but the second is J. B. Priestley, 'the voice of Everyman as opposed to Superman' (1986: 49). Priestley's 'Postscripts', broadcast throughout 1940 and 1941, depicted a conflict in which heroism was the province of 'the ordinary British folk' (1986: 50). He spoke of the everyday and the commonplace, the comfortable and the familiar; seemingly mundane topics, but their very ordinariness was the key to their success. Morgan and Evans agree, seeing the domestic and the martial merge to create a world in which the concept of heroism is demythologised and expanded:

> The idea of heroism was no longer limited to the singular courageous act; it became a generalised quality of all those who endured the deprivations and dangers of both combat and the home front. (Morgan and Evans, 1993: 22)

As heroism moved into the remit of the 'ordinary' individual, so ideals and ideologies were reduced to graspable socio-economic realities. As Aldgate and Richards observe, 'it was the tangible realities of the duckpond and the pieshop for which Britain was fighting as much as the abstract concepts of freedom and democracy' (1986: 50).

Jacqueline Rose, however, has problematised this notion of fighting for freedom. Starting from D. W. Winnicott's claim that although we like the idea of freedom we also fear it, and are 'drawn towards being controlled', Rose observes that '[i]f freedom is the cause we fight for, fear of freedom may also be the origin – the cause in its other sense – of war' (Rose, 1993: 33–4).[5] In order to win the war, 'free' Britain established a regime of unprecedented regimentation – an enforced unity that was to a large extent accepted rather than resented as a repression of personal liberty.[6] Lack of freedom is tolerated and even welcomed in the name of freedom. It could perhaps be argued that the dislocations of war in turn provided an ironic release from a different set of peacetime regulations, but there is none the less an ambivalence evident in the literary responses of even the most certain advocates of wartime conformity.

This ambivalence is powerfully displayed by Margery Allingham's 1941 account of an English village's transition from peace to war, *The Oaken Heart*. In the early chapters of her book, Allingham uses a metaphor of horse and rider to describe the relationship of politicians to the body of the people. This somewhat idealistic idea supposes the rider to be merely the servant of the horse; the man is permitted temporary direction of the horse's far greater power. However, as her argument and her metaphor develop, their implications become not only ambivalent, but sinister:

> I think had we realised then that the Government was nervous of us and was humouring us, as if we were an unbroken colt, while the road was growing wilder and wilder and the storm clouds were piling up like an illustration in the family Bible, we might have panicked badly. As it was, it set us back on our heels when we did see it, but by that time we had immediate danger to steady us and one of the last real statesmen in the nation to gather up the reins and jerk the bit tight in our mouths. (Allingham, 1941a: 19)

The steadying force of danger suggests a tacit acknowledgement of war as a mechanism of social control; while the image of the bit, designed to reassure, more effectively invokes the image of a nation being gagged: the end to free speech and Allingham's notion of democratic control.

There are, however, more radical implications to this newly vocal British identity, some of which are evident in this quotation from one of Priestley's broadcasts:

> The war because it demands a huge collective effort, is compelling us to change not only our ordinary, social and economic habits but also our habits of thought. We've actually changed over from the property view to the sense of community, which simply means that we realize we're all in the same boat. (Aldgate and Richards, 1986: 50–1)

The current of social change was also increasingly evident in the cinema. Aldgate and Richards describe Carol Reed's 1944 film, *The Way Ahead* as an Attlee and Bevin to the Churchill of *In Which We Serve*. It is an interesting analogy emphasising the fact that class co-operation, so long the mainstay of British society, had the potential to become as much a temporary war measure as the coalition of the national government.[7]

The changes embodied by this war, however, were not confined to the familiarity of conflict, a reluctance to fight, or even to social pressures. In the brief interlude between 1918 and 1939, the nature of war itself had undergone a remarkable metamorphosis. The Second World War was, in Annemarie Tröger's phrase, 'a war against civilian populations' (Tröger, 1987: 285). Sacrifice was universalised, and the hierarchies of suffering established by the First World War became an anachronism in this new age of total war.

Along with the nature of the conflict, the nature of the enemy had also undergone a radical change. Nazism presented a very different threat from the earlier claims of German imperialism, and yet curiously, the opprobrium heaped upon the enemy was, like much else in this conflict, distinctly understated. The impression is that although the geographical location of the opposition remained the same, everything else, in particular the names, had been changed. Hitler and Nazism were the enemies, and the manifestation of anti-German sentiment never reached the heights it attained in the heady days of 1914. Tom Harrisson describes this uncharacteristic leniency in the depiction of the 'enemy' in his account of the 1940–1 film season:

> Except in one film, which was made in Russia, the main German characters were always simply misguided people who got lured into Fascism. There were black Germans, really bad, such as heads of concentration camps . . . But at no stage in the war, according to our Mass-Observation archive material, did people ever stop thinking that there were a great many good Germans, despite the violent emphasis of many newsreels. (Harrisson, 1982: 238)

This was a war against an abstract ideal – Fascism – from which, unlike the imperialism of the First World War, Britain could claim to be uncontaminated. That anti-semitism was none the less part of the fabric of British life in the 1930s was conveniently overlooked (Calder, 1969: 512). Jill Liddington's *The Long Road to Greenham* includes a detailed account of the impact of British anti-semitism on one woman's life in the 1930s (1989: 164–5), while George Orwell's essay 'Antisemitism in Britain' provides a contemporary analysis of the problem (Orwell, 1945/1970). Orwell's conclusions are interesting. Determining that although anti-semitism was widespread, it was unlikely to become either violent or institutionalised until it first became respectable –

and so it persisted that in Britain, discretion remained the better part of racism. This lack of serious ideological opposition to the racism of Nazi Germany was complemented by what Morgan and Evans have described as a degree of sympathy for Hitler's attempts to 'redress the grievances that had festered since the Treaty of Versailles', and by the public perception of a greater threat elsewhere:

> Even though his racist policies were formally deplored, they presented no evident threat to Britain and the Empire that justified full-scale war. From this point of view, a confrontation with Germany made rather less sense than a defensive alliance against the Soviet Union. Here was an undisputed opponent of capitalism, dedicated to world revolution, and an ideologically disturbing influence in home affairs. As it appeared from the Right, 'appeasement' avoided alienating Germany as a potential ally against the greater menace of communist influence in the West. (Morgan and Evans, 1993: 19)

None the less, once war began, educated intellectuals feared that the distinction between the 'ordinary' German and the Nazi would soon become blurred. Naomi Mitchison voiced this fear in her diary – 'already some of the young fishermen were saying what they'd do to Germans if they got hold of them – not just Hitler' (Mitchison, 1986a: 36). But in spite of this, there was no repetition of 1914's massive anti-Germanic outburst. This trend appears to have crossed the class divide. Mrs Miniver, the guiding light of middle-class moderation, is found at a lunchtime concert of German music (Struther, 1939/1989: 137), while in Inez Holden's *Night Shift* the specificity of the perceived enemy is emphasised. For the character Mabs, whose home has been devastated by the Blitz:

> Hitler was like a personified god of evil. He was over, he was bombing the East End, he'd gone away again, he'd got tired of sending down flares and suchlike and gone off home, but he'd come back again to-morrow night. (Holden, 1941: 108)

The need to focus hatred on one man is another indicator of the overwhelming totality of this *world* war, the scale of which was impossible to adequately comprehend. In Holden's later novel, *It was Different at the Time* (1943), she presents a fuller description of this attitude in combination with the ever more widespread strategy of understatement. Both represent a means of coping with the enormity of the situation:

> These men and women of work-town often speak of the enemy and even of a whole squadron of bombers as 'he'. Sometimes they mean

> 'Jerry', the collective name for all Germans in war-time, and sometimes they mean Hitler, but, in either case, this personification of the enemy as 'he' is a kind of gigantic debunk of the whole Nazi melodrama of bombs, paratroops, drawling Haw-Haw, screaming Hitler, limping Goebbels, and all the rest of it. (Holden, 1943: 77)

The 'gigantic debunk' is also evident in Allingham's *The Oaken Heart*, where Hitler is quietly ridiculed through absurd comparison; 'there was that chap Hitler looking like Charlie Chaplin and behaving as far as one could gather like Captain Hook' (1941a: 35). The dictator is reduced to a cinema clown and a comic-book villain, comforting strategies that minimise both the extent and the reality of the threat. This persistent use of litotes is an integral part of the 'business as usual' attitude evident in much war writing and consciously propagated by the government war machine. However, beyond its propaganda role, 'business as usual' is also indicative of a significant common denominator shared by the First and Second World Wars – the inadequacy of existing terms of reference to engage with and make sense of the experience of war.

Just as the poets of 1914–18 struggled to find a language adequate to express the unprecedented extent of their suffering, so, in the Second World War, the average person was confounded by the impossibility of articulating the scale of the conflict that confronted them. Robert Graves's rather flippant radio comment of 1941, 'no war poetry can be expected from the R.A.F. . . . The internal combustion engine does not seem to consort with poetry' (Calder, 1969: 518–19), none the less hints at the root of the problem.[8] It was not only the scale of the Second World War, but the technical dimension, that rendered it beyond the scope of existing terminology. Susan Gubar has written of the 'technological depersonalisation' (1987: 229) of the war and Angus Calder suggests that the capacity of machines to insulate their operators from the implications of their actions 'had made the morality of war less clear-cut' (1969: 519). Ironically, while many combatants were often surprisingly insulated, civilians were overwhelmed. Annemarie Tröger's examination of German women's memories of the Second World War emphasises this inarticulacy:

> Even though individuals are compelled to talk about the war, one senses *a painful lack of words* adequate to describe the anthropological meaning of airborne warfare. The most valid expression even for articulate intellectuals appears to be nonverbal; Picasso's *Guernica* is an example. (Tröger, 1987: 285; emphasis mine)

The idea of a non-verbal response can be connected to the massive growth in passive responses to the war situation. In using the word 'passive', I am distinguishing between what might be termed the 'active' response of attempting to write or articulate the emotions created by the experience (primary or secondary) of conflict, and the comparatively 'passive' search for release through the words or pictures of others – that is through reading or the cinema. This non-verbal or inarticulate passivity is also suggestive of problems of identity stemming from the war's capacity to alienate individuals from language, and in consequence, from themselves. I return later to the implications of these responses to war.

Documentary texts of the period thus give the impression that the British response to the literal, metaphorical and geographical 'overkill' of the Second World War was to seek refuge in what Vera Brittain calls 'our national equanimity' (Brittain, 1941: 97). Margery Allingham is more specific:

> The process of hardening up is imperceptible. After the first effort the mental and spiritual muscles get going on their own. The unbelievable gradually becomes a commonplace. The gas-mask loses its nightmare shape and becomes no more ugly than an umbrella. (Allingham, 1941a: 64)

The worse things got, the more traumatic and widespread the destruction, the greater the emphasis on the proverbial 'business as usual'.[9]

Ultimately, however, 'business as usual' becomes a prime example of the chicken and egg conundrum. It is impossible to judge whether the equanimity of *Dover Front Line* was born from the observation of 'British Phlegm' or whether 'British Phlegm' itself was boosted by its presentation as such. Calder comments that '"British Phlegm" had its "Finest Hour" in the Blitz, not only because instances of it made useful propaganda for home and foreign consumption, but also because it had the same kind of use for civilians under bombing as for soldiers under fire: one had to "keep merry and bright"' (Calder, 1991: 17–18).

This façade, or in Calder's term, this 'myth', is undoubtedly a strategy for survival. The danger however lies in its propensity to become a front that cannot be dismantled. The façade has the potential to become too integral a component of a war-endangered identity, and its removal threatens a complete breakdown of personality. This hypothesis suggests the necessity of exploring a less frequently cited explanation for the myth of equanimity. The façade of calm was, quite literally, the blank mask of shock. In *It was Different at the Time,* Inez Holden describes the fate of refugees who seem to fall apart, crumble and die, when they relax their hold on the façade of normality:

> it was just the sense of being able to relax that made it possible for them to react at last against the horrors they had been through, resisted at the time in the only possible way, through suppression of the imagination

> ... It seems that as far as concentration camps are concerned, whether the prisoner ever does get out or not, it must still be the death sentence for him. (Holden, 1943: 86; ellipsis mine)

That the assumed 'normality' had been quite the opposite does not matter. Terms of reference change under the conditions of war, and it is only through the radical alteration of expectations, that impossible conditions can be assimilated, accepted and survived.

MAKING SENSE

This façade of normality is an integral part of the process of 'making sense' that Paul Fussell has identified in many of the myths and rumours of the trenches: 'their purpose is to "make sense" of events which otherwise would seem merely accidental or calamitous' (Fussell, 1975: 121). It has been frequently observed that the home front of the first war became the front line of the second, and on the level of survival and of myth-making, a continuity between the wars becomes evident. Angus Calder takes up the process uncovered by Fussell and applies it to the case of the Blitz:

> except in some parts of London and briefly in a few other places, Blitz was an experience far less extreme than that of the soldiers on the Somme, and to 'make sense' of it, to turn it into 'story', was superficially much less difficult. The language of pre-existing mythologies, including the Myth of the Tommy at the Front, adapted itself to events with remarkable 'naturalness' and fluency, and stories were generated with such success that we, born since, have ignored how frightening and confusing the period from April 1940 through to June 1941 was for the British people. Perhaps we simply cannot comprehend that fear and confusion imaginatively. (Calder, 1991: 18)

In the Second World War people sought practical strategies that would enable them to reorganise their disrupted world into manageable proportions, and, at the same time, many sought imaginative routes through which to escape the constrained and fragile nature of that world. This is the passive response that created the audience for wartime fiction, cinema and radio. The nation of frantic scribblers was replaced by a nation seeking the provision of distraction. People were no longer writing for change, but were instead consuming and creating fantasies that would take them out of a dangerous reality. This distinction applies equally to the many intellectuals who devoted the last years of the thirties to the production of desperate anti-war tracts. Texts such as Virginia Woolf's *Three Guineas* (1938) and Naomi Mitchison's *The Moral Basis of Politics* (1938) had been to no obvious avail; and protest, if not forgotten, was 'de-prioritised', demoted and marginalised by the demands of wartime unity. Even staunch pacifists such as Vera Brittain underwent a literary redirection. *England's Hour*, although frequently lamenting the fact that another war had been allowed to happen, is consumed by a utopian vision of a new post-war world that is as much a fantasy and a strategy for survival as other, more obvious, examples of escapism.

Fussell has called this period the 'Age of Anthologies' (1989: 245). Books were bought at an unprecedented rate (Calder, 1969: 512),[10] and literary magazines, such as *Penguin New Writing*, flourished when their mixture of short stories, articles and poetry was found to be particularly 'war-friendly'. *Penguin New Writing* also enterprisingly adapted to its changing environment:

> The case of *Penguin New Writing* is a striking instance of the way in which what had, in effect, been a literary 'little magazine' before the war, became a widely known and popular institution by 1945. When Lehmann established the magazine, its original purpose was to publish little-known authors. This policy rapidly shifted towards the publications not only of new fiction, but also documentary accounts of real life. (Morgan and Evans, 1993: 93)

This desire to consume the details of everyday life is replicated in the responses to cinema-going recorded by Mass-Observation, and forms a key indication of the complexity of wartime escapism.

Statistics indicate that the growth in popularity of the written text was paralleled by a massive increase in cinema-going. After an initial government clampdown, cinema survived the blackout, sending box office receipts soaring from just under £45 million in 1940 to over £114 million in 1945 (Stacey, 1994: 84). The period even ushered in a 'golden age' for British cinema (Aldgate and Richards, 1986: 3), while the radio became a lifeline to women trapped in the home. Overall, the world of the imagination assumed an unprecedented significance in the realm of day-to-day survival. Elizabeth Bowen encapsulates the situation:

> I wonder whether in a sense all wartime writing is not resistance writing? In no way dare we who were in Britain compare ourselves with the French. But personal life here put up its own resistance to the annihilation that was threatening it – war. Everyone here, as is known, read more: and what was sought in books – old books, new books – was the communicative touch of personal life. To survive, not only physically but spiritually, was essential. (Bowen, 1950: 50)

'Wartime leisure', a Mass-Observation report of July 1940, records the early stages of this transformation. Among its statistics and observations a 30-year-old woman describes her own changing reading habits: 'Actually I don't read a lot. It's only since the war started that I've been reading' (Mass-Observation Archive, FR 290, Women in Wartime III: 165). The survey goes on to suggest that 'amongst most women of the poorer classes':

> the function of the novel is much the same as the function of the film: it takes them out of the dreariness and worries of ordinary life, makes them forget for the moment that they are lonely without their children, or that their husband will soon be called up. It is an antidote to boredom and loneliness. (Mass-Observation Archive, FR 290, Women in Wartime III: 166)

Only a few months later, reading would have to provide a similar antidote to the trauma of the Blitz. Paul Fussell records that W. Somerset Maugham recommended detective stories to American radio audiences seeking advice on 'Reading under bombing', and in one such example of the genre, Dorothy L. Sayers supports the philosophy of escapism. 'Reading *is* an escape to me', comments Lord Peter Wimsey:

> it is to most people, I think. Servants and factory hands read about beautiful girls loved by dark, handsome men, all covered over with jewels and moving in scenes of gilded splendour. And passionate spinsters read Ethel M. Dell. And dull men in offices read detective stories. They wouldn't, if murder and police entered into their lives. (Sayers, 1928b/1989: 216)

But escapism is not as simple as Sayers or the benign overseers of Mass-Observation suggest. The comments of the Mass Observers themselves on their cinema-going habits are particularly revealing. Although their responses frequently echo the desire for escape, the replies to the 1943 survey 'Directive on favourite films' are also surprisingly concerned with 'facts'.

'I like books and films which tell me the facts in the form of fiction', reports a 38-year-old housewife from Lincoln. A schoolmaster from Reading, age 36, liked the film *Tortilla Flat* because 'it was real, and not Hollywoodified'. A 41-year-old social worker from London sums up the prevalent feeling of the observers' reports:

> I tend to like films dealing with the everyday occurrences of life in wartime; films which make the significance of our everyday lives more vivid. I prefer a good British film to a Hollywood production, which, though usually more lavish and sometimes technically superior, is usually more artificial in character. (Richards and Sheridan, 1987: 278)

These comments, from both men and women, indicate a desire for images with which they can reasonably identify – which is perhaps the same desire that fuelled the craving for *Penguin New Writing*'s documentary details of 'ordinary' wartime life. Certainly Hollywood, with its unobtainable aura of glamour, was in the main rejected by the predominantly middle-class Mass Observers. The 1943 directive reveals a considerable similarity between male and female audiences, the films *In Which we Serve* and *The Life and Death of Colonel Blimp* were the top two films amongst both groups. Richards and Sheridan make no claims for the universality of the observers' tastes, but as the same two films topped the box office receipts for the year, it appears that they were not entirely out of step with public opinion. Both male and female respondents rejected the Hollywood image, and it is from a male observer that a particularly telling comment emerges. This anonymous contributor from Portsmouth describes his favourite films by equating 'true to life' with 'a magical quality'. Citing *The Life and Death of Colonel Blimp*, *One of Our Aircraft is Missing* and *The Silver Fleet* he observes, 'All these films I enjoyed for the same reason. They were all absolutely true to life. I could believe everything about them. They all seemed to possess a magical quality which I have never seen in an American film' (Richards and Sheridan, 1987: 231–2). This distinction crystallises the country's paradoxical desire for what can be described as a multi-layered or double-edged realism. There existed both the realism of lived experience in wartime, and an idealised fantasy or 'escapist realism' that drew its imaginative framework from the foundations of its more mundane relative. This idealised realism existed as a parallel state, easily within the grasp of consumers and preferable to the out and out fantasy seen as the province of Hollywood. Effectively this meant that a film's success depended to a large extent on its self-effacement. It should draw attention not to its own artifice but to its role as a 'straightforward' reflection of an external reality. The conception and reception of Noël Coward's wartime propaganda films *In Which we Serve* (1942) and *This Happy Breed* (1944) illustrate this distinction. Commenting on *In Which we Serve*, Aldgate and Richards observe that 'what people at the time were impressed by was the film's realism' (1986: 207). At the root of this realism was the film's audacity in giving 'equal screen time to the other ranks. Even the language had a salty authenticity that would have been censored in the pre-war cinema' (1986: 208).

However, it was not a straightforward issue of documentation.[11] The *Observer* film critic, Caroline Lejeune, explored the complexity of the relationship between cinematic representation and its target audience in her comments upon *This Happy Breed*:

> This film about the suburbs has gone out into the suburbs and the suburbs
> have taken it to their hearts. All the Gibbonses of Greater London have
> flocked to see themselves on the screen . . . Yet *This Happy Breed* is not
> just a photographic and microphonic record of suburban life in the years
> between the two wars. If it were, nobody would care to see it. Art does
> not consist in repeating accurately what can be seen and heard around
> us. Art must try to conjure up, with the help of familiar symbols, things
> that are not perceptible to human eyes and ears. (quoted in Aldgate and
> Richards, 1986: 213)

In a sense, successful wartime cinema encouraged a massive egotism disguised
as a down-to-earth modesty. Surrounded by these 'familiar symbols' spectators
were encouraged to place themselves centre screen, to see themselves in life
playing a role worthy of the cinema. The stature of the individual or the
individual's community was raised to the extent that it seemed able to
stand against (rather than be swamped by) the forces of destruction ranked
against it.

There was, then, a characteristic desire to see small lives revealed as quietly
heroic and events brought to a happy, but not inconceivable, conclusion. When
Dorothy L. Sayers stresses the escapist element of detective fiction she makes
an important point, but she also underestimates the complexity of the genre's
provision. The success of detective fiction as fantasy lies less in its ability to create
another world than in its ability to provide a resolution. Within the pages of the
text the security of a known environment is disrupted through the violence
of murder, but the fear this creates is purely vicarious. The reader remains
safe in the knowledge that before the end of the book the perpetrator will
be exposed, and order and sanity restored. The violation of a society through
the crime of murder can be seen as analogous to the more comprehensive
transgression of war. The solution of the mystery, the provision of an answer
through the courage and intelligence of the individual detective, is a central
fantasy of wartime survival. The social worker's desire to see films 'which
make the significance of our everyday lives more vivid' is the same fantasy
that is enacted in the fiction of Margery Allingham's *Traitor's Purse* (1941) (see
below, Chapter 3) and in other adventure fiction of the war. A typical
example is found in the work of Helen McInnes. Her 1942 novel *Assignment
in Brittany* presents the figure of the single spy, perhaps the archetypal isolated
individual. McInnes's hero, sent on a low-key fact-finding mission, finds the
stakes have unexpectedly risen. Quickly adapting to a changing situation,
his individual intervention achieves not only the short-term disruption of
Nazi plans, but also results in the creation of a whole new network of
Breton resistance.[12] This is a fantasy of control and agency. It empowers

and reassures through its constant assertion that the individual can make a difference.

Thus the centrality of fictions to the process of 'making sense' of war cannot be underestimated. However, it remains essential to uncover the fear and confusion that lay beneath these strategies for survival. When Calder suggests both the impossibility and the necessity of imaginatively comprehending the Blitz experience, he is echoing the concerns of Elizabeth Bowen; 'I do not think that the desiccation by war, of our day-to-day lives can be enough stressed' (Bowen, 1950: 49). In discussing her wartime short stories, Bowen emphasises the vital compensatory role of dreams and fantasies, even of hallucinations:

> The hallucinations are an unconscious, instinctive, saving resort on the part of the characters: life, mechanized by the controls of wartime, and emotionally torn and impoverished by changes, had to complete itself in some other way. (Bowen, 1950: 49)

Bowen's discovery of a 'rising tide of hallucination' reveals her considerable understanding of the predicament of the individual in wartime. Her writing explores the front line of personal defences, and reveals a crucial distinction between how much people can take, and how much they can take *in*. Inez Holden's refugees cannot 'make sense' of their experience. In order to survive they assume an adjusted set of values that enable them to think of war as sense – but when they let go of this façade, they face an inevitable collapse. The extent of war's destruction cannot be assimilated into language. Its 'reality' cannot be acknowledged by the structures of the symbolic order, and as such must be repressed, or as Tröger suggests, find some form of non-verbal articulation. War forms, in effect, the repressed of the symbolic order.[13] Hence its eruption represents not a challenge from without, but rather a threat from within – a manifestation of the forces that society has repressed in the process of its formulation. War is, to use Julia Kristeva's term, the 'underlying causality' of social organisation (Kristeva, 1974: 153).[14] Using Kristeva's terminology of the semiotic, Elizabeth Grosz explains the tensions between the symbolic and its repressed:

> Like the repressed, the semiotic can return in / as irruptions within the symbolic. It manifests itself as an interruption, a dissonance, a rhythm unsubsumable in the text's rational logic or controlled narrative. The semiotic is thus both the precondition of symbolic functioning and its uncontrollable excess. It is used by discourses but cannot be articulated by them. (Grosz, 1990: 152)

This contradictory tension between dependence and rejection can be seen as paradigmatic of the relationship between the patriarchal order and war. In the aftermath of conflict the shaken social order rebuilds its familiar structures over the mass of war's dislocation. The symptoms of war have passed, and memories of the illness are quickly forgotten. In a schizophrenic society divided between peace and war, conscious and unconscious, the controlling factor is represented as the drug of patriarchal control. Within this logic, the emergence of war becomes, paradoxically, both the strength and weakness of society. The drug has failed, war has erupted, but only through a stronger dosage of the same drug can order be restored, and the alter ego of the patriarchal state be returned from whence it came.

Yet whatever the benefits for the regeneration of the symbolic order, the problematic relationship between war and language has considerable repercussions for the individual subject. Constituted through language, the subject is placed in a critical situation through that language's inability to contain or express the experience of war. War disrupts the existing order and, at the same time, by jeopardising stability it increases the value of that order.[15] This disruption challenges the strategies through which the subject makes sense of the world, and prevents the confident articulation of a position within that world. The normal, obscured, workings of language are exposed by the rupture of war, and the ever-present gap between signifier and signified is uncomfortably revealed. This uncertainty creates an instability that situates the fragile structures of identity over a chasm, and demands that a crucial decision be made: to normalise and accept a state of dislocation, or to face the paradox of war. Normalising, the acceptance of a new, arbitrary and fluctuating set of rules as the norm, is the customary technique of survival. Although the subject is situated in the midst of violent destruction, society proceeds as if nothing has changed. The superstructure of social behaviour persists as the only hope of security, and the boundaries of a recognisable patriarchal symbolic order are quickly re-established. Linguistically speaking, the signifiers remain the same, but the signifieds have changed. In 1939, the familiar railway terminology of 'an incident on the line' might have signified anything from points' failure to suicide. In 1941 it almost certainly referred to a bomb – as Vera Brittain succinctly recounts in *England's Hour*: 'In consequence of the line being obstructed by MISHAP Passengers are warned that trains will be delayed' (1941: 120).

The alternative to this adjustment rejects the security of linguistic strategies for survival. Here is the fate of the refugee, who, in letting go of the framework of normality, experiences the full weight of repressed experience, and is brought face to face with the unbearable 'reality' of war. The rationale of war is antithetical to the logic of existence and its 'reality' does not bear too close an inspection. Holden's dead refugees, like Lot's wife looking back at the destruction behind them, were long-distance victims of war.

There is, then, in all war writing and recollections of war experience, a story that cannot be told – something that will not 'make sense'. This is the 'fear and confusion' behind Calder's myth, and the 'desiccation' behind Bowen's dreams and fantasies. It is the unbearable and inarticulable 'reality' of war, ever present behind the fictions of literature and of day-to-day existence.

ENGENDERING WAR

Where is the woman in wartime? If war problematises the (invariably male) subject's relation to the symbolic order, what then will be its impact on the uncertain relation of women to the patriarchy? Do women in war risk sharing the fate of the refugee; displaced and disorientated, their fragile hold on the symbolic order destroyed by the disruption of their always already unstable ego identity?

Margaret and Patrice Higonnet have suggested that 'Women experience war over a different period from that which traditional history usually recognises, a period which precedes and long outlasts formal hostilities' (Higonnet and Higonnet, 1987: 46). From the work of women writers in the years immediately before, during and after the war there stands out just such a rejection of the arbitrary parameters of masculine history. Virginia Woolf, Naomi Mitchison and Elizabeth Bowen all explore and challenge the boundaries of the temporal symbolic order. Texts such as Vera Brittain's *Testament of Youth* (1933) have their foundation in the recognition that the wartime experience of bereavement does not recognise the limits of an armistice or a treaty. From the pre-war protests to the postwar grief and readjustments, women writers' engagement with the Second World War far exceeded the six-year span allotted by the rules of history.

Thus the relationship between war and gender is far from straightforward. In the late 1930s women writers attempted to challenge the dominant power structures responsible for war, but the advent of that war and the experiences that came with it, soon made survival a higher priority than subversion. The problematic relationship between war and women was repressed and disguised by the veneer of national unity. Yet beneath this superficial togetherness, the disruption of war was putting women into an impossible situation of 'double alienation'.

War creates a situation in which the gender debate is subsumed by a meta-narrative of power. It represents a conflict that divorces and prioritises the division between activity and passivity from the founding binary opposition of masculine/feminine. War almost represents itself as a constructive reinscription, or even a rejection of the age-old formulations of gender. This indiscrimination, however, is an integral part rather than a beneficial product of the façade of national unity. Its semblance of equality is more accurately a partially sighted blindness to the social, cultural and historical specificity of woman. The dangers of this homogenising force are perhaps best articulated by Naomi Schor in her attack on Barthes's and Foucault's rhetoric of indifference. Schor's concern is that Barthes's attempt to 'debiologize difference' into an oppositional structure notated as 'Animate (masculine/feminine)/Inanimate (neutral)', in actuality merely obscures or ignores the omnipresent and unchanged operation of sexual difference. Moving on to a discussion of Foucault, Schor observes that the history of male sexuality is unproblematically presented as a paradigm for a 'single universal history' of sex:

> The line of demarcation passes here not so much between men and women, or even between homosexuals and heterosexuals, but between active and passive men, with the result that the opposition between men and women and the concomitant obsessive focus on the enigma of femininity is decentered. (Schor, 1987: 108)

In the course of pursuing the division between a non–gender–specific activity and passivity, woman is 'decentered'. If all that these attempts to deconstruct the hierarchy of gender permit us to articulate is an opposition between two types of one, supposedly neutral gender, the danger is that this becomes, in effect, two types of one masculine gender. The woman once again, has become invisible. Schor concludes her argument with Myra Jehlen's ironic observation that it is only in being other that woman assumes an identity:

> In the first place the claim of difference criticizes the content of the male universal norm. But beyond this, it represents a new understanding that if the other is to live, it will have to live as other, lest the achievement of integration be crowned with the fatal irony of disappearance through absorption. (Schor, 1987: 110)

Yet war none the less acts as a disruptive influence on the patriarchal status quo, and its destructive capacity imposes a hierarchy that cannot be ignored. Following Barthes's Animate/Inanimate proposal I suggest the following classification to indicate both the disruption of gender patterns and the potential 'double displacement' of women within the newly imposed schema of war:

Active (MAN/woman)/Passive (MAN/woman)

The relationship to power dominates the paradigm of gender, but a woman's relationship to power cannot be directly equated to a man's relationship to power while both relationships remain within the patriarchal framework of 'western civilisation'.

So long as woman remains the Other, her engagement with the symbolic order will be an equivocal one. To survive, and to find a voice (even if it is not her own), woman conforms to the existing order – but although she enters this order, she can never possess it, and her position is therefore never fixed and stable, but fluctuating and conditional. She is always an employee, rather than a director, of the patriarchal corporation. In consequence, the outbreak of war, with its disruptive impact on the entire structure of gender relations, destabilises her position still further.

The act and idea of war itself is not unproblematic. It represents both the self-destructive impulse of a patriarchal society and the ultimate achievement of its competitive rationale. War can be understood in metaphorical terms as a transcendental deconstructor, with the power to overshadow, disrupt and displace all other discourses. It represents an arbitrary imposition that has a contradictory double impact. On the surface it homogenises – it causes a coming together and a setting aside of differences for the duration of the conflict – but beneath this surface homogeneity it simultaneously disrupts and fragments the known and established order. War threatens a transition from order into chaos and deceptively presents itself as the ultimate crisis of patriarchy.

The appearance of this disruption, however, is not to be trusted. Naomi Schor has observed that 'phallocentrism revolves around the riddle of femininity' (Schor, 1987: 107), a comment which suggests that the outcome of this confrontation between war and gender cannot easily be predicted. What will be the response of a disrupted patriarchy to the wartime metamorphosis of the riddle? One possible solution is appropriately provided by Nancy Miller's exploration of the myth of Arachne. Ovid's story concerns two women, the goddess Athena, described as 'the female guardian of the law' and the mortal Arachne, artist and creator of the 'feminocentric' text. Their struggle epitomises the contrast between the woman who upholds the law and the woman who transgresses it, and Arachne's ill-fated attempt to empower herself through art becomes a metaphor for the fate of women seemingly empowered by war. Arachne is transformed into a spider: 'The artist is returned to "woman"' (Miller, 1988: 95). In the circumstances of war, at the same time that woman attains the agency of the artist, art ceases to signify as an activity, and the discourse of patriarchy remorselessly returns her to the immobility of the passive other.

A second solution to the riddle is formulated by Susan Gubar. In direct proportion to the increase in woman's usefulness to the patriarchal order, there follows an increase in the perception of woman as a danger to that order. Only half understood, she has suddenly become a vital part of the system that fears her. Gubar's reading of the male literature of the Second World War reveals the extent of this fear. Woman has once again been split into the traditional polarities of good and evil. The portrayal of woman as corrupt and corrupting characterises the fiction of writers such as Leon Uris and Norman Mailer, and is embodied in the dominant personification of war as a whore. However, the paradigm of the bad woman was given its most vivid depiction by the poster art of the propagandists. Gubar writes:

> Allied propaganda spoke directly about and to servicemen's fear of their women's betrayal. Posters enjoining silence as a protection against spies implied that women's talk would kill fighting men: a Finnish poster, for example, graphically suggested that women's lips should be locked up, while English cartoons and posters pictured women as irresponsible in their garrulity or sinister in their silence. The female spy, a vamp whose charms endanger national security, was not unrelated to the foreign femme fatale whose enticements threatened the physical security of the fighting forces . . . The danger of female pollution . . . is also evident in British posters in which alluring, feminine accoutrements . . . grace the skull's head that would lure soldiers to dissolution and death. (Gubar, 1987: 240)

The equation of women and death was presented with a terrifying blatancy. The awesome potency of the bad woman was established as a spiritual Fifth Column, perpetually threatening destruction from within.[16]

Yet ironically, the paradigm of the good woman embodied an even greater potential threat. The woman on a pedestal; wife, mother, or 'best girl', protecting the home, was elevated to the status of guardian to the cherished values and social order of a vanishing pre-war world:

> the dead German soldier in Keith Douglas's poem *'Vergissmeinnicht'* is not saved by his talisman [a picture of a girl] . . . As the only witness who would weep to see 'the lover and killer . . . mingled' and mangled, the girl he left behind is a repository of the humane values that men must suppress in wartime, and she is therefore rarely present except as a fleeting image or a trace memory. (Gubar, 1987: 246; first ellipsis mine)

If woman has become the guardian of order and values, she has moved dangerously close to the source of the law. The potential power of such a central position (although a guardian can never be mistaken for an originator) renders her marginalisation obligatory. Hence woman guards the now defunct laws of peace, while the symbolic order defends itself through the assumption of a new code of war.

Woman, then, is both guardian and infiltrator, upholder and betrayer of the law. She is the archetypal foreign body – necessary and yet reviled: a dualism that allies her with that most ambivalent of contemporary figures, the spy. The spy is a complex and multiple signifier, simultaneously occupying the space of both hero and traitor. Operating within a perpetual dynamic of betrayal, the spy offers both the greatest risk and the greatest reward. Woman becomes a passive version of the active agent, perceived as being both reward and risk to the man at war. The alien status of woman exists as a threatening undertow beneath the calm façade of wartime togetherness. As I suggested earlier, this 'coming together for the duration' is only made possible through the projection of a clearly defined Other who is the enemy. In the specific instance of the Second World War, this legitimate Other is predominantly defined as the Nazi. Yet as Gubar has observed, woman remains as Other *within* the framework of national homogeneity. She is perceived and portrayed as a 'foreign body', which intentionally or unintentionally has the potential to betray the 'masculine' body politic.

The Otherness of woman, then, complicates the operation of domestic homogeneity, and this complexity is evident in women's writing. Agatha Christie exploits the worst fears of misogynistic nation in *N or M?* (1941), a wartime spy thriller featuring the seemingly inexhaustible Tommy and Tuppence Beresford. The novel offers up the usual suspects, archetypal ousiders such as the refugee and the Irishwoman; but resists the construction of an easy scapegoat, suggesting instead that the cancer of betrayal lies at the very heart of Britishness. The perpetrator is a young middle-class mother – symbol of all the nation is fighting for, and supposed guardian of home and hearth. The improbably named Mrs Sprot is indeed a fiendishly clever spy, playing on the gender assumptions of the nation to ensure her freedom from suspicion. By adopting a child as camouflage she becomes effectively invisible, transformed into a cultural non-presence described by Tuppence as 'that milk and water creature we just thought of as – Betty's mother' (Christie, 1941/1962: 209). Mrs Sprot certainly feels no compunction about betraying her country and *N or M?*, along with the wartime novels of Margery Allingham and Elizabeth Bowen, raises profound questions of loyalty. After all, what incentive is there for Tuppence to save a nation that rejects her brains in favour of her husband's brawn? In the 'spy' novels of Margery Allingham and Elizabeth Bowen women must choose between private desires and public good. In a patriarchal society that tells women they have no remit beyond the private, there can be no easy assumption that they will 'do the right thing'.

It is, however, in a short story by Jean Rhys that this fear of woman is most tellingly revealed. 'I spy a stranger' (reprinted in Boston, 1989: 114–27) disturbingly depicts the sinister implications of domestic homogeneity and deconstructs the supposedly benevolent national character to reveal a monster, rotten at the core. Even the legendary British sense of humour is exposed as vicious, destructive and xenophobic. Within the tight-knit community of an English village, Laura, a non-conforming woman, becomes the target of abuse. Easier to reach than the offical enemy, she becomes the localised other, on to which the resentments and anxieties of wartime England are projected. Yet, the most significant element of Rhys's story is not its illustration of the negative stresses of a wartime community, but rather its suggestion that this is a matter of continuity not change. The village's capacity for evil was not caused but merely intensified by war. The evidence lies in Laura's confiscated journals that focus on the gender relations of British society. She, like Virginia Woolf, sees misogyny and war as intimately connected:

> There is something strange about the attitude to women as women. Not the dislike (or fear). That isn't strange of course. But it's all so completely taken for granted, and surely that is strange. It has settled down and become an atmosphere, or, if you like, a climate, and no one questions it, least of all the women themselves. There is *no* opposition. The effects are criticized, for some of the effects are hardly advertisements for the system, the cause is seldom mentioned and then very gingerly . . .
>
> But no one can go against the spirit of a country with impunity, and propaganda from the cradle to the grave can do a lot. (Boston, 1989: 120–1; ellipsis mine)

Laura's cousin, Mrs Hudson, hovers on the brink of seeing through the gender propaganda, and its connection to the hostilities of war, but sinks back into banality by the story's gothic ending. Laura, the 'madwoman', is incarcerated, repressed along with the truth that nobody wanted to hear.

Yet the impact of war on gender is not confined to an intensification of institutionalised misogyny. The work of Paul Fussell and Eric Leed on soldiers' responses to the First World War has uncovered what the editors of *Behind the Lines* term a 'crisis of masculinity', and this crisis raises significant questions regarding war's reconstruction of gender relations. The editors observe that:

> The discovery of the crisis of masculinity reveals that so-called masculine traits are not universal, natural attributes of men; the perception that women's subordination persists despite profound changes in their economic and political activities suggests that status does not depend on reaching a fixed position in the social order. How, then, is gender designated? (Higonnet *et al.*, 1987: 3)

One answer to this question lies in the Higonnets' image of the 'double helix'. This model permits an understanding of the curious progressions and regressions of women's emancipation in wartime, and it also reveals the structure which ensures that men's alienation becomes women's double alienation:

> This image permits us to look at woman not in isolation but within a persistent system of gender relationships. The female strand on the helix is opposed to the male strand, and position on the female strand is subordinate to position on the male strand. The image of the double helix allows us to see that, although the roles of men and women vary greatly from culture to culture, their relationship is in some sense constant. If men gather and women fish, gathering will be thought more important than fishing; in another society where men fish and women gather, fishing will be more prestigious. The actual nature of the social activity is not as critical as the cultural perception of its relative value in a gender-linked structure of subordination. (Higonnet and Higonnet, 1987: 34)

A crisis of masculinity, then, is far removed from a crisis of the patriarchy. The patriarchal system, like the structure of the double helix, stands firm despite the chaos of war. It may be the eye of the storm, but it is those around it who must bear the brunt. Julia Kristeva has suggested that 'when he flees the symbolic paternal order . . . man can laugh' (Kristeva, 1974: 150). Nancy Miller expands and clarifies this distinction: 'only the subject who is both self-possessed and possesses access to the library of the already read has the luxury of flirting with the escape from identity' (Miller, 1988: 83). Both observations emphasise the relative security of men. However, within the context of war, Elaine Showalter's work on male hysteria adds a more complex dimension to Kristeva's idea. Showalter sees shell-shock as 'the body language of masculine complaint' (Showalter, 1987a: 64).[17] Disempowered and placed in an untenable position, many soldiers of the First World War manifested the symptoms of hysteria, previously seen as an almost exclusively female complaint. The symptoms of hysteria vary, often according to external factors such as class and education, but, however the problem is revealed, it represents a physical manifestation of a trauma that cannot be verbally articulated. The deprivation of agency resulting from war places men in what would otherwise be seen as a 'feminine' position of powerlessness.

In the light of this feminisation, Kristeva's image of the laughing man assumes a new dimension. Displaced through war from the centre of his logocentric universe, man temporarily becomes the Other. However, as the heir apparent of the symbolic order, man has the freedom to jeopardise his position. He is free to come and go, to explore the boundaries and the margins – thanks to the privilege of movement, in wartime man theoretically becomes a superwoman. This potentially positive emancipation of man from the tunnel vision of phallocentrism is, however, negated by two factors. First, the power structures of war can be seen to assume the form of a rationalised, revitalised patriarchy. The hegemony of the masculine is therefore replaced by a selective hegemony of masculine *power*. The political juntas that cause and co-ordinate the dance of war are far removed from the disenfranchised, feminised soldier who follows orders. For the duration of the conflict, he too, has become an employee of the patriarchal corporation.

The second factor that negates the potential of wartime gender disruption, is that woman, following the pattern of the double helix, is displaced still further, into another otherness – a double alienation. How can women survive this? The answer would seem to lie in a complex process of masquerade; the adoption of a multi-layered façade, created partly out of impulses of self-preservation and partly at the behest of the propaganda machine. The ideological undercurrents that manipulated the transformation of women's lives in the Second World War are clearly in evidence in the workings of this double alienation. How is it possible, asks Maureen Honey, that 'a crisis that necessitated radical revision of traditional views' should provoke 'the paradoxical spawning of a reactionary post-war feminine mystique'? (1984: 1)[18] Honey's conclusions in the main suggest that the 'feminine mystique' never went away, and traditional images of femininity remained throughout the war, contradicting and undermining the powerful figure of the female war worker. 'Beauty is your duty' declared a 1940 advertisement for Icilma Beauty Aids, while Vinolia Soap offered the following information that 'Women in uniform should know':

> Because many women are now in uniform, it doesn't mean that they should abandon their femininity and charm. On the contrary, men expect them to be just as attractive as ever. But many women are finding that their service duties make the maintenance of their personal daintiness more difficult. (Waller and Vaughan-Rees, 1987: 99)

The advice was not confined to the double-edged pleas of advertisers. The columns of the women's magazines, although decorated with images of women in uniform, offered warning articles under headings such as 'Don't get slack!' This piece continued with the advice, 'The wise woman realizes what a tonic she can be to men on active service – and so she looks her best' (Waller and Vaughan-Rees, 1987: 81), but other articles focused less on the altruistic benefits of femininity and more on the shame associated with a loss of womanliness. Ursula Bloom, writing in *Woman's Own* in February 1941, sounds an ominous note:

> Have you thought what it will be like if, after the war, men came home to wives and sweethearts who have let themselves go? If you let go now,

you may not get the chance to pull up afterwards. Stay lovely. (Waller and Vaughan–Rees, 1987: 80)

Thus, the editors of *Behind the Lines* conclude that wartime propaganda:

stipulated that women's new roles were 'only for the duration' and that wives and mothers must make heroic sacrifices 'for the nation in its time of need.' Propaganda reminded female defense workers that they were not themselves – that is, not 'natural' – but behaving temporarily *like men*. (Higonnet *et al.*, 1987: 7)

Women, never comfortable in a symbolic order that situates them as other, are no longer even the possessors of their customary otherness. Instead they are asked to assume temporarily the *semblance* of masculinity – to act like men, but to remain constantly aware of their femininity. They have not, and never can assume a masculine position. That some women were a little confused by the complexity of this dual role, and hoped after the war to continue their 'masculine' employment, is not altogether surprising.

Ironically, for a force of destruction, war seemed to provide a potentially creative space in which women and men could challenge the constraints of rigid gender definitions. This space, however, was illusory, for the flux of war was firmly contained within the boundaries of a stronger rather than a weaker patriarchal organisation. This anti-climactic lack of change can be seen as part of a twenty-year cycle of decadence, destruction and renewal. The 'liberation' inherent in the widespread social criticism engendered by feminist and pacifist discourses of the 1930s has an air of *fin de siècle*. They represent an evolutionary process of change that is usurped and destroyed by the discourse of war. When conflict begins the 'freedom' they represent can be 'legitimately' repressed by the demands of martial law. None the less, in the 'decadence' of the late 1930s, existing outmoded patriarchal structures are under attack, particularly from a wide cross-section of feminist writers. The 'apocalypse' of war does not save these institutions, but neither does it benefit their attackers. The process of war rather metamorphosises the impotent old patriarchy into a new and virile war machine – and at the same time silences all criticism in the name of national security.

Once again, the patterns of war deflect and undermine the progress of women. Rosie the Riveter's enforced postwar retreat into the home and the family should not be a surprise – it was inevitable from the onset of hostilities. War must be seen not as the demise but as the rebirth of patriarchy. Between 1930 and 1950 the cycle comes full circle from the decadence of the old, through the apocalypse of war, to the birth of the new. The new, however, is not different; it does not represent change. It is instead the infant patriarchy, nurtured on the breast of women's wartime labour – a breast which it must inevitably reject. In the new era of the 1950s women are safely back in the home, stabilising the shaken male ego, and effectively marginalised from the concerns of the symbolic order. As an attribute of government, the prime achievement of war is that it enables the patriarchy to 'scrap the argument'. Under the rule of war, the terms of debate are easily changed, and the lines of conflict redrawn. It is a case of moving the goalposts, which regressively redefines the role and position of women.

Gail Braybon and Penny Summerfield conclude their analysis of women's experiences in two world wars with the comment:

> After 1945 what was important in life was still emphatically male, whether one was looking at work, leisure, politics, language or for that matter the way that historical accounts were written. (Braybon and Summerfield, 1987: 287)

The important things in life have never been anything else, and most current feminist researchers support this pessimistic view of women's 'progress' in wartime. Dorothy Sheridan, for example:

> Most feminist historians, myself included, agree that progress was limited. Challenges to women's subordination were contained within an overarching nationalist rhetoric which positioned woman at the heart of the family in her idealised role as wife and mother. (Sheridan, 1991: 3)

Socially and politically women were allowed to play at rewriting the gender rules, but their games were kept firmly within the schoolroom of patriarchal authority. Ultimately, and in spite of all the problems of articulation associated with the war, the only potential space that could offer any challenge to the homogeneity of masculine discourse was that of the text.

NOTES

1. The reluctant public was none the less subjected to a deliberate campaign of misinformation, the crowning glory of which was the policy of 'self-censorship' indulged in by the press barons. Richard Cockett's article 'Saluting Hitler' (*Guardian*, 17 May 1989) indicts not only the collusion of the Conservatives Rothermere and Beaverbrook, but also the co-operation of Lord Southwood, owner of the Labour *Daily Herald*. Acting at and beyond the government's behest, and ignoring the advice of their own correspondents, the press summarily removed any criticism of the Nazis from its pages. It is also interesting to note that unflattering portraits of Hitler's Germany were banned from the cinema in this period (Richards and Sheridan, 1987: 187).
2. Although not as widespread as in the First World War the expression of grief continued to be a focus of much published poetry. Vera Bax's sonnet 'To Billy, my son', with its careful measured use of structured poetic form, is perhaps more characteristic of earlier writers' attempts to use poetry to impose a concrete and manageable shape on to their otherwise uncontainable grief (Plain, 1995). The sense of loss in Bax's insistent repetition of 'the end' also associates this poem more closely with 1918 than 1945.
   Now comes, indeed, the end of all delight,
   The end of forward-looking on life's way,

The end of all desire to pierce the night
For gleam of hope, the end of all things gay.
(Reilly, 1984: 13)

3. George Orwell's essay 'The lion and the unicorn' also provides a comprehensive overview of the national persona.

4. Mass-Observation was founded in 1937 to observe and record the ideas, attitudes and processes of daily life in Britain. The movement's creators, Tom Harrisson, Charles Madge and Humphrey Jennings, set in motion an unprecedented exercise in people-watching, the results of which are houses in the Mass-Observation Archive at the University of Sussex. Although the project began by using teams of trained observers, perhaps its most fruitful dimension was the later recruitment of thousands of volunteer observers who contributed diaries and provided answers to the monthly questionnaires or 'directives'.

5. Rose refers here to Winnicott's (1950) article, 'Some thoughts on the meaning of the word "democracy"', published in his *Home is Where We Start From*, Harmondsworth: Penguin, 1986.

6. In her curious combination of memoir and opinion piece *Me – In War-Time*, the novelist Naomi Jacob offers a clear-sighted and succinct acknowledgement of this fact: 'Much as we dislike the idea of a totalitarian government, much as we may dislike dictators and autocrats, we must face the fact that a nation at war is a nation ruled not by one dictator but by several, whatever form of government it may have favoured before the declaration of hostilities' (Jacob, 1941: 80).

7. The social changes that followed the cessation of hostilities – the Labour victory of 1945, the birth of the welfare state and the implementation of the 1944 Education Reform Act – might seem to contradict the ultimately rather pessimistic conclusions that are drawn from this study. I would suggest, however, that positive social change is not necessarily synonymous with benefits for women, or indeed with any reinscription of traditional gender relations.

8. Graves's talk was an attempt to explain the much lamented absence of the war poet, and his pessimistic conclusions reveal the familiar assumption that war is an exclusively masculine arena. There is something almost bizarre in the following lament for the loss of the Soldier's privileged relationship to death, that would seem to support critics who suggest that the Second World War was a crisis of masculinity. The soldier, Graves observes, 'cannot even feel that his rendezvous with death is more certain than that of his Aunt Fanny, the fire-watcher'. That Aunt Fanny might feel inspired to poetry is quite out of the question!

9. In order to maintain this environment it was necessary not to make waves. Once the conflict began there was more widespread criticism of BBC programming than of the act of war.

10. In spite of paper shortages, book sales increased by 50 per cent. However, Calder is at pains to point out that with over 400 libraries blitzed, it's not surprising that book-buying increased, and that this figure alone cannot be taken as an indicator of changing reading patterns. None the less he does concede the immense popularity of the relatively new paperback Penguins, whose sales in 1941 averaged over 100,000 per volume.

11. Achieving an effective balance between the real and the fictional was not easy. Aldgate and Richards also explore the reception of two 1943 films about the Auxiliary Fire Service – Humphrey Jennings's Crown Film Unit documentary *Fires were Started* and Ealing Studio's fictional *The Bells go Down*. Although both films featured remarkable documentary fire-fighting footage, the critical and public response favoured Jennings's use of real firemen over the actors and romantic embellishments of *The Bells go Down*.

12. A curious contrast can be noted between wartime and postwar representations of masculinity. Texts written during the war, such as those of Allingham and McInnes, offer a curious fantasy of masculine rejuvenation to their readers. A new, and improved, version of the familiar man returns from the experience of war. In Allingham's case, Campion's amnesia leads to a re-evaluation of both his own behaviour and his feelings towards his neglected fiancée Amanda, while in McInnes's novel, Anne's prospective husband is quite literally replaced by a better version of the same man. These wartime representations of benevolent change are in marked contrast to the picture of postwar emotional scarring depicted in novels of the 1920s and 1930s. Storm Jameson's *Mirror in Darkness* trilogy is just one example among many, featuring a cast of literally and metaphorically emasculated men, irredeemably emotionally damaged by war. Such a change of emphasis seems an integral part of the problem of looking directly at the Medusa's head of war.

13. There is a useful ambiguity in the word 'form'. War forms, or becomes, the repressed of the symbolic order, but it can simultaneously be seen to create (to form) the repression which upholds that order.

14. Kristeva describes this 'underlying causality' as 'a figure of speech that alludes to the social

contradictions that a given society can provisionally subdue in order to constitute itself as such' (1974: 153).

15. Phyllis Lassner has also identified this dynamic in which the prospect of change gives a new, and largely unmerited, value to the security of the old. Discussing Elizabeth Jane Howard's *The Long View* (1956) she describes how, 'with internal and world war threatening her every movement' Antonia, the central character, 'sacrifices a sustained enactment of her desires to a futile hope for continuity' (Lassner, 1990b: 92).

16. Margery Allingham's *The Oaken Heart* sheds fascinating light on the literal and metaphorical status of women. This quotation utilises the two crucial signifiers of femininity in the period: the domestic helpmeet and the transgressive, sexually powerful woman who carries with her the threat of illness and decay: 'If we can keep Courage as it were a wife, an ordinary well-appreciated darling helpmeet, as she is to-day, we shall at least have got one great sound thing, but if we make either a remote all-powerful goddess of her or a false little strumpet of her to parade and grow sick of, we shall forsake her again . . . Courage, . . . is not by herself enough. She cannot stand alone. She is a part, not a whole, a wife not a man and wife' (Allingham, 1941a: 239; ellipsis mine). This seems extremely revealing in terms of Allingham's gender assumptions, but somewhat less revealing with respect to her point about courage.

17. Male hysteria is discussed by Showalter at greater length in *The Female Malady* (Showalter, 1987b), and in Chapter 3 below.

18. Honey's excellent introduction to the state of current historical research on the relationship between women and war includes this very pertinent summary of the work of Ruth Milkman and J. E. Trey: 'both contend that tying war work to traditional female images was a logical direction for capitalist ideology to take because it reinforced women's inferior position in the work force at a time when material conditions challenged sexist work divisions' (Honey, 1984: 4–5).

Part One

If we keep on speaking the same language together, we're going
to reproduce the same history. Begin the same old stories all
over again.

Luce Irigaray, *This Sex Which Is Not One*

2

Prelude to War

The temporal span of any war cannot be confined to its literal historical duration, and the exact shape of the 'prelude' to the Second World War is similarly difficult to define. At a conservative estimate it would cover the six-year period between Hitler's appointment as chancellor of Germany in January 1933 and the outbreak of war in September 1939; but, for many writers, the Second World War has its origins as far back as the 1919 Treaty of Versailles. The first part of this study is, then, focused predominantly on the 1930s, but in accordance with this historical uncertainty, its boundaries are necessarily flexible. The reasons for dividing the book into two parts will, I hope, become clear, but the titles of these parts might benefit from some explanation. Metaphorically, 'prelude' and 'storm' are unashamedly mixed. In the years before the outbreak of war, invocations of the 'storm clouds gathering over Europe' were legion, and 'weathering the storm' pays tribute to this venerable, but not inappropriate, old cliché. Traditionally storm is preceeded by calm, but such a term seemed unable to encapsulate the integral connection between pre-war and war. The prelude thus suggests that although the 1930s may be temporally located before the outbreak of war, they cannot be conceptually divorced from the conflict they preceed. Yet, although the first part of this book is concerned with events leading up to the war, and the second with the actual onset of hostilities, there remains a sense in which prelude and storm are inappropriate. Indeed, it could almost be argued that their inversion would be more fitting to the contrasting climates of impending doom and imminent disaster that characterised the literature of the 1930s, and the aura of calm stoicism and understatement that formed the dominant public discourse of the early 1940s.

The literary climate of the 1930s is, then, a curious conglomeration of opposites, and its literature is both that of peace and war. The roots of this duality extend back beyond the literal manifestation of war in Spain, and are grounded instead in an all-pervasive war consciousness stemming from the national trauma of the First World War. The decade was shadowed not only by the threat of a second world war, but also by the omnipresent memory of the first. This perpetual war consciousness had a considerable impact on the literary world, and few would argue with Samuel Hynes's claim that this was a decade in which literature and politics were fundamentally connected (Hynes, 1976). Yet much of the early, and influential, work on the thirties as a cultural concept was androcentric in the extreme, focusing almost entirely on the so-called 'Auden Generation'.[1] This narrow perspective has left us with a skewed perception of the period, a limited conception of the literary landscape, and a reinforcement of the age-old assumption that women have no place in either politics or art. This supposition of exclusive masculinity has achieved the status of orthodoxy, a status scarcely challenged until the appearance of Alison Light's *Forever England*. Light's exploration of 'conservative modernity', however, presents a vigorous challenge to 'those who are content to work with a map in which what they call the popular and what they deem the high cultural are seen as poles apart' (1991: ix–x), and her analysis of the gaps in British cultural and literary history is as applicable to a consideration of war writing as it is to the literature of the interwar years:

> The largest gaps in our histories of British life this century are still those which the careless masculinity of its writers continue to create. It is extraordinary how much the literary history of 'the inter-war years', for example, has been rendered almost exclusively in male terms: whether it be the doings of right-wing aesthetes or the radicalism of the 'Thirties poets', the dying moments of English liberalism, the late flowerings of high modernism, or the making of social documentary and social realism – it has been male authors who are taken to represent the nation as well as those who are disaffiliated from it. This has been at least as true of commentators on the left as on the right . . . but in most cases the reading habits of the majority of the British people, let alone the women among them, are rarely mentioned. (Light, 1991: 6)

Who, then, were the women writers of the 1930s, and how did they respond to the threat of war? Marion Shaw does much to answer the first question in her brief survey of feminism and fiction between the wars. Reconsidering the definition of 'women's writing' in the 1930s, Shaw observes that '[r]ecent feminist criticism, and the recuperative publishing activity accompanying it, has tended to concentrate on those novelists who chose experimentalism and who were most obviously the "new" feminists of the literary world of the war and interwar years: Woolf, Sinclair, Richardson, Lehmann, Rhys, for example' (Shaw, 1986: 179). In contrast to this tradition of women's writing, Shaw examines those writers who 'adhered more or less to the realist traditions of documentary verisimilitude' (1986: 179), writers frequently considered 'conservative', who often chose the epic form of the awesomely researched historical novel as their arena. It is vital, she argues, to resist the temptation to pronounce one branch of women's writing radical and another reactionary, purely on the basis of formal considerations. After all, '[h]istorical fiction provided (and still provides) a means by which women could appropriate a past that had largely been denied them' (1986: 181). Shaw's work on Winifred Holtby and Light's rehabilitation of writers such as Agatha Christie and Daphne Du Maurier are crucial interventions in the 1930s debate, challenging the still widely-held assumption that Virginia Woolf was the only British woman writer of the interwar years. It is one of the central projects of this book to continue that challenge by breaking down the boundaries that divide Woolf the modernist from Woolf the feminist and considering her work alongside that of her less highly-regarded female contemporaries.

Women's writing was, then, an integral, if critically marginalised, part of the 1930s and the work of both popular and highbrow novelists frequently engaged with contemporary debates.[2] In political terms, one of the most cogent analyses of the contradictory tensions of interwar life comes from Storm Jameson's *Mirror in Darkness* trilogy. The three novels, *Company Parade* (1934), *Love in Winter* (1935) and *None Turn Back* (1936) focus on both the idealism and divisions of the left, while also exploring the human motivations and postwar trauma that fed the ruthless creed of capitalism. Jameson's trilogy, written in the 1930s, but set in the 1920s, seems to contract the interwar years. The time of writing and the time of setting collapse the period between the wars into a short, sharp downhill run from the harsh retribution of Versailles. In contrast to Hynes's focus on the rise of the Hitler tyranny as a focaliser of war anxiety (1976: 131–3), Jameson takes a longer historical view. In *Company Parade*, David Renn, an ex-soldier turned advertising copywriter, observes in 1919 that 'a bad treaty doesn't settle anything – except the causes of the next war' (Jameson, 1934: 99). For Jameson, the inevitability of a second world war does not begin with the inexorable rise of European fascism, rather it is most profoundly located in the botched closure of the First World War.

Over the course of the decade, the prospect of war steadily encroached upon the terrain of fiction. Enterprising detective-story writers sent their heroes to avert it (Blake, 1939), while less optimistic novelists from Rosamund Lehmann (1936) to Elizabeth Bowen (1938/1962) reflected a complex climate of uncertainty and lost direction. George Orwell's Gordon Comstock even, temporarily, longs for what he imagines will be a liberating apocalypse

(1936/1989: 93, 257). But beyond this tangential engagement with the impending crisis, there existed a whole genre of fiction dubbed the 'next war' novel (Ceadel, 1980; Croft, 1990). Women were amongst the many contributors to this most topical of literary forms, although writers such as Naomi Mitchison and Storm Jameson were more concerned with the moral implications and the aftermath of conflict than with the graphic depiction of gassed corpses. Indeed, Mitchison's *We have been Warned* (1935), in spite of its title, is not exclusively or wholly a 'next war' novel. The majority of its pages offer a classic Mitchison blend of myth, folklore and the supernatural with documentary social realism. The novel follows the lives of a group of middle-class, left-wing intellectuals as they try to put theory into practice, experimenting with communism, free love and art. However, the instability of their world is radically revealed in the final pages of the novel where the optimism of Dione's pregnancy is set against a series of nightmare visions of the future. In contrast to this prophetic approach, Jameson's *In the Second Year* (1936) explores not the threat, nor even the advent, but rather the consolidation of a fascist dictatorship in Britain. Here the domestic details and spiritual confusion of living in a familiar yet utterly alien world are explored in an impressively understated manner. The story is narrated by Andy Hillier, who is both a part of and yet detached from the events in Britain. An academic living in Norway he returns to a Britain ruled by the 'National State Party' under its leader Francis Hillier – who turns out, somewhat uncomfortably, to be Andy's first cousin. This is a radically altered Britain, governed by a subdued state of fear and a system of euphemistically entitled 'training camps'. The parallels with Nazi Germany are not difficult to detect. The dicator Francis Hillier exudes a Hitlerian magnetism that draws people towards him into a system of simple unquestioning belief, while his right-hand man Richard Sacker represents the initially useful but rapidly obsolescent Ernst Röhm. As Andy is interrogated by his erstwhile first cousin, he witnesses the mechanism of personal metamorphosis that has brought Hillier to power:

> He had begun to work himself into a voluptuous excitement. His eyes were glazed and turned upward, and his gestures became looser, like a drunken man. I saw the saviour of his country emerge from him and take full possession. Even in my desperation I was partly fascinated by the sight . . .
>
> This, I thought, wearily, is how he did it. People wanted to believe. More than they wanted anything they wanted belief. Just that – belief. Not reasons or facts. The narcotic of belief. (Jameson, 1936b: 259–60; ellipsis mine)

Most painful, however, within Jameson's world is the perceived impossibility of the situation. Andy cannot reconcile the world he has known with the surreal scenario now confronting him:

> As most men in my circumstances would, I believed in the reality of the world I was born into, a world kept in order by a known compromise between force and goodwill. Offenders were punished lawfully. A man was not shot in a room with an oilcloth-covered sofa, a coloured calendar on the wall, and a mahogany table bearing a trayful of broken cups. (Jameson, 1936b: 252)

Yet, in spite of the prevalence of popular fictive accounts of imminent world destruction, it is difficult to gauge the exact extent of public awareness or anxiety regarding the prospect of a second world war. Tom Harrisson's *Living Through the Blitz* suggests an all-party political anxiety about both the threat of aerial attack and the likely civilian response to such an event:

> A continuing, deeply ingrained contempt for the civilian masses had major effects, too, on preparations for the receipt of bombs at the British end. The proletariat were bound to crack, run, panic, even go mad, lacking the courage and self-discipline of their masters or those regimented in the forces. The alternative view – that a Belfast plumber might manage as well as an Irish Guards officer – was rarely seriously advanced. (Harrisson, 1976: 22)

In contrast to this alarmism, the evidence of the early years of Mass-Observation suggests that 'few took the grim published messages either wholly or lastingly to heart' (Harrisson, 1976: 26) – not least because of an ingrained distrust of the very authority that dispatched the warnings. The historical evidence of popular awareness is, then, difficult to decode – as, indeed, is the literary. For some writers it was a case not of too little but of too much trust in an omnipotent authority. This belief that someone, somewhere was taking care of everything is reflected in the early chapters of Margery Allingham's *The Oaken Heart* (1941), and in spite of the propagandist intent of the work, the dominant tone of book swiftly becomes one of betrayal. How could a trusted government have let things come to such a pass? Thankfully, from Allingham's point of view, the 'fixed compass' (1941a: 169) of Churchill was waiting to steer Britain to safety – and once the rightful leader is installed, the book soon subsides into the customary wartime trope of 'business as usual'.

It seems clear, then, that public awareness of, and attitudes to, the prospect of war varied considerably. It is none the less difficult to deny that the air of the 1930s was thick with a sense of uncertainty. What was also uncertain was the status of women's writing within a literary establishment that consciously privileged masculine experience. In the introduction to her collection of women's writing from the Second World War, Jenny Hartley quotes Cyril Connolly's rejection of 'domestic' experience:

> We take the line that experiences connected with the blitz, the shopping queues, the home front, deserted wives, deceived husbands, broken homes, dull jobs, bad schools, group squabbles, are so much a picture of our ordinary lives that unless the workmanship is outstanding we are prejudiced against them. (Connolly, *Horizon*, January 1944; quoted in Hartley 1994: 8)

The woman's perspective, Hartley observes, was 'largely outlawed by the literary world of the time' (Hartley, 1994: 8). Connolly's prejudices, however, were not confined to the 1940s. This catalogue of the unacceptable could equally have been applied to the 1930s, where the domestic can be seen as one of the primary focalisers of the paradoxical tension between war and peace that characterised the pre-war dynamic.

I suggested in Chapter 1 that the onset of war is marked by radical changes in the familiar demarcations of role and place. Value systems are not so much revised as reallocated, and the boundaries of 'masculine' and 'feminine' behaviour are redrawn in accordance with the needs of the moment. Thus, while wartime issues of *Horizon* continued to abhor the domestic, *Penguin New Writing* opened its arms to the minutiae of day-to-day life. This transition, however, does not represent a victory over dominant androcentric attitudes, nor even a re-evaluation of specifically female experience, rather it is indicative of the newly 'active' and uncertain nature of home-front life. The literary value of shopping exists in direct proportion to the perceived dangers of that occupation. As the home front became fit for heroes, so it also became fit to print.

This transition becomes all the more remarkable when viewed from the 1930s, a decade in which the domestic was the object of unprecedented revulsion and ridicule. Gordon Comstock, the 'hero' of George Orwell's *Keep the Aspidistra Flying* (1936), is obsessed and oppressed by what he sees as the soul-destroying forces of advertising and domesticity. Advertising services and symbolises the superficial business ethic that had triumphed while all others lost in the First World War, and is depicted by Orwell as a mindless, hungry deception practised on an unwitting population. Domesticity, meanwhile, is represented as the province of women, and in Orwell's case, it assumes almost phallic proportions. This remorseless domesticity threatens to consume and defeat Gordon's cherished desire to be an heroic, angry individual. Such a vision of the domestic was remarkably widespread in the 1930s. Alison Light comments on the characteristic Woolworth-phobia of many male writers, concluding that:

> What is striking too ... is the sense of wounded masculine pride which emanates from these writers. Driven into exile, many modernist prophets and minor *cognoscenti* lament both the proletarianisation and the domestication of national life. Since war, whatever its horrors, is manly, there is something both lower-class and effeminate about peacetime. (Light, 1991: 7)

The emasculated man is a central metaphor of the 1930s. From the wounded soldiers of Vera Brittain's *Testament of Youth* (1933) to the economically emasculated unemployed on the periphery of Jameson's *Mirror in Darkness*, the postwar period became associated with the demise of some mythical masculinity. However, while women writers such as Jameson laid the blame for this impotence firmly at the feet of war itself, male writers tended to portray it as a product of peace. The perception of a national 'feminisation' was not confined to fiction. When Ngaio Marsh united Inspector Alleyn with Agatha Troy, the *Times Literary Supplement* reviewer recoiled in horror:

> *Death in a White Tie* has only one serious defect. The Chief Inspector is made to pursue his love affair with the lady artist unprepossessingly called Troy which began in an earlier novel. It would be a pity if the example set by Miss Sayers with Lord Peter Wimsey of entangling her detective of seemingly settled and delightful bachelor habits in a serious-minded love affair were to be regularly followed by all writers of detective stories. (*Times Literary Supplement*, 10 September, 1938)

Perhaps a light-minded dalliance with a decorative object would be more acceptable?

The snare of domesticity everywhere awaited the unwary male, and in Gordon Comstock's outcry, sex, death and advertising are monstrously conflated:

> You can see our whole civilization written there. The imbecility, the emptiness, the desolation! You can't look at it without thinking of French letters and machine-guns. Do you know that the other day I was actually wishing war would break out? I was longing for it – praying for it, almost. (Orwell, 1936/1989: 93)

Gordon's response to the looming face of his nemesis Rolland Butter is on one level absurd, but it is also typical of the contradictory impulses of the 1930s. Storm Jameson's ex-soldier David Renn yearns for action – even the

futile action of briefly opening a doomed newspaper – to relieve him from
the impotence of postwar passivity:

> Renn did not believe in this ridiculous paper which was to blow up
> society, but he was going to work for it until all hours and to give up his
> evenings, and that with joy. The thing was to have found something to do
> at last. An exquisite happiness and relief filled him. (Jameson, 1934: 99)

Action provides relief from the necessity and responsibility of thought – a relief
provided on a national scale in 1939. However, a more disturbing example of
this developing opposition between a virile activity and a compromised passivity
is found in the chilling paradox that marks the poet Julian Bell's rejection of
pacifism. Described by Samuel Hynes as being 'belligerently' anti-war, Bell
declares that 'the war-resistance movements of my generation will in the end
succeed in putting down war – by force if necessary' (quoted in Hynes, 1976:
195). This seems painfully ironic. A generation's perceived disempowerment
by war can only be rectified by the (mis)perceived empowerment of a
second war.

However, for the women writers considered here, there was no danger of
conflating a desire for action with a desire for war. For Dorothy L. Sayers,
Stevie Smith and Virginia Woolf the prelude was a period of intense change,
and amongst the common trends identifiable in their works is a growing
awareness of the threat of war. Their respective responses to this situation,
however, can be sharply contrasted. For Virginia Woolf it was a period in
which writing was, at first, intensely difficult. She struggled for five years
over the composition of *The Years*, a finely crafted novel which attempts
to challenge the phallocratic view of patriarchal history. The completion of
this novel, in 1937, only became possible after Woolf's decision to divide
in two her original vision (which has since been published as *The Pargiters*).
The second part of 'The Pargiters' became *Three Guineas* (1938), a scathing
critique of domestic and political tyranny, rapidly written in an new spirit
of anger described by Caroline Heilbrun as an 'extraordinary release' (1989:
126). Thus in Virginia Woolf's immediately pre-war work there is a complex
dialectic of fear and daring which combined to produce her most explicitly
political feminist work.

The prospect of war also significantly changed the nature of Dorothy L.
Sayers's literary work. In 1937 Lord Peter Wimsey and Harriet Vane were
dispatched to retirement. A serial narrative that had steadily evolved over
nearly fifteen years was brought to an end in the closure of domestic bliss.
Sayers went on to write more 'serious' works, in particular the wartime radio
success *The Man Born to be King*; but my concern is less with Sayers's long
postponed transition from the 'triviality' of detection to the weightier matter

of Christianity, than with the nature of her disposal of Peter and Harriet. There is a transition from male to female evident in the final Wimsey novels that is not unconnected to Woolf's movement from *history* to *herstory* in *The Years*. This gradual marginalisation of the hero is one manifestation of the state of flux and uncertainty that grew apace as the 1930s drew to a close. It is worth noting that this transition from male to female is not confined to women writers. Nicolas Blake's 1939 novel *The Smiler with the Knife* sees the almost total marginalisation of his detective hero Nigel Strangeways, in favour of his intrepid wife Georgia. In almost single-handedly saving Britain from a fascist takeover, Georgia's exploits prefigure the many fantasies of agency that would be enacted during the war.

The disruption of gender is also central to Stevie Smith's 1938 novel *Over the Frontier*. The reader is presented with a nightmare transition, in which the wilfully undisciplined, meandering mind of Pompey Casmilus assumes the secretive, deceptive and brutal uniform of the spy. Pompey appears to take on or reveal something more than the semblance of masculinity, and within the novel, Smith weaves the endemic uncertainty of the 1930s into a frightening vision of spiritual decay. This bizarre narrative of apocalyptic absurdity is arguably this period's most chilling indictment of war.

Thus, in spite of their strongly contrasting literary and political allegiances, the writers of the prelude are linked by profound concerns with questions of gender and power. Their novels may utilise very different techniques to explore the prospect of war, but within all these pre-war texts – and within those of the wartime 'storm' – there exists a story which cannot be told. Behind the wartime fantasies of escape and the confident pre-war predictions, there lies a substratum of fear and anxiety that manifests itself in the dislocation, and even the fragmentation, of the text. The difference between prelude and storm is perhaps only one of degree. The direct engagement with an unthinkable future that characterises Woolf's *Three Guineas* and Smith's *Over the Frontier* is not qualitatively different from the strategies of avoidance I consider in Part Two. Both disguise a profound anxiety about a problematic present and an uncertain future – but, paradoxically, within the Cassandra cries of the prelude, there exists a belief in the possibility of change that is absent from the later wartime texts. While the war remains a theoretical proposition, prophets have a vital role to play. When war becomes reality, they are silenced: their predictions have materialised and survival lies in evading rather than imagining the full weight of this reality. The first part of this book considers the utterances of three prewar Cassandras. Sometimes direct and sometimes oblique, their works combine ominous prophecy with pleas for change. Their visions of the future are not uniform, but their texts are profoundly and inescapably connected through their anticipation, and confrontation, of the Second World War.

NOTES

1. The problems arising from this exclusively masculine focus are perhaps less to do with critics such as Hynes and Bergonzi (1978), who at least make their agendas clear, than with the absence of primary materials from which to build alternative perspectives on the 1930s. Robin Skelton's *Poetry of the Thirties* (1964), which has long been the standard collection, is almost totally devoid of women writers. However, the publication of Jane Dowson's (1995) anthology of women poets from the period should help to redress the balance, as in critical terms should the appearance of Jan Montfiore's work on the 1930s.
2. The extent of female marginalisation and the power of a masculine critical orthodoxy is ably illustrated by John Lehmann's 1940 anthology *New Writing in Europe*. In an index of authors comprising nearly 150 writers, there are only seven women.

3

Safety in Sanctity:
Dorothy L. Sayers's Marriage of Convenience

I read detective stories, too. They were about the only thing I could read. All the others had the war in them – or love . . . or some damn' thing I didn't want to think about.

Dorothy L. Sayers, *The Unpleasantness at the Bellona Club*

We are lost and unhappy in a universe that seems to make no sense, and cling to science and machines and detective fiction, just because, within their limited fields, the problems do work out, and the end corresponds to the intention.

Dorothy L. Sayers, *Begin Here: A War-Time Essay*

The exploits of Lord Peter Wimsey are not generally regarded as a narrative of war. Yet reading them as such can augment our understanding, not only of the novels themselves, but also of the tensions and strategies of the late 1930s. The threat of war was ubiquitous, and in the fiction of Dorothy L. Sayers it is manifested through a complex dialectic of fear and resignation, abhorrence and patriotism. Sayers's work articulates both an acceptance of the need for war and a rejection of the nature of war. This contradiction, in some respects typical of the Second World War, creates in her work a series of tensions which are not so much resolved as overriden by her persistent emphasis upon the importance of individual responsibility. To this end, her novels, whose dominant moral theme could perhaps be described as 'all things in moderation', present a rejection of extremes, be it of belief or behaviour, and a movement towards the stability Sayers believed was inherent in the idea of tradition. None the less, this stability was more easily desired than achieved. As the increasingly complex Wimsey novels draw closer to the critical moment of war, Sayers's desire for security is persistently undermined by an undercurrent of chaos and absurdity. Tradition and modernity, the old and the new, come face to face in a paradoxical prelude to the Second World War.

R. L. Stock and Barbara Stock (1979) have observed that Sayers's early villains tended to be professional, gifted individuals, who turned almost thoughtlessly to crime because they considered themselves above the dictates of conventional morality. Opposed to tradition, their amoral intellectualism was no compensation for their lack of humanity. As Sayers's criminals became more ambiguous figures, the weight of their crimes mitigated by outstanding circumstances, so Lord Peter evolved into a more complex and less superhuman character. Beginning as a collection of clichéd surfaces, he was gradually given the depths of a personality until, by *Gaudy Night* (1935), he seemed to have attained a balance between his still remarkable outer strengths and his manifold inner weaknesses. This dichotomy foreshadows the dynamic at the centre of the final completed Wimsey novel, *Busman's Honeymoon* (1937), in which the external circumstances of war demanded the reconciliation of a self divided by the conflicting demands of the private and public spheres. It can thus be said that, as a body of texts, the Wimsey novels chart a progress from an outward-looking but selfish denial of the private, through a more inward acknowledgement of personal need, to the recognition of and submission to the law of public service – represented here by the duty of war.

With the notable exception of a couple of minor reincarnations, Lord Peter Wimsey lived from 1923 to 1937. His arrival, development and demise were all contained within the brief twenty-one-year respite that separated the two world wars, and indeed, war casts its shadow over the entire corpus of Wimsey novels. From the embittered veterans of the Bellona Club to Harriet's fear of the Abyssinian crisis, it leaves its unmistakable stamp. 'I can't help it. I suppose I've never really been right since the war' (Sayers, 1937b/1988: 379) confesses Peter in the grip of the depression which attacks him after the conclusion of every murder investigation. The earliest depiction of Peter's shell-shock is found in *Whose Body* (1923), and from this point Sayers creates a careful and effective portrait of the survivor as hero. Wimsey's neurosis stems from the guilt of the First World War officer charged with the task of repeatedly authorising the death of his own men. It manifests itself as a fear of responsibility which at its peak left him, in his mother's words:

so dreadfully afraid to go to sleep . . . and he couldn't give an order,
not even to the servants . . . I suppose if you've been giving orders for
nearly four years to people to go and get blown to pieces it gives you
a – what does one call it nowadays? – an inhibition or an exhibition, or
something, of nerves. (1937b/1988: 379)

Detection is an occupation which satisfies Wimsey's intellect; but, as the end
product of his investigations is not simply the apprehension but the death
of the convicted criminal, it also remorselessly returns him to the same crisis
of responsibility from which he is trying to escape.

This pattern indicates in Wimsey a compulsion to repeat the trauma similar
to that which Elaine Showalter has identified in Siegfried Sassoon. Showalter
sees the symptoms of war neurosis as a physical manifestation of gender anxieties
intensified beyond control by the demands of combat:

> If it was the essence of manliness not to complain, then shell shock was the
> body language of masculine complaint, a disguised male protest, not only
> against the war, but against the concept of manliness itself. (Showalter,
> 1987a: 64)

Sassoon spent the second half of 1917 in the care of the psychologist
W. H. R. Rivers at Craiglockhart hospital outside Edinburgh. Rivers was
an early advocate of Freud and the use of psychoanalytic techniques in the
treatment of hysterical symptoms – into which category Sassoon's protest
against the 'political errors and insincerities' of an 'evil and unjust' war was
conveniently slotted. A pioneer of the 'talking cure', Rivers's approach to
shell-shock was both more sophisticated and more humane than that of the
majority of his contemporaries, but as an officer of the Royal Army Medical
Corps this humanity was tempered by the demands of a war economy.
Showalter describes Rivers's 'talking cure' as a strategy to emphasise the
femininity of Sassoon's emotional response to war. Shamed by the rational
masculinity of Rivers's discourse, Sassoon made a guilty return to the troops he
had 'deserted'. The immediate impact of Rivers's psychology is evident from
Sassoon's letters. On 17 October 1917 he writes to Lady Ottoline Morrell that
having 'made my protest on behalf of my fellow fighters . . . the fittest thing
for me to do is to go back and share their ills' (Sassoon, 1983: 190). The
long-term effects of Sassoon's trauma, however, would seem more accurately
to be reflected in his postwar literary inability to put the past to rest.[1]

Sayers indicates from the start that Wimsey is constantly reliving the horrors
of his past experience – there are nightmares, outbursts of compulsive dangerous
activity and an overwhelming blank exhaustion. The process of detection
both distracts Wimsey's attention from the ghosts of the past while leading

him inexorably back into the reworking of the very depression he seeks to assuage:

> It's a hobby to me, you see. I took it up when the bottom of things was rather knocked out of me, because it was so damned exciting, and the worst of it is, I enjoy it – up to a point. If it was all on paper I'd enjoy every bit of it. (Sayers, 1923/1989: 122)

A constructive model for the analysis of Peter's behaviour is provided by Dianne S. Hunter's essay, 'Hysteria, psychoanalysis and feminism: the case of Anna O' (1985). In her description of Bertha Pappenheim's hysterical symptoms, observed to have originated in a rejection of 'the cultural identity offered her' (1985: 100), Hunter surmises that Bertha 'restaged the origins of her symptoms in order to undo them. This is ritual as Catharsis.' (1985: 102).

Detection for Peter is 'ritual as catharsis'. Wimsey recreates, through the action of detection, the situation of responsibility for another's death. The repetition of this action provides the opportunity to re-enact the moral dilemma, but it cannot remove the guilt. In consequence, Wimsey remains suspended in a form of 'emotional limbo', a state of paralysis disguised by the mask of his foppish façade. This front acts as an hysterical symptom comparable to Pappenheim's loss of her native German speech and her fluency in the foreign tongues of English, French and Italian. In Hunter's words, 'She made a spectacle of herself in order to resolve the tension between her guilt and her desire to escape familial exploitation' (1985: 101–2). Wimsey seeks escape not from familial, but from social, exploitation (although the one is perhaps merely a microcosmic reflection of the other). He too is making a spectacle of himself as the 'silly ass about town', and his natural language of seriousness is masked by the meaningless babble of his affected, self-conscious idiocy. Unfortunately, until the creation of Harriet Vane, there is nobody able or willing to translate the symptoms of Wimsey's hysteria, and this translation is essential if the endless cathartic ritual is to be turned into an effective release of long-repressed anxieties.

Ironically, in the context of escapism, the fabled 'purpose' of detective fiction, Wimsey's investigations can be seen as doubly cathartic. They re-enact and release emotions not only for the detective, but also for the reader, who endlessly consumes the same narrative of danger and its resolution, creating a fantasy of agency in an uncertain world. For Wimsey, however, the intellectual exercise of detection cannot exorcise the persistent presence of a reality founded on the knowledge of pain and death, and the ultimate manifestation of this reality is war. In what can be seen as a meta-narrative running throughout the individual puzzles that disguise it, Peter's war story awaits detection. Appropriately the full extent of his trauma is not revealed until the final novel. None the less, the clues are there throughout Sayers's serial narrative, and a sophisticated groundwork is laid in the deceptively straightforward debut *Whose Body?*

The beginning of the novel does not augur well. The criticisms of class snobbery frequently levelled at Sayers are easily justified by the opening pages of *Whose Body*. The unfortunate Mr Thipps, in whose bath a naked body has been found, is patronisingly discussed through a catalogue of diminuitives ranging from the 'little architect man' (1923/1989: 12) to the 'poor little beast' (1923/1989: 13). Lord Peter also seems an improbable creation. Caught between two hobbies, he is at his most affected; consoling the distraught Mr Thipps he comments:

> 'I'm sure it must have been uncommonly distressin',' said Lord Peter, sympathetically, 'especially comin' like that before breakfast. Hate anything tiresome happenin' before breakfast. Takes a man at such a confounded disadvantage, what?' (1923/1989: 14)

However, having established the credentials of her aristocratic detective, Sayers then begins the process of developing and explaining Wimsey, making her hero both more complex and more likeable. The characterisation of Wimsey properly begins once the process of investigation is over. While sitting in front of the fire, late at night, Peter finally feels the pieces of the puzzle fall into place. As the tension of the plot moves towards a resolution, Sayers immediately expands the narrative through the tantalising introduction of another Wimsey. This first glimpse of his past, and more complex, personality is provided by a brief shell-shock scene. Wimsey's breakdown follows a childhood memory which synthesises the disparate elements of his adult guilt. His memory is of the curiosity which prompted him to tug at a table-cloth until an entire breakfast service crashed to the floor 'in one stupendous ruin' and of 'the horrified face of the butler, and the screams of a lady guest' (1923/1989: 132). The product of his curiosity was pain. This is combined with the guilt that he feels as a figure of authority sending men to their death. This typical experience of guilt could also be seen as a strategy for coping with the loss of individual agency commensurate with war. The belief in responsibility for death represents a particularly desperate fantasy of control. None the less, for Wimsey the action of detection and the action of participation in war have a common end product: death on the battlefield becomes interchangeable with death on the scaffold. The result is a vision of responsibility in which the curiosity that provokes Wimsey's detection causes only the pain of others.

The weight that Sayers attaches to the idea of individual responsibility and the social obligations of class, status and education are also evident from the outset.[2] In *Whose Body?* Wimsey's fear of responsibility (a fear inappropriate to his class), is manifest in his amateur status – encapsulated by the never to be repeated overlooking of evidence later discovered by the policeman, Parker. It is Parker's duty to remind Peter of his responsibilities and to speak the home truths which, combined with Wimsey's identification of the culprit, bring on the attack of shell-shock:

> You want to be consistent, you want to look pretty . . . Well, you can't do it like that. Life's not a football match. You want to be a sportsman. You can't be a sportsman. You're a responsible person. (1923/1989: 124)

Wimsey never entirely loses this anachronistic desire to see fair play, and on one level he is a relic of a pre-war past where 'the stridently athletic ethos of the late Victorian and Edwardian public school produced an atmosphere in which soldiering and games were equated' (Cannadine, 1981: 195). A belief in the nobility of death could scarcely emerge unscathed from the carnage of the First World War, but it could be argued that elements of this national heroic ideal were transmuted into a hardly less destructive code of individual loyalty. Sacrifice co-existed with the acknowledgement of its futility – duty continued to be done, but it was performed less out of deference to authority than out of respect for comradeship. It is interesting to find this vein of 'fair play' and 'honour' still being dissected over twenty years later by the Second World War poet Keith Douglas. In his 1943 poem 'Sportsmen' (Douglas, 1979) he sounds the death knell of a class of soldier already presumed dead. Focusing on the contrast between the power of the killer and the vulnerability of the individual, Douglas goes on to catalogue the tragically outmoded attitudes of heroism that are, once again, exploded by the reality of war. Wimsey, however, seems caught between the cynicism of Douglas's killer and the naivety of his victims. In the context of this transition, Alison Light's distinction between an older generation of 'vintage port' and a new generation of 'bubbly' is useful for identifying the contradictions of Sayers's hero. Armistice Day at the Bellona Club places Wimsey firmly in the ranks of the younger, anti-heroic generation (1928b/1989: 18), but later in the same novel his culinary values (the rejection of lobster and champagne) are used to symbolise a clear resistance to modernity.

The framework that Sayers establishes for the exploration of Wimsey's shell-shock corresponds to contemporary medical assumptions regarding the incidence of male hysteria. Showalter's *The Female Malady* convincingly demonstrates the class-based assumptions that distinguished the diagnosis, explication and treatment of hysteria in officers from that of its occurrence amongst the other ranks:

> In sum, then, the hysterical soldier was seen as simple, emotional, unthinking, passive, suggestible, dependent and weak – very much

the same constellation of traits associated with the hysterical woman – while the complex and overworked neurasthenic officer was much closer to an acceptable, even heroic male ideal. Interestingly, mutism, which was the most common shell-shock symptom among soldiers and non-commissioned officers, was very rare among officers. To be reduced to a feminine state of powerlessness, frustration, and dependency led to a deprivation of speech as well, just as it had for Anna O. (Showalter 1987b: 175)

Showalter is perhaps inaccurate when she limits this feminisation to the lower ranks. War disempowers in a much less class-specific sense and it is only the symptoms of this lack that can be catalogued according to status. What is clear, however, is that war disrupts the construction of gender. It exceeds and transgresses the boundaries of class and education and makes a mockery of pre-war assumptions of masculine superiority. Encoded within Sayers's novels are the ambiguous and contradictory results of war's disruption. A faith in the social responsibility of the educated (rather than the strictly upper) classes, channelled into a belief in the integrity of the individual, is combined with the creation of a hero whose self is clearly not a unified and coherent whole, but who is instead a fragmented, unstable and bisexual subject protected by the façade of a fluctuating defensive mask.

In 1935 Sayers added the 'Paul Austin Delargardie' postscript, which appeared as a biographical note in later editions of her novels. Ostensibly claiming to fill in the missing pieces for readers attempting to construct the puzzle of the 'real' Wimsey, the note itself is something of a red herring:

In 1918 he was blown up and buried in a shell-hole near Caudry, and that left him with a bad nervous breakdown, lasting, on and off, for two years. After that, he set himself up in a flat in Piccadilly, with the man Bunter (who had been his sergeant and was, and is, devoted to him), and started out to put himself together again.

As befits his role in the meta-narrative, Delargardie is a distinctly unreliable narrator. The most significant omissions of his story make it a defence of the social status quo that suggests that Sayers was perhaps a more perceptive critic of class than is usually assumed. Delagardie completely ignores the central role played by Bunter in Peter's recovery – an assumption of control in an isolated, closed environment which is reminiscent of J. M. Barrie's role-reversal satire *The Admirable Crichton* (1902/1914). Interestingly it is Peter's mother who finally acknowledges the debt to Bunter in a conversation with Harriet (who has become the detective of Peter's story) at the end of *Busman's Honeymoon*.

Clearly it is only amongst women that such a potentially threatening topic as the inversion of the dictates of class can be discussed!

That Wimsey did not put himself together, but was in fact reassembled by another, suggests that his recovery should rather be read as a rebirth. In the case of Wimsey's postwar recovery, it is Bunter who assumes the nurturing role normally associated with the biological mother. Entering into the womb-like environs of Peter's darkened room 'he turned on the lights and drew the curtains and took charge from that moment. I believe he managed so that for months Peter never had to give an order about so much as a soda-syphon.' (1937b/1988: 380). Once established in a new London flat, Bunter protects Peter from unwelcome intrusions and gradually nurtures him back to a state in which he is able to face the outside world. In the early novels however, Peter remains safely under the cover of Bunter's protective wing. Thus with Bunter as mother and Peter as child, the two exist as a self-contained pre-symbolic dyad protected from the world through the creation of a mask, a façade which some critics have found almost too convincing; P. D. James, for example:

> the change from the Wooster-like, monocled, man-about-Town of *Whose Body?* to the sensitive guilt-oppressed scholar sobbing in his wife's lap at the end of *Busman's Honeymoon* is less a development than a metamorphosis. (Brabazon, 1981: xiv)

The extent of the change, seen like this, is enormous, but it is not a metamorphosis. Margaret P. Hannay's perceptive essay 'Harriet's influence on the characterisation of Lord Peter Wimsey' suggests that in *Gaudy Night* Sayers uses Harriet's perspective to facilitate the rewriting of the earlier psychologically shallow Peter. Quoting Harriet's confusion as to why it had taken so long for the inner Peter to be revealed, Hannay concludes that:

> By her skillful use of Harriet's perspective Sayers lulls the reader into thinking there is good reason for *them* not to have seen this side of Peter before. The truth is, of course, that these weaknesses did not exist before this novel, but they have been skillfully projected back into the past. (Hannay, 1979b: 48; Hannay's emphasis)

This is a persuasive argument, and Sayers undoubtedly makes good use of Harriet as a narrative device for explaining and augmenting Peter's personality. However, to situate the entire creation of Wimsey within the pages of *Gaudy Night* is to ignore the evolutionary details that emerge from the eight preceding novels. Even to suggest, as Sayers does, that the conclusion of *Strong Poison* (1930) was the turning point, is an unnecessary act of closure. The technique described by Hannay is only possible because the gaps are there to be filled, and in consequence, the sequence of novels as a whole resists the imposition of a definitive moment of transition. Sayers herself observed that Peter had always had the 'embryonic buds of a character of sorts. Even at the beginning he had not been the complete silly ass: he had only played the silly ass, which was not the same thing' (Sayers, 1937a: 211).

Thus the Wimsey stripped bare at the end of *Busman's Honeymoon* was always potentially present, and the 'monocled, man-about-Town' can be seen as a construct, designed to protect through the creation of an elaborate charade, in which initially only Bunter is complicit. Bunter is the essential component of Peter's mask. Although acting the part of the dependant, in actuality he bears the responsibility for his 'child'. The extent to which Bunter parents Peter is clear from the shell-shock scene, in which Peter is dosed and put to bed. Fifteen years later the roles have not changed as Bunter confides to his mother on the eve of Peter's wedding, 'I took the liberty to prescribe a dose of bromide and got him to sleep at last' (1937b/1988: 12).

It is only after seven years and four novels that Sayers disrupts the secure homosexual economy of the Wimsey/Bunter dyad and begins what is both a heterosexual reclamation (the beginning of a movement towards conformity and security which will culminate in marriage), and the beginning of an Oedipal struggle that reintroduces the child, Wimsey, to the wider social environment. This complex proceeding begins with the advent of the father – Harriet Vane.[3] Her appearance disrupts the comfortable mother child dyad because she brings with her the structures of the patriarchal social order. Ironically it is Harriet who reintroduces Peter to an awareness of the weight of the law, even though (or perhaps especially because) her first appearance is as a powerless victim of that law. Once Harriet has been introduced, Wimsey has to 'get serious' – he has to pay attention to the outside world, put away childish things and leave the security of Bunter's nurturing environment – in order to save her from death. *Strong Poison* thus becomes Wimsey's mirror stage. Leaving the prison, exhilarated and excited after his first meeting with Harriet, Wimsey's vanity causes him to stop:

> He paused before a shop window to get a surreptitious view of his own reflection. A large coloured window-bill caught his eye:
> GREAT SPECIAL OFFER
> ONE MONTH ONLY
> 'Oh, God!' he said, softly, sobered at once. 'One month – four weeks – thirty-one days. There isn't much time. And I don't know where to begin.' (1930/1989: 45)

As he stares at his own reflection, the unchallenged unity of Wimsey's world collapses and, entering into the symbolic order, he becomes at once aware of the awesome imperative of time.

Harriet, then, provides the initial impetus for the breaking down of existing structures and façades, but this process is accelerated and exacerbated by Wimsey's need for security in the face of a growing political threat. By the time of the publication of *Gaudy Night* in 1935, this uncertainty had crystallised into a clear and unequivocal acknowledgement of the proximity of war:

> I thought – at one point we all thought – something might be going to happen. All the old filthy uproar. I got as far as saying to Bunter one night: 'It's coming, it's here; back to the army again sergeant.' (1935/1990: 268)

The gradual revelations of *Gaudy Night* function in accordance with the process of a psychoanalytic cure. The 'talking cure' of Anna O., used to such effect on Siegfried Sassoon, has its beginnings in *Strong Poison* and culminates in the disclosures of *Gaudy Night* and the discoveries of *Busman's Honeymoon*. Harriet, in addition to her role as the detective of Peter's story, also becomes the analyst of his narrative. On another level, however, the dynamics of psychoanalysis are also present within the process of detection itself. In her analysis of Agatha Christie, Alison Light has convincingly united the processes of detection and psychoanalysis. Discussing *Appointment with Death* (1938) she concludes that 'Both the murder and the crime of family life are to be solved by talking' (Light, 1991: 103). Wimsey, long unable to talk, has taken instead to detection. In this context, his compulsion to repeat the trauma behind his shell-shock also becomes a compulsion to review the evidence. A repeated search for answers to relieve him of his guilt can be seen as a displaced attempt at self-analysis. Peter wants, but is unable, to cure himself.

However, the analyst/analysand dynamic is not confined to the Peter/ Harriet relationship. Harriet too is troubled by unresolved tensions and the ghosts of the past, and in *Gaudy Night* she must also retrace her steps through a return to the security of a pre-symbolic dyad. In *Gaudy Night*, the paradigm of the secure homosexual environment that exists between Peter and Bunter, is recreated and paralleled by the microcosm of order and integrity that is college society. The contrasting uncertainty of the outside world, destabilised by the threat of war, makes explicit the perils of engagement with the patriarchal symbolic order. Just as Peter took refuge in the dyadic security of his relationship with Bunter, so Harriet would willingly have retreated into the pre-symbolic represented by the women's college. Shrewesbury College serves as mother to Harriet, nurturing her as Bunter has nurtured Peter.[4] Indeed, it is only after Harriet has been 'reborn' through her return to Shrewesbury College that she feels able to undertake the social and emotional responsibility of a relationship with Peter. Yet these enclosed environments can only offer an illusion of security. While Peter and Harriet can refuse or delay the transition into the social, they cannot ignore the disruption of their security by the encroachment of the 'law' in the form of war. War has the capacity to enforce commitment to the symbolic order at the same time as it threatens the very existence of that order.

The multiple layering of selves created by Sayers complicates the unravelling of the interaction between Peter, Harriet and war. As a victim of war, the Peter beneath the mask retains the emotional state loosely defined as feminine. His silly-ass persona, while outwardly effeminate, served as adequate protection against unwelcome intrusions, making it in effect a traditionally masculine defence against the danger of being seen to be less than appropriately stoical. However, this strategy can also be identified as the typically female defence of the masquerade (Riviere, 1929). Stephen Heath (1986) suggests the Lacanian term 'parade' for the incidence of this male display, but it seems simpler to apply Riviere's original term of masquerade to Peter as well as Harriet. Although the threat of war places their respective gender identities in a state of flux, both Peter and Harriet are, in one sense, feminised by war. Superficially war's disruption might seem to enable Harriet, providing increased agency in proportion to Wimsey's increasingly ambiguous position. However, as Higonnet's image of the double helix shows, a direct inversion of masculine and feminine norms is impossible (see Chapter 1). Harriet is empowered only within the terms of the language of peace. Within the new, and superior, discourse of war, her gains are effectively meaningless. Thus in the equation of war, both Peter and Harriet are rendered passive and, in consequence, both must ultimately resort to the masquerade of gender conformity as a strategy for survival.

The issue of conformity is raised by this psychological equation of shell-shock with hysteria, and its implications can be illuminated by further recourse to Showalter's model of Rivers and Sassoon. Showalter stresses that Rivers's job, irrespective of the love with which it was performed, was to repair the damage so as to return soldiers to the war from which their hysteria had removed them.[5] The completion of an hysteric's cure, then, necessarily involves a return to the conditions that preceded and provoked the symptoms of the illness. Treatment therefore becomes a denial of the right to escape – the cure is an ironic negation of the imperative of survival. The cure also represents a return to 'normality' – a normality defined by a patriarchal symbolic that exists through the oppression of the non-conforming Other and whose *modus operandi* is war. Nineteenth-century women, the 'archetypal' hysterics, were emphatically made aware of the obligation of conformity. Their body language of hysterical resistance represented an unacceptable challenge to patriarchal hegemony. Male hysteria constitutes an even greater threat to the social contract through its blatant illustration that this 'dis-order' is not the other of woman, but the other of the apparently unified self. It is, in Kristevan terms, the 'underlying causality' that must be repressed in order to 'enter the socio-symbolic contract'.

The potential of the threat is encapsulated in Kristeva's belief that it is 'capable of blowing up the whole construct' – a painfully appropriate metaphor for the discourse of war (Kristeva, 1974: 153).

In the case of shell-shock, then, a vicious circle is created in which the repressive terms of social 'normality' become both the cause of the symptoms and the end product of the cure. The individual's attempt to escape from participation in the destructive order is invested in the process of creating the drama of an escape into hysteria. That a cure be undertaken is the demand of a society constituted on the subjugation of disruptive elements, but ultimately a cure is also the only feasible strategy for the survival of the individual. 'I've been running away from myself for twenty years, and it doesn't work', observes Peter in *Gaudy Night* (1935/1990: 292). Hysteria represents the marginality of silence and the deprivation of agency. In the dialectic of power, silence can be seen as a metaphorical death. Escape into hysteria is only a fantasy of escape, the meaningless act of an individual which can only end in self-destruction. Ultimately, only through speaking in the symbolic is it possible to challenge the symbolic. This is the impasse of a politics of marginality – a politics which Sayers neither supported nor understood, but which the fantasies of her fiction suggest she unconsciously desired. As with the character of Wimsey, Sayers's texts run aground on the contradictory tension between the desire for escape and the call of duty. Sayers had found it impossible for her newly created Harriet to accept Peter Wimsey without a loss of face: 'I could not marry Peter off to the young woman he had (in the conventional Perseus manner) rescued from death and infamy, because I could find no form of words in which she could accept him without loss of self-respect' (Sayers, 1937: 211). Similarly it is inconceivable that Peter should wholeheartedly embrace the prospect of a second world war – and yet his duty (as dictated by the social pressures of class, patriotism and education), alongside Sayers's beliefs, demanded that he do so. This contradiction remains unresolved within the Wimsey novels, erupting most disconcertingly and persistently within the multi-faceted narrative of *Busman's Honeymoon*.

However, it is not only hysteria that represents an escapist strategy. The 'cure' of hysteria is also a fantasy (and a necessary one for survival). It represents the illusion of a return to agency, to articulation, and to the essential delusion of a coherent self. But, in the terms of the social order that effects this cure, it is simply a readjustment of the 'deviant' individual to the 'normalising' codes of patriarchal society. The Wimsey/Vane/Bunter triad operates within this framework, and in consequence the metaphorical opposition of homosexual and heterosexual economies becomes part of this imperative of conformity.

In a socio-political context, hysteria can be defined as a refusal of cultural identity, while its cure is a dutiful resumption of that same cultural identity.

Hence within Sayers's work a contradiction is created. The closer Peter comes to emotional honesty and the more he drops the façades and affectations of his hysterical persona, the more he simultaneously readopts the personae and practices of the very cultural institutions his unconscious had rejected. By *Gaudy Night* he has reassumed his interaction with the patriarchal order, performing the duties prescribed to a man of his class and education. This reintegration is a painful process. Each of Peter's forays into that world leave him looking ill and exhausted. He develops a fine line in almost apocalyptic pronouncements – 'our sands are running down fast' (1935/1990: 271) – and to Harriet, the 'psychic' detective, or indeed the analyst, layer after layer of Wimsey's vulnerable ego–identity is exposed:

> Harriet could find nothing to say to him. She had fought him for five years, and found out nothing but his strength; now within half an hour he had exposed all his weaknesses, one after the other. (1935/1990: 271)

The normalisation of Peter represents a neutralising of his potentially dangerous otherness, and there is also in the text a parallel normalisation of Harriet. Carolyn Heilbrun (1989: 57) raises the question of Sayers's decision to abandon Harriet to 'the fate of a married woman' and concludes that the remarkable independence of Harriet would have been impossible to sustain. Although interesting, this answer seems insufficient. It is my contention that in the fate of Harriet Vane, Sayers unwittingly presents a prime example of war's ability to change and dominate the terms of reference: to demand that otherness and other debates be put aside in order to concentrate on the priority of conflict. Thus in the late 1930s, Sayers's characters are gradually, but inexorably, brought into line. Peter rejects homosexuality for heterosexual marriage. Harriet rejects her independence and non-conformity for submission and marriage. In so doing, both adopt the masquerade – Harriet of womanliness, and Peter of manliness.[6]

That Harriet should adopt the masquerade is not altogether surprising. Riviere's essay concerns itself with the analysis of 'a particular type of intellectual woman' (1929: 34) and the techniques used by this woman to disguise her possession of the phallus of intellectual achievement. Discussing the strategies of her woman patient, Riviere observed:

> Womanliness therefore could be assumed and worn as a mask, both to hide the possession of masculinity and to avert the reprisals expected if she was found to possess it – much as a thief will turn out his pockets and ask to be searched to prove that he has not the stolen goods. (1929: 38)

Harriet is particularly well qualified to identify the potential repercussions of the possession of masculinity. Carolyn Heilbrun encapsulates her position:

> Here is a woman who has, metaphorically speaking, killed and abandoned
> her lover when she outgrew him. So realistic, so 'unfeminine' is her
> scorn of him that she is tried for his literal murder in *Strong Poison*.
> (1989: 57)

The penalty for failure to masquerade is death, yet the threat of war
increasingly places Harriet in a relatively masculine position. Her situation is
an impossible one, and in this context the conformity of her marriage can be
seen as an increasingly necessary deployment of the mask of womanliness.[7]

The prospect of war and the ensuing rise in the temperature of international
relations are presented as the factors that conspire to push Harriet from her
'feminine' position of absolute helplessness in *Strong Poison* to a relatively
masculine position of centrality in *Gaudy Night*. The result is the existence
within the text of a counter-current running against the surface conformity of
the romance plot. It is important to stress, however, that even the conformity of
the Wimsey/Vane marriage is not straightforward. *Gaudy Night* posits a conflict
between a 'traditional' woman's devotion to her man and a non-gender-specific
devotion to the intellect, and Harriet Vane's love story occupies an uneasy space
between the two. Within the dominant framework of middle-class values that
shape both the genre of detection and the formula of romance, Harriet and
Peter represent the ideal. A respectable doctor's daughter is offered the ultimate
fairytale: marriage, for love, to an attractive, intelligent, wealthy aristocrat.
Sayers refuses to sanction this fantasy of perfection, not least in her removal
of Harriet's respectability, and she struggles to reject the option of 'safety and
closure' which Heilbrun identifies as the customary female fate:

> Safety and closure, which have always been held out to women as the
> ideals of female destiny, are not places of adventure, or experience, or
> life. Safety and closure (and enclosure) are, rather, the mirror of the
> Lady of Shalott. They forbid life to be experienced directly. Lord Peter
> Wimsey once said that nine-tenths of the law of chivalry was a desire to
> have all the fun. The same might well be said of patriarchy. (Heilbrun,
> 1989: 20)

Sayers refuses to condemn Harriet unconditionally to such a fate, and by
Gaudy Night the shadow of war is already preventing Peter from having all
the fun. Rather, Sayers attempts to reclaim the institution of marriage as a
sanctuary, and extends the option of its safety as much to the beleaguered
Peter as to the self-sufficient Harriet. It is essentially a conservative strategy,
but it must be seen as a rehabilitation and a rewriting of the old, rather than
simply a reactionary return to 'traditional' values. Sayers's novels constantly
pose this conflict between resistance to change and desire for change, and in

consequence her response to the threat of war is ambiguous. While deploring the prospect of war, she is not above using the implications of conflict for a distinctly feminist purpose. The Harriet Vane novels form a paean to a woman's right to self-determination. The argument here, as in her 1938 essay 'Are women human?', is couched in largely individualist terms. The overall scheme of Sayers's individualism is undoubtedly liberal-bourgeois in character, but her essay does not deny the need for collective feminist action, and her refusal to homogenise women can be seen as a surprisingly radical assertion of difference. It is within her fiction, however, that Sayers's feminism is most clearly articulated, and in the novels of the 1930s she uses the detective genre to undermine the traditional gender roles of the formula novel.

There is a change of perspective evident in the novels after *Strong Poison* (the first to feature Harriet Vane). Wimsey remains central in *Murder must Advertise* (1933) and *The Nine Tailors* (1934), but in *Have his Carcase, Gaudy Night* and *Busman's Honeymoon*, the reader is struck by the increasing absence of the expected hero. He is absent at the beginning of *Have his Carcase*, and shares the burden of investigation throughout (although his position as top detective is not undermined). He is noticeably absent throughout the greater part of *Gaudy Night*, and moreover he is not available when he is needed, indicating a 'greater' priority elsewhere. Finally, he is absent throughout the Prothalamion of *Busman's Honeymoon*, involved in this higher priority which has been created by the threat of war.

Harriet's usurpation of the role of hero is an important departure in terms of both detective fiction and the prelude to war. In this context she represents a transition from male to female, which combined with the absence of the male, can be seen as indicating the onset of crisis – a preparation for war which demands the disruption of traditional patterns and the abandoning of old concerns. This trend of gender disruption is not confined to Sayers. A spirit of transition – or at least an increased female presence – can be discerned in many of the crime writers of the late 1930s. While in Nicholas Blake's *The Smiler with the Knife* (1939) Georgia Strangeways totally eclipses her husband, the detectives of Margery Allingham and Ngaio Marsh are steadily, if discreetly, drawn towards the safe haven of marriage. In Marsh's 1938 novel *Artists in Crime*, Roderick Alleyn meets his future wife, Agatha Troy; while in Allingham's novel of the same year, *The Fashion in Shrouds*, Albert Campion is reacquainted with his future wife – the plucky and capable aircraft engineer, Amanda Fitton. Yet it is in Sayers's work that this disruption is most comprehensively catalogued. By *Gaudy Night* the threat of conflict has forced Peter to abandon his old priorities and his place as hero of a detective novel. Women, in this instance Harriet, must come forward and assume the roles of men for the duration of the crisis. War work might be an extravagant description, but Wimsey's distraction undoubtedly enables her to break new ground in the detective genre. With Peter's movements at the arbitrary whim of the Foreign Office, Harriet must provide the concentration and stability at the centre of *Gaudy Night*. Her active position as catalyst and controller is emphasised first, by the attack on her property, the chessmen; and secondly, by the ultimate accolade of the adventure novel, an attack on her person. According to the conventions of the genre, the typical villain will attack that which threatens him most seriously. Harriet survives the attack and is thereby elevated from the traditional superfluity of female characters. Instead of woman as helpless victim or manipulative villain she attains the usually male prerogative of the protagonist's role.

This is not the only convention which Harriet disrupts. 'You are the most unwomanly woman I ever met' (Sayers, 1935/1990: 199) declares Peter's wayward nephew Viscount St. George. Indeed so overwhelmed is he by Harriet's peculiarities that by the end of the novel he has to say it again, this time drawing attention to the issue of priority: 'What an unnatural woman you are! He [Peter] ought to be here, weeping into the sheets and letting the international situation blow itself to blazes' (1935/1990: 408). Both the radicalism and the perils of Harriet's position are evident. The mask of womanliness, seldom worn in *Gaudy Night*, is becoming conspicuous by its absence.

Gaudy Night thus encompasses a blurring of gender boundaries, creating an ambiguity which undermines and diffuses the authority of the established patriarchal system of distinctions. This ambiguity is symptomatic of the tensions of the period. The prospect of a seemingly inevitable war dominated intellec-tual activity, and engaging with this threat created the belief that only some form of radical change could put an end to the self-destructive impulses of patriarchal society. The result, for better or for worse, was a change of priorities for women writers. The desire for a deconstruction of patriarchal binary oppositions was transformed into an attempt at a positive reconstruction of existing gender roles. 'All change' was replaced by 'all together' and explorations of difference became a denial of gender – with the ironic result that outside the sphere of its political influence, Fascism had a homogenising effect on the dynamics of gender. Sayers herself contributed to this trend. Claiming that the time for an 'aggressive feminism' had passed, she proposed a comparatively radical deconstruction of gender roles on the grounds that 'a woman is just as much an ordinary human being as a man, with the same individual preferences, and with just as much right to the tastes and preferences of an individual' (Sayers, 1938: 107). While Fascism itself relegated women to the domestic sphere, maintaining traditional gender polarities, its impact elsewhere was one of (temporary) liberation. The necessity of revolution was replaced by the imperative of survival, and the discourse of gender was usurped by a discourse of power. Virginia Woolf, in juxtaposing the private brother and the public father, acknowledged that rigid gender specifications destroy men as well as women, and in her society of Outsiders she conceives of a space – a neutral ground – where the minds of men and women can meet in an ideal realm of communication. The metaphor of the 'poor college' proposed in *Three Guineas* epitomises her conception:

> The aim of the new college, the cheap college, should not be to segregate and specialize, *but to combine*. It should explore the ways in which mind and body can be made to *co-operate*, discover what new combinations *make good wholes* in human life. (Woolf, 1938/1986: 40; emphasis mine)[8]

It was perhaps a utopian vision, but the prospect of war demanded radical thinking. For writers of the 1930s, war cut an arbitrary swathe across existing terms of reference, and the dominant response was the creation of an alternative system of oppositions – roughly speaking, the distinction between those who run wars and those who have wars run over them. The terms 'masculine' and 'feminine' remain useful signifiers for this distinction, and to a certain extent the established division of active/passive was reinforced, but the progression to a male/female, combatant/non-combatant demarcation was disrupted by what Susan Gubar (1987) has termed the 'technological depersonalisation' of the Second World War. Power, though largely in the hands of men, was not gender-inclusive, and the average soldier or male civilian found himself effectively emasculated by the arbitrary imposition of war. Gubar suggests that:

> Because European Fascism evolved as a reaction against the emasculation associated with the First World War and the Depression, the fascist 'father' regarded his leadership as a sexual mastery over the feminized masses. (1987: 230)

On a superficial level a gender-based opposition is still in evidence. As Peter is feminised or unmanned by the combination of recurrent shell-shock, repeated absence and the gradual loss of the role of hero, so Harriet is empowered (and hence rendered 'unwomanly') by her assumption of the traditional male position of controller. Yet however much gender roles change, the fact remains that in the situation of war both Harriet and Peter are powerless. Harriet's assumption of control within the environment of the novel does not make her one of the war party. Her metamorphosis occurs in a different area which is related to war through contact, but is otherwise situated on an entirely different axis.

After its development in the background of *Gaudy Night*, the threat of war is made clear and undeniable in the opening pages of *Busman's Honeymoon*. The dowager duchess's diary records:

> Harriet's book finished and sent to publisher. This unfortunately leaves her mind free to worry about Abyssinia, so tiresome. Convinced civilisation will perish and Peter never be seen again. Like cat on hot bricks saying she wasted five years of P.'s life and can't forgive herself and it's no good saying he's over age because he has M.I. [Military Intelligence] written all over his conscience and if he were seventy he might still be gassed or bombed in an air-raid. (1937b/1988: 23)

This is the backcloth against which Wimsey's last detection is played – and the performance is a unique and disturbing one.

In *Busman's Honeymoon* Sayers takes two serious and carefully developed characters and entombs them in the midst of a sordid and absurd rural farce. Why? The answer lies in the novel's subtitle – 'A love story with detective interruptions'. Interruption or disruption is the key to an understanding of the novel's role in the preparations for war.

The union of Harriet and Peter is a strategy for survival. It represents the double fiction that it is possible to withdraw from the threat of an increasingly chaotic and disordered world by entering into the 'normality' of domesticity. The apparent cure of their deviance, through the ritual of marriage, renders them victims of the bourgeois delusion of fair play. They think that together they are safe. Peter and Harriet are seeking a refuge from the storm about to break over Europe and seemingly they find it in the Englishman's symbolic castle – the archetypal home of classical detective fiction – the country house. This strategy is similarly explored by Virginia Woolf in *Between the Acts* (1941); both novels expose the corruption at the heart of Englishness, and in *Busman's Honeymoon* this is achieved through the symbolic violence of murder. To continue the analogy with Virginia Woolf, Peter and Harriet's ideal, 'feminised' union and their retreat to Talboys can be seen as a desire to situate themselves as Outsiders. The problem is that the patriarchal order will not let them. A tension is evident between the social responsibility into which Peter was born and the individual he has become through the experience of war. His desire is for the creative unity represented by his marriage to Harriet, but his duty is to the destructive force of war. This conflict is central to the structure of the narrative and it manifests itself in the constant disruption of order and unity. The Prothalamion and Epithalamion should frame the tranquillity of the marriage bed. Instead the nuptial celebration becomes a state of fragmentation. The 'detective interruptions' and the intrusive, oppressive presence of the villagers become absurd to the point of farce – indeed to the point where a man is killed by a low-flying cactus. This is the descent into chaos that war will bring; only the reality will not be so comic.

For the duration of the detecting, the fragile division between the sublime and the ridiculous is under a constant state of siege. Peter's intimate confession of love and dependence, coming in a moment's calm after a farcical day, is shattered by the inadvertent presence of the irritating Miss Twitterton and her tale of blighted love. The pace of the novel is exhausting. Events and characters crowd into Talboys, leaving Harriet and Peter with only the code of literary quotation as a means of communication across the competing claims for their attention. Even here they are denied their privacy as Sayers introduces a literary policeman, capable of matching them quote for quote, and in so doing reducing their private code to a communal parlour game. So close indeed is the novel to chaos that in an unprecedented moment of revelation we witness the first inadvertent dropping of Bunter's mask – an emphatic indication of a civilisation on the verge of collapse:

> 'Gawdstrewth!' cried Bunter. The mask came off him all in one piece, and nature, red in tooth and claw, leapt like a tiger from ambush.
>
> 'Gawdstrewth! Would you believe it? All his lordship's vintage port!' He lifted shaking hands to heaven. 'You lousy old nosy-parking bitch! You ignorant, interfering old bizzom! Who told you to go poking your nose into my pantry?' (1937b/1988: 273)

Although we are never permitted access to Bunter's fears, the collapse of his mask reveals a fragmentation of his identity commensurate with the disruption of his world, his increasing marginalisation and the loss of his role as primal nurturer. Both his class and the homosexual economy he represents make Bunter powerless to challenge this marginality; but none the less he continues to have some influence within the family unit. The balance of power is illustrated in an exchange with Harriet over the welfare of the distraught Peter that concludes in an acknowledgement of their parental role: 'Their eyes met with perfect understanding' (1937b/1988: 391).[9]

However, within the dislocation created by the novel's absurdity, Harriet and Peter alone create a mock-heroic world which removes them effectively from the sordid reality of the day. Within this fantasy of absence Peter looks to John Donne for words to express his love, finding himself 'vexed at his own impotence' when it comes to the responsibility of finding his own words. The merging of fairytale romance with farce is encapsulated by a chapter heading which, in sharp contrast to Sayers's usual poetic inclinations, effectively sums up the forces of chaos, madness and wrongheadedness which confront the narrative:

> So Henny-penny, Cocky-locky, Ducky-daddles,
> Goosey-poosey, Turkey-lurkey, and Foxy-woxy
> all went to tell the king the sky was a-falling.
> (1937b/1988: 84)

Thus Sayers conducts a symbolic struggle to rationalise the forces of chaos within the structure of the detective novel. Her experiments with the absurd acknowledge the endemic uncertainty of the period and stretch the normally inelastic formula to the bounds of the possible. Ironically, the very conservatism of the detective novel offers the ideal arena for the expression of pre-war anxieties. In *Gaudy Night* the college represents a microcosmic haven of order and tranquillity juxtaposed against the scarcely contained chaos and false values of the outside world. Cherished traditions are seen to be under attack, and the greatest fear of the novel is that the college should succumb to the threat of the new. Frequent comment is made regarding the detrimental change in the attitudes and behaviour of undergraduates; 'Before the War they passionately had College Meetings about everything. Now, they don't want to be bothered . . . They don't want responsibility' (1935/1990: 101). Again Sayers presents the double bind. The students, in a postwar rejection of values that they see as contaminated, endanger the educational parity established by the previous generation. War is not simply a harbinger of violent change, it also destroys the focus required for the pursuit of constructive change.

In his analysis of the formula novel, John G. Cawalti identifies the isolated setting of the classical detective story, and the 'pageants of local color' which accompany them, as both technically useful devices and highly relevant symbols:

> they symbolise the normally peaceful and serene order of society disrupted by the anomaly of crime and restored when the detective isolates the guilty individual. Many twentieth-century writers of classical detective stories reflect the nineteenth-century novel in their treatment of society in the form of nostalgic fantasies of a more peaceful and harmonious social order associated with the traditional rural society of England. (Cawalti, 1976: 98)

Thus the detective novel represents a middle-class fantasy of order, which Sayers paradoxically resists and embraces. This re-establishment of security and stasis in the face of external influences of violence and change can be seen as highly desirable by readers under the shadow of war. If our fears of social disorder can be vicariously controlled through the resolutions of crime fiction, then cannot war, the ultimate violent crime, be similarly reduced to manageable proportions? The cancer of evil or conflict can be reassuringly removed by the surgical skill of the detective. Such a strategy also has the useful side-effect of avoiding the necessity of interrogating our own society, and thereby conspires with the tunnel-vision ideology of war. Ultimately, however, the formula reassures because it reinscribes the authority of the individual. If the detective alone can solve the crime, then the individual must have the capacity to make a difference.

This fantasy of control is most clearly articulated not by Sayers, but by her contemporary Margery Allingham. Allingham's 1941 novel, *Traitor's Purse*, sees the fate of the nation resting literally in the hands of one man, the detective Albert Campion. Single-handedly, and without the aid of his memory, Campion saves the war economy, restoring order in the face of chaos. Sayers's approach may have been more subtle, but the appeal to 'each man's personal responsibility', in the wartime Wimsey Letters, indicates her fervent belief in the value of individual, or communal, integrity.[10] In spite of this it is difficult to discern an overall moral scheme within the Wimsey novels. They are not apparently motivated by a simplistic idea of good and evil, and Sayers is certainly more sophisticated, or subtle, in her treatment of crime than contemporaries such as Margery Allingham. With the exception perhaps of the aptly named Sir Julian Freke, villains are seldom immediately recognisable. There are no evil auras, and there is considerable sympathy for characters such as Will Thoday in *The Nine Tailors* and Mr Tallboy in *Murder must Advertise* – a sympathy that recognises the existence of grey areas in the division between right and wrong. Nonetheless, Thoday meets his maker in a freak fen flood and Tallboy walks out with very British pluck to a certain death from waiting assassins. Providential justice is seen to be dispensed in a manner that recognises the demands of the genre: 'she writes detective stories, and in detective stories virtue is always triumphant. They're the purest literature we have' (Sayers, 1930/1989: 114). That *Gaudy Night*'s Shrewsbury College is saved as much by its own integrity as by the intervention of Lord Peter Wimsey is perhaps Sayers's most gratifying manipulation of this convention.

Thus by engaging with the discourse of war through the tactical deployment of a shell-shocked hero dependent on his wife, Sayers attempts to move the detective genre away from its customary glib oppositions. Whatever the virtue of the cause, the ultimate product of detection – or war – is always destruction: 'It's getting uncommonly easy to kill people in

large numbers, and the first thing a principle does – if it really is a
principle – is to kill somebody' (1935/1990: 317). Sayers wrestles with
the irreconcilable contradictions of a war that nobody wanted but which
had to be fought, and Wimsey articulates this dilemma when faced with
a conflict of conscience against inclination in *Busman's Honeymoon*. The
idea of war was unbearable but it would have to be borne: 'I hate
violence! I loathe wars and slaughter, and men quarrelling and fighting
like beasts! Don't say it isn't my business. It's everybody's business'
(1937b/1988: 128).

Sayers resists the inevitability of handing Peter over to the authorities,
allowing the illusion of sanctuary to persist for the duration of *Busman's
Honeymoon* – but the disruptions are always there to remind us that this
cannot last. The outside world cannot be denied, and neither ultimately
can the imposition of war. War in this context rejects the identification of
biological men with patriarchal power. It presents instead the remorseless
power of a literal and metaphorical Fascism, which can be seen to feminise
all who are not *actively* associated with it. In the process of feminisation, war
deprives the individual of executive power, leaving only the marginality of
hysteria as an illusory arena of escape. *Busman's Honeymoon* presents a complex
transition in which the discourse of detection, ostensibly usurped by love,
is in fact transformed into a narrative of war. That Sayers both subscribed
to and resisted the necessity of this cultural imposition is evident in the
tensions and disruptions of this final novel. In her fear of chaos, Sayers falls
into the trap of an ailing but still potent patriarchy. Survival is presented
as conditional upon the abandonment of change and a return to 'basics' –
the basics of a patriarchy that will not be depleted, but intensified, by the
experience of war. Within this schema, the production and consumption
of detective fiction can only persist as a strategy for survival, representing
the feminised individual's constrained and lonely fantasy of masculinity
and power.

NOTES

1. Elaine Showalter's *The Female Malady: Women, Madness and English Culture, 1830–1980* (1987b)
   provides a fascinating and detailed account of the variety of medical opinion regarding the occurrence and
   treatment of male hysteria.
2. Sayers tends to subscribe to stereotypical models of class, duty and education, as she does to prevalent
   ethnic stereotypes, for example, when discussing the nature of gigolos in *Have his Carcase* (1932/1989:
   83). Yet Alison Light is perhaps harsh when she compares Sayers unfavourably with Agatha Christie
   on this subject. Racist attitudes in Sayers are usually attributed to their logical owners, and she is
   equally capable of presenting a more positive attitude towards racial issues, as in the case of the
   cross-cultural marriage of Freddy Arbuthnot and Rachel Levy.
3. The timing of this transition corresponds with contemporary literary and social developments. Harriet's
   first appearance in 1930 is situated in the midst of the flood of memoirs and autobiography that began
   in 1928 with Graves and Blunden and was still progressing in 1933 when Vera Brittain's *Testament
   of Youth* appeared. Many commentators have remarked upon this ten-year delay in the transition

from repression to expression, and the similar evidence of more recent conflicts – Vietnam, the Falklands – would suggest this phenomenon is a powerful indicator of the extent of personal and national trauma.

4. Janice Rossen has also considered the mothering role of Shrewesbury College: 'What is fascinating about all these references to Freud and psychoanalytic theories is that Sayers seems to be defining the main conflict in the novel as one centering on repression and fear of emotions, whereas its real battleground is Oedipal, and has to do with the relationship of the heroine to her respective parent figures of Shrewesbury College and Peter Wimsey' (1990: 141).

Undoubtedly the college does assume a mothering function, and at the end of the novel Peter effectively removes Harriet from this maternal sphere; but, by describing Peter as 'so palpably a patriarch' (1990: 154), Rossen oversimplifies the complexity of Sayers's construction, negates the many strengths of Harriet and denies the ambiguities of a genre novel in which the gender roles have been so blatantly reversed.

5. The new fulfilment and consequent happiness experienced by Rivers (a single and probably homosexual man) through his nurturing role is remarkably similar to the satisfaction Sayers portrays in Bunter when circumstances enable him, also a single man, to assume the role of carer and confidant.

6. Stephen Heath makes the observation that hysteria is nothing other than *'failed* masquerade' (1986: 51).

7. This situation is ironically reminiscent of nineteenth-century practices: some schools of thought regarded hysteria as a moral ailment for which the recommended cure was a return to the twin icons of compulsory heterosexuality – marriage and the family. It is also possible, as Sayers's biographer James Brabazon suggests, that many of Sayers's actions were motivated by a persistent sense of sin resulting from the secret of her illegitimate child. Certainly her belief that conformity is a duty in time of crisis plausibly could be connected to her own guilt at transgressing the moral dictates of her faith; and it is possible that in normalising Harriet's relations she atones for the unresolved 'sin' of her own. More recently, Barbara Reynolds's biography has sought to undermine this guilt-ridden image of Sayers by suggesting that the ritual of the Anglo-Catholic confessional relieved her of this burden. Yet, in spite of Reynolds's absolution, Sayers's enormous sense of responsibility becomes evident in the extracts from her letters: 'I don't want to be helped. J.'s my look-out entirely, and it's feeble if I can't manage without help' (quoted in Reynolds, 1993: 150).

8. Interesting comparison can be made with Harriet's fantasy at Shrewesbury College: 'that whole wildly heterogeneous, that even slightly absurd, collection of chattering women fused into a corporate unity with one another and with every man and woman to whom integrity of mind meant more than material gain . . . their personal differences forgotten in face of a common foe' (Sayers, 1935/1990: 31; ellipsis mine).

9. Indeed Sayers's depiction of the Wimsey/Bunter intimacy is suggestive of a more than symbolic homosexuality. The following exchange between the dowager duchess and Harriet sets the stage for a remarkably camp performance:

'I do hope Bunter isn't being difficult or anything.'

'He's a marvel – and quite amazingly tactful.'

'Well, that's nice of the man,' said the Duchess, frankly, 'because sometimes these attached people *are* rather difficult . . .' (1937b/1988: 379)

The duchess continues in detail, from the meeting in the trenches when they 'took a fancy to one another', through Bunter's assumption of control, to Peter's return to mastery over the issue of a sausage; from which, she concludes, he has never looked back.

10. The Wimsey Letters appeared in *The Spectator* between November 1939 and January 1940, and are both an exercise in propaganda and an example of the use of comic relief in the dissemination of information. The final letter, from Peter to Harriet, presents a fascinating statement of Sayers's creed and moral foundation:

Tell them, this is a battle of a new kind, and it is they who have to fight it, and they must do it themselves and alone. They must not continually ask for leadership – they must lead themselves . . .

It's not enough to rouse up the Government to do this and that. You must rouse the people. You must make them understand that their salvation is in themselves and in each separate man and woman among them . . . the important thing is each man's *personal responsibility*. They must not look to the state for guidance – they must learn to guide the State . . . It is the only thing that matters.

4

Faith in a 'Watching Brief':
Stevie Smith and the Religion of Fascism

> [I]f you have achieved peace in your own mind when the worst happens (if it does) you will have reserves of strength to meet it. And if you have not achieved peace in your own mind how can you expect the world to do better. You are the world and so am I.
>
> (Stevie Smith, letter to Naomi Mitchison, 1937)

Stevie Smith's response to the threat of war can more accurately be termed a response to the threat of an unquestioning, all consuming belief. In the religion of fascism she saw a mesmerising ideology that threatened to destroy the diversity of the world she cherished. Smith's fears are voiced in two pre-war novels; *Novel on Yellow Paper* (1936) and *Over the Frontier* (1938). My particular concern is with *Over the Frontier*, which presents a striking and intensely pessimistic indictment of the impulse to war. Beginning where her first novel ended, and following closely in style and content, Smith's second novel undergoes a bizarre transition from dreamy inaction to nightmarish action. The light-hearted intimacy that characterised *Novel on Yellow Paper* is gradually developed into a brittle surrealism, culminating in the transformation of the absurd into a shocking and deadly seriousness.

Both novels follow the thoughts and actions of Pompey Casmilus. Something of a chameleon, Pompey revels in a triumphant multiplicity – going, thinking and being where, what or whoever she pleases. Yet even from the outset of *Novel on Yellow Paper,* this freedom is seen to be problematic. Pompey is both every man and no man – a contradiction of self and gender that permeates the fabric of both novels. On one level, Pompey's significance lies primarily in her individuality. The question of gender, although of interest to Smith, is secondary to her concern to establish Pompey as the archetypal 'I'. Pompey responds as one, as the selfish individual, to the lure of power – and yet her response can also be seen to symbolise a general human failing. Smith believes that the individual is essential to a healthy society and fears its absorption into a reductive group ethos, governed by the lowest common denominator of human experience. Pompey is presented in both situations. Her angry response to what she terms the 'männlicher Protest' (Smith 1936/1980: 99) of Nazi Germany sets her outside the masculine order – at the same time that her own angry and violent impulses are situating her firmly within the tradition she abhors. The 'masculine' fascination with power is not represented as a sex-specific trait. Here, as throughout her work, Smith is ultimately more concerned with exploring the individual's relation to power than with linking this relationship to essentialist categories of sexual difference. Pompey, then, is a multi-faceted creation who moves effortlessly across the frontiers of class and religion, rejoicing at her admission into the separate worlds of her very different friends. Her meditations on the 'happy accident of Nordic birth' (1936/1980: 12) which form the extremely discomforting opening to *Novel on Yellow Paper,* establish the serious intentions which underlie the superficially light-hearted tone of the novel. Pompey, for all that she loves her Jewish friends, cannot escape from her inbuilt, irrational racism. On the surface, superior claims of friendship and rationality may defeat the impulse, but it is always there and always dangerous. From the opening of the novel, Pompey offers us her confidence and tests the limits of our willingness to identify with the narrative voice. Hers is a comfortable welcoming voice, it draws us in, offering easy friendship and asks us to privilege this friendly tone over a dubious moral content. This concern with underlying motivations, with hypocrisy and the dark substratum of human life, sets the pattern for the Pompey Casmilus novels and thereby articulates Smith's understanding of the European predicament.

Significantly Pompey defines herself through her friends – an act which emphasises the ambivalence of her character, and which potentially enables her to situate herself in the position of both the oppressor and the oppressed:

> How greatly I enjoy for a week-end, for a week perhaps for a fortnight, to savour the lives of my friends. They are all so very different from each other my friends, they are not at all alike, and cannot even safely be set down in front of each other. Show me a man's friends and I will show you the man. Then what sort of a *man* is Pompey whose friends are 'all of different kinds'? Is there any Pompey at all? (Smith, 1936/1980: 196–7)

Pompey does not represent a single unified self. She has a characteristic voice, but that is only a surface, a common denominator that connects, but does not homogenise her many personae. This multiplicity enables her to engage with an endless potentiality of physical and metaphorical areas of experience. In each genre that Smith explores in *Over the Frontier*, Pompey takes on and subverts a new leading role. She has access to everywhere; but, significantly, she belongs nowhere. In her biography of Smith, Frances Spalding (1988: 19) discusses the infant Stevie's capacity to be both a leader and an outsider, essential and yet outside, and this same duality is central to the nature of Pompey Casmilus. Surrounded by friends and yet always alone, ('the talking voice that runs on' (Smith, 1936/1980: 39) is always a monologue) we see her watching and recording, coldly condemning the passion of belief, exposing those who become too deeply involved and thereby lose their perspective:

> Oh how deeply neurotic the German people is, oh how it goes right through and isn't just the leaders, like they pretend in *The Times*. Oh they are so strained and stretched and all the time they are wanting something so yearningly, it is something they don't quite know, like a dream or something that is out of focus. (1936/1980: 102)

There is perhaps nothing particularly radical in the role of the observer, indeed the slightly superior authorial recording of the weakness of others often tends towards the didactic. Yet when this distance is challenged, when the observing eye gets too close to see the whole picture, the responsibility falls on the reader to observe the remorseless absorption of the narrator into the guilty rituals of belief. The reader becomes a witness to the conversion of the sceptical observer into the most fervent disciple. To see this happen to a close confiding 'friend', the narrator, is an attack on the complacency of the reader. The character with which we identified has been corrupted – an act which throws our superiority into doubt, questioning not only our knowledge of others but also our knowledge of ourselves. Through *Over the Frontier*, Smith illustrates that our security is illusory: the potential for Fascism lies within us all.

The previous chapter illustrates Dorothy L. Sayers's symbolic struggle to rationalise the forces of chaos within the structure of the detective novel. Both Sayers and, I argue, Virginia Woolf attempt to cut across a definition of war that necessarily identifies biological men with patriarchal power. War can be more clearly identified in their works with a type of literal and metaphorical fascism, which can be seen to feminise all who are not *actively* associated with it. Yet they find a faint hope in ideas of the immutability of a common humanity – something transcending the impulses of the essentially socially constructed evil of Fascism. Stevie Smith presents an altogether bleaker and more pessimistic vision. She takes war's sexual indiscriminacies for granted and situates the threat of war in a different area altogether. A loss of humanity is central to *Over the Frontier,* but Smith's critique is focused not on society's implication in the process of war, but on the guilt of the individual. In a disturbing reversal Smith identifies the forces of chaos and evil as internal rather than external.

Over The Frontier toys with the absurd and with surreal images of frenzied action, but the light-hearted intimacy that characterised the earlier *Novel on Yellow Paper* soon disappears and the life of Pompey Casmilus is transformed into a coldly compelling and alienating allegory of Fascism. Needing to recuperate in the aftermath of a broken engagement, Pompey, the narrator, accompanies her friend Josephine to the mysterious Schloss Tilssen where she meets the dashing, but inane, Major Tom. What is his dark secret, what lies behind the deceptively foolish exterior? Is he the proverbial bad egg or will he turn up trumps? The enchanting Major Tom is accompanied by the fascinating Miss Pouncer and the bumbling Colonel Peck, creating a bizarre cast of characters who, in the course of the novel, are remorselessly revealed to be not quite what they seemed. Pompey, wandering naively into an incomprehensible web of intrigue, finds herself embroiled in the shady amoral world of espionage from which it is only a short step over the frontier into war. Recruited as a spy for her ability as a code-breaker Pompey undergoes a terrifying transformation which can almost be described as a change of identity. This new persona, implicated in the evils of war and power, is the product of Pompey's belief in an unspecified cause, and it dominates her mind until she finds an ironic salvation in a later loss of faith.

Frances Spalding catalogues Smith's postwar reading and her involvement in contemporary debates on Catholicism, both of which illustrate her early awareness of the attractions of ritual and belief. In the aftermath of the First World War the intensely structured nature of high church ritual seemed to offer a comforting, perhaps even anaesthetising, framework from which to rebuild shattered lives. The pre-war social order had been transformed beyond recognition, and the enormity of the death toll had dampened the joy of victory, leaving a sense of uncertainty which prompted people to search for something that could provide a new infrastructure for their lives. It is difficult to establish whether there was an overall growth or decline in religious belief in the immediately postwar years, but it does seem clear that the nature of belief underwent a radical transformation. David Cannadine's (1981) study of mourning rituals in Britain initially seems to suggest a decline in traditional forms of worship – their credibility weakened by their inability to provide answers in the face of so much mortality and grief. Yet in opposition to this must be set the unprecedented growth of the spiritualist movement, which as a search for contact with the dead developed a hitherto unimagined relevance for the bereaved. The huge and unexpected popularity of the

Cenotaph and the Armistice Day ritual would also seem to be connected to this need. The government had been reluctant to implement both of these memorials, but their popularity bears witness to the huge public desire to manifest their grief. Cannadine concludes that these rituals 'made public and corporate those unassuageable feelings of grief and sorrow which otherwise must remain forever private and individual' (1981: 222).[1]

In such a climate, the ascendency of highly structured religious systems over more private forms of worship seems a logical development. In 1919 Smith received a letter from her soldier friend 'Tommy' Meldrum in which he described himself as 'ravenously hungry for Catholicism' (Spalding, 1988: 34). Through the preoccupations of their friends, both Stevie and her sister Mollie were immersed in the religious debate. But as Mollie moved ever closer to an acceptance of Catholic dogma, Stevie remained aloof. She situated herself outside this need for an unquestioning religious belief, just as in the 1930s she would distance herself from the growth of political belief. Smith's position was remarked upon by Naomi Mitchison in her review of *A Good Time Was Had by All* in 1937:

> Because I myself care passionately about politics, because I am part of that 'we' which I am willing to break my heart over, and can no longer properly feel myself an 'I' . . . I see no reason why everyone has got to. Stevie Smith can still be an 'I'. And that's good. (quoted in Spalding, 1988: 131–2)[2]

Smith, then, was determined to stand outside the factions of belief, and the connection she makes between religious and political fanaticism emphasises her central concern – it is less a problem of what people believe, than the fact that they believe at all. 'Death to all ideologies', cries Pompey in *Over the Frontier*. Belief blinds people. They cannot see otherness and therefore desire to reduce difference to a crippling, conforming sameness. Here Smith's sentiment is that of Virginia Woolf in *Three Guineas* (1938). Only as an Outsider, as a non-believer, can we avoid implication in the cruelties of ideology – political or religious. Ideologies, be they organised religion, Fascism or communism, are united in one thing – their demand for faith. Only through non-belief can we survive.

As Pompey becomes implicated in the power structures of Fascism, *Over the Frontier* becomes increasingly vivid in its depiction of cruelty. However the real concern of the novel lies less with the content of Fascism than with its techniques. It is the language of Fascism that fascinates Smith and she equates its capacity to capture minds with the dominance of religious ideologies over our perception of right and wrong, good and evil. Fascism is empowered through language; words are its most powerful weapon and because it manipulates them so successfully it is able to disguise its true intentions. Smith graphically illustrates this in *Over the Frontier* by turning Pompey's open-ended, free ranging, non-phallogocentric narrative into a closed and brutal narrative of Fascism. The transition seems initially abrupt, but her concern with the deceptions of language is evident from *Novel on Yellow Paper* where she identifies in Shakespeare a contradiction between the secure conventionality of the language and the disturbing nature of its implications. Smith calls this dislocation an antithesis and in *Over the Frontier* she examines this phenomenon in detail through the language of Milton and Crashaw:

> But reading these poets, and sensing the magnificent power of this swift-running, counter-running, wrong ever wrong magic of their poetic vision, the sympathy of the reader too … has to go running in this contrary current, that goes sweeping and licking up in a way that is contrary to truth and an abomination; but a sweet abomination and a very exceedingly delicious contrariness that is at the same time so dangerous. (1938/1980: 31–2; ellipsis mine)

This division of form and content is at the heart of Fascism, and Smith continues to define the dangers inherent in this mesmeric language:

> For suddenly running swiftly after this deceitful sweetness of the verse, you go running too far, too far, too far altogether, and suddenly you come to where it is getting dark, and very excessively dark and gloomy are these parts. And perhaps then suddenly you are there, and you are there. And there too are suddenly these great devils. And no, absolutely, there is nothing noble-in-defeat about them at all, nothing sweet, nothing to be desired. (1938/1980: 32)

This is the technique which Smith will use in the concluding third of *Over the Frontier* where Pompey's language assumes an incantatory rhythm of almost visionary power which numbs the reader into what I'd like to describe as a 'false sense of poetry'. By this I mean a language, like that exploited by the speeches of Hitler and the automatic responses of religious ceremonial, as much as by the verse of Shakespeare, in which the cadences of the narrative voice create a hypnotic beauty which distracts attention from the implications of the content. These displays of technical virtuosity are integral to Smith's text. This is a novel about disguise and it can be seen to be operating on three levels: the linguistic, or perhaps more appropriately 'euphemistic', level; the narrative level, in which the text adopts, adapts and abandons genres with almost the facility that the novel's characters wander in and out of disguise; and finally the individual level, where Smith explores the masks – and uniforms – with which we conceal our 'real' selves. The nature of the self is central to *Over the Frontier*, for beneath the novel's concern with projected selves and role play, lies a search for 'the heart of darkness' (1938/1980: 49) – where the seeds of Fascism are stored. Ultimately the novel poses and answers a single fundamental question: does the emergence of Fascism represent a loss or an exposure of self?[3]

But the reader must journey to the 'heart of darkness', and in *Over the Frontier* the route is camouflaged by a multiplicity of textual digressions and façades. Around the central motif of the frontier, the novel comprises a narrative voyage through almost the entire gamut of literary genres. The characteristic features of romance, detective, adventure and spy fiction are all developed within the bounds of a larger fairytale motif. It is a fantastical world, and textual references to the 'scale gargantuan' (1938/1980: 139) of Schloss Tilssen and to the code-breaker's 'looking-glass' world are suggestive of a Pompey in Wonderland. Everything is out of proportion and slightly sinister. The narrative is peopled by grotesque characters easily identifiable as witches, sorcerers and fairy godmothers. The fascinating Pouncer who hides behind the mask of her 'freshly enamelled look' (1938/1980: 189) is addressed by Pompey as 'dear Mrs Witch' (1938/1980: 193), and in the tradition of all good witches she offers doom laden prophesies to Pompey the neophyte spy: 'There will be winter in the air, and death in winter upon the wind from the north. Do well, do well' (1938/1980: 195).

As with all fairytales the narrative treads a narrow line between fantasy and horror. Throughout the novel the distinction between dreaming and reality is blurred and the constant sense of foreboding leaves every dream on the verge of becoming a nightmare. Pompey's dream dance (1938/1980: 49–50) is a nightmare premonition of her wild dance with Josephine at Schloss Tilssen, where the two girls whirl around the dance floor, ignoring the insistent presence of Tom waiting on the sidelines with 'so much an expression of violence hardly to be restrained' (1938/1980: 213). Tom is waiting to whisk Pompey away to her military career, the threat of which is foreshadowed in the early dream-dance sequence by ominous images of war:

> And within the music there is moving now a more insistent clamour, a harsh grating sound, a clash of steel on steel. It is very menacing, very military, this rapidly increasing metallic clamour, thrusting, driving, marching. (1938/1980: 50)

Tom's role in this fairytale is ambiguous. He variously fills the parts of Prince Charming, the Fairy Godmother (Pompey, you shall go to the war!), the Ugly Sister (who would hold Pompey back from the ball of military triumph) and the Knight in Shining Armour who plans to rescue her at the end (1938/1980: 269). For Pompey, the Cinderella of the tale, everything changes at midnight, a fact to which Pompey herself draws attention with a certain touch of irony – 'How romantic and melodramatic is Pompey at midnight' (1938/1980: 175).

It is at midnight, creeping down the stairs, oppressed by the harsh electric light of her room, that Pompey first meets the 'real' Tom Satterthwaite, who in true fantasy style is gradually transformed in Pompey's eyes from mild-mannered major to incisive spy. Most importantly, it is during her midnight escape from the claustrophobia of an evening at the Schloss that Pompey undergoes the central loss of innocence which makes her military career possible. Pompey's understanding of what is happening at the Schloss (information to which the reader is never made party) draws her into a conspiracy with Tom which shrouds her life in codes, obliging her to mask her words in a new language of exclusion which alienates her from both her past experience and character: 'I try to say a Christian prayer but I am come very far from that and it falls athwart my memory stumbling slantwise into consciousness' (1938/1980: 162). This is a central moment of loss, the crossing of a metaphorical frontier and it prefaces the metamorphosis of Pompey the dreamer into Pompey the practical:

> Oh war war is all my thought. And suddenly I am very alert and not dreaming now asleep at all, but very awake and for ever more, and not dreaming again at all, to wring my hands and cry, but very practical I am become. Achtung, achtung! I hope that I am very practical. (1938/1980: 163)

However, before examining the implications of Pompey's transfer of allegiance, the constantly shifting framework within which her adventures proceed needs to be considered. What contribution does the textual use and abuse of formula fiction make to a reading of Pompey's journey?

Within the fairytale framework, other genres appear and in turn are undermined. Pompey appears as an unwilling detective whose insatiable curiosity leads her to stumble across all manner of clues which point inevitably towards intrigue. Overhearing the bumbling Colonel Peck speaking fluent, incisive German on the telephone, she quickly assumes the characteristic vocabulary of the detective. Before discreetly moving to feign interest in the aptly named 'Bystander' magazine she finds herself compelled to listen:

> I am amazed and so in my great surprise at this uncharacteristic voice that is so completely foreign to the picture we have built up on the very most circumstantial evidence the picture of this distracted Colonel Peck (1938/1980: 153)

Similarly, it is with considerable irony that Smith assembles in *Over the Frontier* all the ingredients of the traditional romance, the 'woman's story' that Pompey condemns so scathingly in *Novel on Yellow Paper*:

> I cannot tell you about the stories for unmarried girls, the ones that are so cleverly and coyly oh. And they are so bright and smiling, and full of pretty ideas that are all the time leading up to washing-up. You will know how they go but I cannot tell you. I am already feeling: No, I should not have said all this. It is the ugliest thing that could ever have been conceived, because it is also so trivial, so full of the negation of human intelligence, that should be so quick and so swift and so glancing, and so proud. (1936/1980: 154)

The genre is there with good reason, as it is an essential component of the business of constructing selves. In the world of magazines, of which Pompey is a part, an artificial self is created, prescribed for and ultimately imposed upon women. Yet for all her scorn, Pompey is employed by this industry, and her most explicit condemnation is saved for the so-called 'lady novelist'. As befits the novel's delight in gender transgressions, this dubious character is a man. With a world-view based on a heady concoction of Swinburn, Kipling and the Bible, he is shown to represent the symbolic order that defines self and other, man and woman.

However, within *Over the Frontier,* the working out of the 'romance plot' and the threat it contains to Pompey's sense of self is entirely subverted by Pompey's becoming the dominant party in the relationship. She not only takes over Tom's job, as Colonel Peck had warned she might (1938/1980: 220), but there is also a gradual shift in the dynamic of power between the two (1938/1980: 243) which culminates in a bizarre exchange of characteristics, illustrating that only one person can lead, be it in love or war (suggesting by implication that the other, usually the woman, will conform to a certain negative pattern of developed characteristics) – 'And as I grow stronger Tom grows weaker, on occasion petulant, frivolous, irrational and obstinate' (1938/1980: 246). All of these are characteristics of which the old Pompey could have been accused. This seemingly parasitic transition illustrates the ways in which power corrupts, and forces us towards extremes, either of strength or weakness, to fill the roles of victor or victim. However Smith's concern is less with exploring the gulf between the powerful and the powerless, than with illustrating the changes manifested in the self by power. This internal relationship acts as a key not only to the differences between individuals, but also to the terrifying thing we all have in common – the capacity for Fascism.

Tom, then, has undergone a transition of self from 'masculine' to 'feminine' – he has lost his place in the hierarchy of power – and his 'decline' is paralleled by Pompey's 'progress' from 'feminine' to 'masculine'. The empowering of

Pompey is a gradual and insidious process, which begins when she transfers her allegiance to the realm of the rational:

> For suddenly my sleeping dreaming eyes are open very wide, and my thoughts that left me on a wide high upreaching flight, to shoot so high and curve downwards on a long trajectory to the beginning of my thought, have come home to me to wait, very tensed, very alert and practical. (1938/1980: 164)

The implications of this transfer of allegiance start to become clear when Pompey visits the old Jew Aaronsen, who is already the subject of abuse from Nazi students. Initially Pompey ironically juxtaposes the barbarity of the Germans against her own anger at their cruelty, but her own language becomes increasingly disturbing:

> I find myself slipping into his mood that does not come at all foreign to me . . . it rouses in me such a fury to destroy, to be so cruel, with more than battle cruelty, to be so cruel to tread upon the ecstatic face of this *idealismus barbarus*. (1938/1980: 197; ellipsis mine)

For a moment Pompey wonders if there is not 'a little of this very *barbarismus*' in herself, but she rejects this thought and succumbs instead to a belief in the frightening concept of a 'righteous pure intolerance'. The final stage in Pompey's transition from a feminine to a masculine ethos is a symbolic act of renaming. Already embarked on her adventure with Tom, she experiences a moment of doubt. In his joking response Tom calls her 'Pompey die Grosse', which she mentally repeats and then changes to 'Pompey *der* Grosse' (1938/1980: 228). Her identification with the military is complete. In making this transition from 'feminine' to 'masculine', Pompey illustrates that masculinity is a naming process – another mask or façade assumed to protect the delicate self. As with Sayers's revelation of the many-layered selves of Peter Wimsey, masculinity is seen to be a social construct rather than an inherent characteristic; something assumed in order to participate in the rituals of the symbolic order. This too involves a question of belief. For Pompey to identify herself with the 'masculine' ethos, she must have faith, and must undertake a belief in the divinity of patriarchal power. Pompey makes this commitment, but the conclusion of the novel ostensibly challenges the power of belief by presenting her with a second revelation – a double-edged image that I discuss later. Pompey returns from the edge of war, and *Over the Frontier* can be understood to comprise two frontiers: the frontier represented by Pompey's loss of innocence and acceptance of belief, and the frontier represented by her subsequent loss of faith.

The loss of innocence which enables Pompey to understand what is happening at the Schloss, also enables her to assume the mask of the 'good soldier', one of many façades employed by the text, and a position which demands a certain economy with the truth. Pompey was never the most reliable of narrators – the distinction between the work of her imagination and the reporting of events had always been blurred – but by the time she has crossed the first frontier it becomes a mask of deliberate obfuscation. Pompey the dreamer had longed to take action, to regain the control she had felt deserting her in the stifling prospect of marriage to Freddy. Her meandering thoughts develop into a double fantasy of action and control, but these dreams turn to nightmares with the realisation of the dubious moral basis (of a desire for power) from which they spring. Pompey discovers that her two fantasies are, in fact, incompatible. In her desire to take action, Pompey ends up taking orders, and in consequence relinquishes control of her action and indeed loses narrative control of the novel. Her close and confiding relationship with the reader is steadily undermined until the reader becomes obviously excluded from whole areas of her thought – including information essential to the understanding of exchanges and choices Pompey must make in the development of her military career. In conspiring with Tom, she takes orders from another and in accepting this 'uniform' denies the non-uniformed reader access to a whole encoded area of her mind. A substantial part of Pompey has been invaded and occupied by the military. This newly practical Pompey finds relief in the prospect of action and tells us, in chilling contrast to the old Pompey who revelled in the scope of her imagination, that her thoughts can no longer fly, they 'cannot rise up and be off to no good purpose' (1938/1980: 166). Indeed, she continues, 'it is a relief to me what he is saying, it is a *direct orientation* of my thought' (1938/1980: 167; emphasis mine).

As Pompey matures in her new profession, the reader is made increasingly aware of the corrupting nature of uniform. 'I harden my heart' (1938/1980: 233) she announces, looking down from the 'high tower' of the 'becloaked commander' upon the miserable existence of the foot soldier, and rejoices in the power that makes these men 'ours, to move this way and that, to command and to visit with rewards and penalties' (1938/1980: 234). The harshness within Pompey is made equally explicit by the changing narrative tone. There is a moment of absurdity, typical of the old Pompey, in her description of her midnight assailant:

> My eye travels over his face, the flat nose, the nostrils splayed and broken at the edges, the saliva dripping from too slackly open lips, the teeth, long, yellow, filthy, like dog's fangs upon the edge of a really shockingly illkept moustache. (1938/1980: 249)

Otherwise the passage leading up to the extermination of 'Ratface' is remarkable for the cold brutality of the writing and for Pompey's attempt to justify her action by suggesting that Ratface is somehow less than human. This dehumanisation echoes the logic behind fascism's final solution. The process of the crime is inverted; responsibility is displaced from the perpetrator to the victim, whose 'inadequacy' is presented as the eminently reasonable cause for their persecution. Yet within Smith's novel, the façade of uniform and its attendant power has not brought Pompey the individual control, the power of self-determination, that she desires. It has simply raised her position within a hierarchy of pawns.

Smith's use of codes and masks is designed to emphasise the spiritual proximity of the art of deception and the military ethos. Pompey's likely susceptibility to the lure of the military is suggested by her aptitude for codes. Her talents in this area have long been in evidence:

> By and by I'm going a step further on the upward grade and going to invent a code that doesn't need a code sheet, but you do it in your head, standing on your head, with one hand tied behind, and altering the run of numerals according to the date, see? Simple? Of course it's simple. (1936/1980: 19)

In *Over the Frontier* this ability assumes a central importance. Pompey deciphers codes, and at the same time the novel presents the reader with codes which must be deciphered in order to follow the tortuous journey of Pompey through alienation to self-awareness. The frequent use of German words within the text contributes to the smokescreen and once more emphasises the concern with masks, deception and disguise. German words are used within the text to give added emphasis to a literal meaning. The use of *unruhig* (1938/1980: 160) disrupts the flow of the English text in a disquieting manner entirely appropriate to the word's meaning – restless or uneasy. On other occasions, German words are used to suggest a possible secondary emphasis, for example, *Kurhaus* – meaning guest-house or sanatorium (literally curehouse). In the context in which *Kurhaus* is used, its meaning is manipulated by implication to the much more sinister idea of curbing and restraint: something restrictive as befits the Schloss: 'In this famous Kurhaus the light is always being so particularly hard and brilliant, so death and destruction to happy thought and the sweet doze that waits upon it' (1938/1980: 142). For the non-German reader the desired meaning is usually clear and the technique remains a simple one of drawing extra attention to a phrase. However in the use of the word *Blödsinnigkeit* Smith extends the idea to a more subtle and complex level. The literal translation of *Blödsinnigkeit* is not immediately clear and is therefore of secondary importance to the actual appearance of the word. It is used in the midst of a particularly impassioned passage on cruelty and intolerance, where Pompey, discussing the persecution of Aaronsen exclaims, 'Ah the Zurückkehren of the barbarismus oh the Blödsinnigkeit of the idealismus, that is all of what cher Aaronsen is not' (1938/1980: 197). The word seems clearly to have been chosen for its English-language connotations. *Blödsinnigkeit's* visual and aural proximity to the words 'blood' and 'sin' loads it with a greater weight of condemnation than is appropriate to its literal translation – 'imbecilic', 'silly' or 'idiotic'. The result is an implication, not of foolishness, but of evil.

A final code indulged in by the narrative is that of the euphemism. It is not just Shakespeare and Milton who are guilty of irresponsible use of language. Pompey unmasks the words which disguise or water down unpleasant realities for general consumption. The word 'war' is too crude, too unsubtle, and is promptly replaced by the ambiguous, ill-defined 'arrangement':

> My dear chap don't be hysterical. War? We've got past all that, we are not so crude nowadays, we are not so crude at all. But there has been this Turkish arrangement and this Egyptian arrangement. (1938/1980: 156)

Pompey's fascination with the military is in a sense the attraction of opposites: an obsession with an ostensibly alien brutality which yet touches an inner chord. Her military career represents the rise to domination within her of another, alien self, and this self is only able to attain this position because it represents a strong and previously denied part of Pompey which demands to be acknowledged. War enables this dark side to be channelled into the military, but it has always been present. In *Novel on Yellow Paper*, Pompey imagines replacing her beloved Freddy with a chimera, but the chimera contains a monster, and in escaping from its grasp she tears herself as well as the creature (1936/1980: 222). The chimera forms a multi-faceted image within the text. Like the ideology of Fascism it has a seductive, mystical aura that enchants and enamours Pompey. But suddenly and terrifyingly the chimera disappears leaving only a 'little monster' (1936/1980: 222) behind. This seductive/destructive force is also representative of Pompey's inner self. Her reference to the chimera in *Over the Frontier* indicates that she will not find the control she desires in an external relationship with an alternative Freddy, but inside, in a pact with the other side of her self; 'Eheu Chimera, I will track you down yet, I will hunt you to earth in some green forest of Deutschland, be sure that you shall not escape me' (1938/1980: 114–15). This creature is not Tom, but Pompey herself.[4]

That Pompey's military self is an integral part of her, and not a temporary mental aberration, is perhaps best illustrated by the curious developments of Smith's final novel *The Holiday* (1949/1979). Initially written and set during the Second World War, by the time of its eventual publication in 1949 Smith had been obliged to alter all the war references to the rather more ambiguous 'postwar'. The narrator of *The Holiday* is Celia Phoze, a postwar manifestation of Pompey Casmilus, and although the published version of this novel is set after the war, the uniformed self is still very much in evidence. The difference here is that Smith effectively creates two characters that are one, instead of two opposing selves within one individual. The military/brutal side finds its own character in the shape of Celia's cousin Casmilus. Celia, like Pompey, cries a lot, is devoted to her aunt and has an all encompassing, free-ranging mind. Also like Pompey she is magnetically drawn towards the cruelty within Casmilus and his world. Their attraction is clearly sexual and their closeness is further emphasised by the absence of speech marks within the novel. In conversation it becomes difficult to distinguish between them and, at the end of the novel, Caz articulates Celia's earlier unspoken thoughts in a voice that could easily be hers: 'Oh, said Caz, shivering, there is a feeling of evil in this house to-night, oh, it is the laughter and what runs in the echo, oh. He put his hands to his face' (1949/1979: 198). The pain of this relationship however lies not in the disunity of one inner self but in the impossibility of the two separate selves uniting – there is a hint of incest which suggests that Celia and Casmilus are brother and sister. They represent the two sides of one inner debate, but while their thoughts may be interchangeable, they must ever remain at a physical distance. Ironically, the figure of Tom has, by the time of *The Holiday*, been pushed out into madness. He drifts through the novel, inarticulate and vaguely threatening, the man that Celia is told she should marry to restore his equilibrium.[5] As in *Over the Frontier*, Celia/Pompey does not need Tom. Her two selves, interior or exterior, are quite self-sufficient.

In a letter to Naomi Mitchison, written in 1937, Stevie Smith observed that:

> I don't think we can pass the buck to forces of evil or to anything but our own humanity. We are bloody fools. But then we are hardly out of the eggshell yet. I think we want to keep a tight hand – each of us on our own thoughts. (Mitchison, 1979/1986: 155)

In the final third of *Over the Frontier* there is a subtle change of emphasis which indicates that this was still Smith's concern in the writing of her novel – and which provides an answer to the underlying question of whether Fascism represents a loss or an exposure of self. The metaphors of costume parties, masks and disguises are turned on their heads to reveal not a taking on but a stripping-off of façades. Paradoxically the taking-on of a belief in Fascism does not involve the taking-on of a new self. Rather it represents the taking-off of an old self or mask – the façade of civilisation which society demands that we hold in place. Fascism reveals a naked inner self, devoid of all humanity, which is safer left concealed. This is a crucial distinction, and it marks the point at which the novel changes from the faintly absurd to the deadly serious. As Pompey reaches the pinnacle of her military career – joining the archbishop at Mentz – she turns the pages of a 'brilliant picture book' (1938/1980: 261) filled with images of soldiers, kings and princes:

> How lovely, how dark and brilliant these pages are, how entirely absorbing, how fascinating and how dangerous . . . Ah for instance if they were only absurd, if I can only see that they are, in the exigeance of their pride, laughable, ridiculous, mice in motley, infinite in pretence, in value nothing. (1938/1980; 262 ellipsis mine)

At this point the use of ridicule would be appropriate to Stevie Smith's usual penchant for bathos, but instead the novel crosses yet another frontier: 'But they do not appear to me to be so ridiculous at all; they are the flower of our humanity, the poison flower that is not less lovely for all its venom' (1938/1980: 262).

There is no happy ending to *Over the Frontier*. Once Pompey has crossed the literal and metaphorical frontiers that divide active and passive participation in war, the novel becomes dominated by the paradoxical image of the poison flower. This forms a symbol both of language's untrustworthiness and of our essentially divided selves. The final section of the novel is filled with passages of vivid, striking poetry, the brilliance of which cannot quite disguise the terrifying proximity of beauty and ugliness, good and evil:

> Outside of our room is the cold frozen cold dark night fields, and upon them the war that goes backwards and forwards, and the fighting men by day-time give their scarlet blood to the white snow and the golden sunshine. (1938/1980: 252)

Only when the poison of uniform's corruption begins to leave her system is Pompey able to cross back from the frontier of her commission and remember her other self, her 'former dream life' (1938/1980: 261). In the course of the novel Pompey undergoes two important revelations. The first is the loss of innocence that enabled her to become a soldier and the second is the loss of belief, or faith, in the creed of war that accompanies her returning memory.

Over the Frontier concludes with a chilling insight, 'power and cruelty are the strength of our life, and in its weakness only is there the sweetness of love' (1938/1980: 272), which is reinforced by Pompey's earlier growth in self-awareness:

> I may say I was shanghaied into this adventure, forced into a uniform I intuitively hated. But if there was nothing in me of it, nothing to be called

awake by this wretched event, should I not now be playing, in perhaps some boredom, but safely and sanely enough, with those who seem to me now beyond the frontier of a separate life. (1938/1980: 267)

War taps into the hidden cruelty and intolerance that Smith sees as present in us all and this conclusion forces the reader to consider the validity of the moral assumption that action in a good cause is necessarily a 'good thing'. The novel asks whether there is anything we can do without risking the destruction of our personal integrity and whether in the long run it is indeed better to lose this than to acquiesce in evil.

It is in the transition from loss of self to revelation of self that the novel presents its most threatening indictment of the human impulses that lead to war. Through the revelation that Fascism is not something that we choose, something picked up and put on, but something present within us all, waiting to emerge if we let our guard slip and drop the façade of civilisation, *Over the Frontier* ultimately challenges the system of oppositions that define the individual's relationship to power. Smith recognises the existence and the power of binary oppositions, but she sees their real significance as internal, not external. The two extremes of power and exclusion co-exist within the individual. Either may dominate, but for society to survive, the individual has a duty to wear the mask of civilisation – even if motivated only by a selfish fear of mutual destruction.

In *Novel on Yellow Paper*, the threat of Fascism is first introduced through a metaphor of disease. Society is afflicted by the twin plagues of 'Cenobites' and 'Dictators' (1936/1980: 123). Pompey recovers from the sickness of her Fascism, but that she was ever ill, that she became contaminated is a disturbing indictment of the corruption at the heart of the self. The implication is clear – if it could happen to Pompey, it could happen to anyone. We cannot even take comfort from Pompey's recovery. Her second revelation may appear to be a metaphor of hope – the forces of unreason will come to their senses and wake up from the bad dream of European war – but a closer look at Pompey's name reveals that optimism would be self-deceptive. Casmilus or Hermes, the winged messenger of the Gods, enjoyed free access to and from the underworld. Pompey identifies herself with Casmilus/Hermes.[6] Like Dante, she *can* return from hell and other mortals cannot. We can only, in the enigmatic words of Tom, 'hold a watching brief', and choose not to drop the façade of civilisation – choose not to go to Fascism or to Hell.

Ironically, for all their use of fairytales and the fantastical, Stevie Smith's novels are ultimately anti-escapist. For Smith, the consolations of a blind belief were far closer to escapism than any appreciation of what Martin Pumphrey (1986: 93) describes as the 'imperfect alternative' of the fairy world.[7] Religion offers rewards and punishments for variously interpreted codes of behaviour, but it would deny Pompey her chameleon element – her right to define herself as multiple. Pumphrey describes the magic world of Smith's poetry as being 'consistently associated with self-discovery, transgression and art', concluding that 'the freedom it offers is ambiguous. Though alluring, it is also frightening and dangerous' (1986: 92). Fairytales teach us to accept the consequences of our actions – there is no God to mitigate our suffering or to forgive our sins. Threats materialise in this world, and Smith feared that the threat she identified as early as 1931 (her first visit to Germany) would indeed come to pass. Like Sayers she sees the world spinning out of control and uses absurdity to indicate this perilous state, but her novels demand that we counter the threat of chaos rather than attempt to escape from its forces. We must acknowledge and restrain the Fascism of our 'true' selves – a task that requires not the fantasy of a saviour, but the reality of self-control.

NOTES

1. Cannadine's observations are based on comments in *The Times*, 8 November 1919, and the dynamic described paradoxically seems to suggest both a constructive communality, and the more ambiguous vision of easily-manipulated mass emotion that would be exploited by the National Socialists in Germany.
2. This concern with the relationship between individual and community was also central to both Sayers and Woolf. All four writers came to distinctly different conclusions as to the nature and benefits of the interaction.
3. Smith's development of this central idea is interestingly prefigured in *Novel on Yellow Paper*, where Pompey, describing Germany succumbing to the lure of National Socialism, observes that 'the people were stripping themselves too naked' (1936/1980: 102). Smith devotes a considerable amount of attention to the transformation of Germany, announcing that 'a whole race was gone run mad' (1936/1980: 103). These passages are remarkably prescient, forming a powerful, and largely ignored, political focus within *Novel on Yellow Paper*.
4. The prospect of marriage represented a threat to the stability of Pompey's façade of self. Her rhetorical question 'Is there any Pompey at all?' (1936/1980: 197) emphasises the fragility of her persona, and the loss of self associated with marriage disrupts her equilibrium. This is perhaps another factor in Pompey's susceptibility to Fascism, a threat to her individuality against which she overcompensates and gives free reign to the darker side of her psyche.
5. Here, as in Sayers, the idea is suggested that marriage somehow represents a force capable of restoring sanity. While it seems to have been popularly adopted as a refuge in the face of war, in the postwar age it loses its appeal, and is never seriously considered by Smith.
6. Although Smith seems to find the association between Hermes and Casmilus self-evident, its mythological roots are somewhat less obvious. The *Encyclopaedia Britannica* connects the two, but tells us nothing about the actual figure of Casmilus. None the less the identification of the two figures is central to the scheme of Smith's novel and she reiterates it in *Over the Frontier* through the medieval figure of Hermes Trismegistus:

   > Remember the so-famous first conductor of conducted parties, the great Trismegistus, whose name by a punic sleight is yours, who was himself the only one of those conducted parties that ever, laughing softly up his sleeve, came back again from hell. So remember and remember to be wary and watchful. (Smith, 1938/1980: 32)

   It is perhaps also worth mentioning that Mercury, the Roman manifestation of Hermes, is also the God of eloquence!
7. Pumphrey observes that Smith's poetry rejects the comfy sentimentality of later fairytales, and bases itself firmly in the 'cruel, destructive laughter' of the brothers Grimm.

5

'Breaking the Mould':
Virginia Woolf and the Threat of War

Now again I pay the penalty of mixing fact & fiction: cant
concentrate on The Years. I have a sense that one cannot control
this terrible fluctuation between the 2 worlds.

Virginia Woolf, *The Diary of Virginia Woolf*,
1 November, 1935

Virginia Woolf's response to the prospect of war was, of necessity, divided.
The Years was published in 1937 and *Three Guineas* a year later in 1938;
together they comprise Woolf's attempt to engage with and represent the
endemic fear and uncertainty of the late 1930s. Ambiguity, dislocation and
fragmentation shape *The Years*, while anger and polemic are neatly contained
within the tightly argued structure of *Three Guineas*. The world of *The Years* is
devoid of moral certainty and characters are hard pressed to communicate with
each other, let alone engage with the implications of Fascism; *Three Guineas*
confidently and ruthlessly exposes the patriarchal conspiracy at the heart of
all dictatorships. The contrast is considerable, but it is also revealing, for both
the divided response and the individual texts are indicative of the impact of
the crisis on Woolf and the influence of war on the structure and shape of
her narrative.

The roots of both works, however, reach back as far as 1932, when Woolf
undertook an experiment with what she called a 'Novel-Essay'. Mitchell
Leaska's edition of this unfinished project was published in 1978 as *The
Pargiters*, and this text offers a valuable insight into Woolf's creative process,
revealing an exciting, if overambitious, attempt to unite fiction and polemic.
Yet the experiment was abandoned. The novel section underwent a long and

painful transition, finally emerging as the 1880 chapter of *The Years*[1] and the information gathered for the essays was absorbed into *Three Guineas*. This joint beginning emphasises a connection between the two works that is reinforced by their shared concerns, and it is possible to see *The Years* as fuelled by the same question that motivates *Three Guineas*: 'How are we to prevent war?' This question pervades the novel, hovering unasked above the individual anxieties that beset the Pargiter family. The answers are harder to discern. Grace Radin (1981: xxi) observes that Woolf compared the writer's art to an iceberg, the text representing merely the tip of a much larger submerged mass. In the case of *The Years*, the shape of this mass becomes clearer when considered in conjunction with *Three Guineas*. Yet even the polemical certainties of *Three Guineas* cannot entirely resolve the contradictions of *The Years*, which confound any attempt to impose a theory of narrative or thematic unity upon the text. Each segment of the novel offers multiple interpretative possibilities and my analysis will at times suggest contradictory decodings of Woolf's work. In consequence, this chapter is focused not on the definition of a single strategy for assimilating the threat of war (a task that would be neither possible nor desirable), but rather on Woolf's iconoclastic challenge to the dangerous inertia of the entire socio-cultural status quo. Woolf's response to the threat of war would seem to have been a desire to 'break the mould' – an ironically aggressive urge to deconstruct the destructive forces of society. Her prewar fiction resists consistency and conformity, demanding through disruption the possibility of change.

ONLY CONNECT . . . ?

The narrative structure of *The Years* can be seen as a jigsaw puzzle. The overall framework is present, but there are crucial pieces missing – gaps and elisions that must be filled by the reader. This is a novel made up of short scenes, excerpts from much larger unexplored lives, offering the bare minimum of narrative strands to be grasped. This narrative of omission also results in a lack of certainty, creating a novel that both upholds and fragments the paradigm of linear progression. The only apparent unity is the family, the Pargiters, but the novel paradoxically yet persistently refutes the feasibility of a coherent family unit. Martin's cynicism is consistently supported by the events of the book:

> It was an abominable system, he thought; family life; Abercorn Terrace. No wonder the house would not let. It had one bathroom, and a basement; and there all those different people had lived, boxed up together, telling lies. (Woolf, 1937/1977: 171)

The isolation of individuals is extreme to the point of alienation. Characters talk at each other or into a void, fearing rejection, and yet each is asking the same unanswerable questions, never recognising that it is their very isolation which stands in the way of change. It is probable that an answer is never expected. The eternal questions have become reassuring clichés and it would require a new question before there could be any hope of an answer:

> she could not find the word she wanted – about the old couple, talking, as they had talked for the past fifty years . . . They were all talking. They had all settled in to add another sentence to the story that was just ending, or in the middle, or about to begin. (Woolf, 1937/1977: 200)

Yet, paradoxically, in *The Years* as in the earlier *A Room of One's Own* (1929), it is a vision of unity and a sense of the necessity of community that conclude the novel. There is more than a thematic bond uniting the ends of these two texts. The final chapter of *A Room of One's Own* opens with an image of the invisible river of London life, which flows into a vision of a future in which gender is perceived as a positive rather than a destructive force:

> Now it [the river] was bringing from one side of the street to the other diagonally a girl in patent leather boots, and then a young man in a maroon overcoat; it was also bringing a taxi-cab; and it brought all three together at a point directly beneath my window; where the taxi stopped; and the girl and the young man stopped; and they got into the taxi; and then the cab glided off as if it were swept on by the current elsewhere. (Woolf, 1929/1977: 92)

A man and a woman come together in a taxi cab and *proceed together* to an unknown destination. Perhaps the end of their enigmatic journey into the future is found in the final pages of *The Years*:

> [Eleanor] was watching a taxi that was gliding slowly around the square. It stopped in front of a house two doors down . . . A young man had got out; he paid the driver. Then a girl in a tweed travelling suit followed him. He fitted his latch-key to the door. 'There,' Eleanor murmured, as he opened the door and they stood for a moment on the threshold. (Woolf, 1937/1977: 330–31; ellipsis mine)

The threshold of what? Another war, or a brighter future in which the unity of male and female in the form of the politically androgynous 'outsider' creates a new day, dawning like the vivid sunrise whose image finally concludes *The Years*?

BREAKING THE HOLD OF THE PAST: HISTORY AND THE YEARS

The Years is a novel on the brink. Published on the verge of war, its creation brought Woolf to the edge of despair, and the lives it encapsulates are left poised at the gates of an unknowable future. This borderline status creates a central tension within the novel. It has rewritten the past, undermining the dominant history of masculine 'progress' through that history's own strategies of marginality and exclusion. But it cannot rewrite the present, for the present is always already inscribed by the ideologies of the past that have shaped its existence. We are perhaps too close to the present to see how it can be changed, a problem of which Woolf was not unaware. Gillian Beer draws attention to Woolf's critical demand that we 'stand further back from life', an aesthetic observation which can be usefully connected to her political vision of the Outsider. Beer, however, sees the problem of writing about the present most clearly articulated in *Orlando* (Woolf 1928/1977):

> If *Orlando* seems to have run out of steam at the end, that can be taken as the problem of making the present real on paper. The past is realised most fully in language. The present exists as body and as a semiological mass so current that our acts of interpretation are barely conscious. (Beer, 1987: 100)

This is the impasse that confronts Woolf in the final chapter of *The Years*. Not only does the present in general resist the imposition of interpretation, but the particular present of the 1930s seemed already to have been inscribed with the inevitability of the Second World War. 'All determined on war' (20 September 1935; 1977–84: vol. IV, 343) writes Woolf in 1935, revealing the underlying fear that persists beneath her fierce public insistence on the possibility of preventing conflict. To prevent war, to change the future, radical action must precede the inscription of a conflict which seemed to Woolf to be already predetermined. Thus, as a radical rewriting of history, when it reaches the present day, *The Years* inevitably comes to a dead end.

If *Orlando* is, in Gillian Beer's description, 'a sensory history of England' (1987: 99), *The Years* is Woolf's political history. Formed in its deviance from the 'facts', it runs aground when there are no facts to subvert, and it is at this point that the novel undergoes its seemingly arbitrary transition from pessimism to what might be defined as optimism. *The Years* is also Woolf's imaginative illustration of the process she describes in *Three Guineas*:

> in imagination perhaps we can see the educated man's daughter, as she issues from the shadow of the private house, and stands on the bridge which lies between the old world and the new, and asks, as she twirls the sacred coin in her hand, 'What shall I do with it? What do I see with it?' (Woolf 1938/1986: 19)[2]

These are impossible questions to which Woolf could offer only a pessimistic reply, and thus it is that the conclusion of *The Years* must undergo a final transition. The *her*story that has replaced history is ultimately usurped by fantasy. In no other way could Woolf reconcile the potential of her newly emancipated 'daughters of educated men' with the bleak reality of imminent world war. Thus it is that a novel which consistently undermines the illusion of patriarchal family life concludes with a party scene that presents the provisional, and doubtless extremely conditional, unity of that same unstable structure. Throughout, Woolf has emphasised the inadequacy of the outmoded and inflexible construct that is the family, but at Delia's party this temporary enforced togetherness gives rise to a sense of optimism that turns the novel round. This enables the Present Day section to conclude with the only indisputably positive image of all the novel's chapters. Many of these sections end with death, or the memory of a death – be it the king (1937/1977: 147), the unknown Miss Pym (1937/1977: 123) or the burial of Rose Pargiter (1937/1977: 69). Some end with a sense of hopelessness or with an image in which nature conspires to create an aura of despair and decay. Abel Pargiter's experience of the impotence of old age concludes the 1891 section:

> It was quite dark; lamps were lit; the autumn was drawing in; and as he marched up the dark windy street, now spotted with raindrops, a puff of smoke blew full in his face; and leaves were falling. (Woolf, 1937/1977: 99)

But the last lines of the Present Day section, and of the book, stand out in dazzling contrast to the dominant mood of the novel: 'The sun had risen, and the sky above the house wore an air of extraordinary beauty, simplicity and peace. (Woolf, 1937/1977: 331).

This seemingly incongruous ending affirms the possibility of survival, of overcoming chaos, and suggests that *The Years* became an attempt to find hope in the form of a positive, communal response to the threat of renewed division and conflict. This represents a marked contrast to the responses of both Dorothy L. Sayers and Stevie Smith to the prospect of war. Sayers is ultimately unable to assimilate the impending crisis, and avoids it through a retreat from the 'real' world. Smith follows Sayers into the realm of the absurd, but her bleak vision avoids nothing in its exposure of the roots of evil within us all. Woolf, however, manages an assimilation of the crisis by means of a metamorphosis whereby fear of war is transmuted into a plea for change. In so doing, it is possible that Woolf, like Sayers, ultimately avoids engaging with the realities of war.

This problem is most clearly marked in *Three Guineas* in which Woolf can neither accept nor articulate the Janus face of war: conflict is about killing as well as dying. Su Reid finds evidence of this inability to assimilate aggression in Woolf's use of photographs from the Spanish Civil War; photographs which,

unlike the images of ceremonial dress which bedeck the text, are absent from
Three Guineas:

> Killing, when it does appear in *Three Guineas*, is something men, but
> not women, do to pheasants. *Fighting* appears often, and it's something
> women do too, in their fight for university education for example: but
> fighting, in *Three Guineas*, does not mean killing. I have to suggest that
> the whole of *Three Guineas*, all its argument about the relationship of
> patriarchy and of the oppression of women to tyranny and to war, rests
> on a continuing silence about what war actually is, and what makes it
> different from other, certainly wicked, forms of oppression: war is people
> killing people. (Reid, 1991)[3]

Reid's argument is persuasive, but Patricia Laurence (1991) suggests a plausibly
simple alternative reading in her article 'The facts and fugue of war: from *Three
Guineas* to *Between the Acts*'. Laurence's primary concern is with genre, and the
relationship between Woolf's exploratory notebooks, the public arena of the
media, and the finished text of *Three Guineas*. Much of the material collected in
these notebooks was garnered from *The Times*, which in the winter of 1936 was
filled with vivid reports and terrifying photographs of the Spanish Civil War.
The photographs that are absent from Woolf's text were shockingly present
in the powerful and pervasive texts of the media, and from this site, argues
Laurence, they would undoubtedly have permeated the public consciousness.
None the less, the absence of these photographs from *Three Guineas* is
significant. Woolf is not afraid to describe violence: 'This morning's collection
contains the photograph of what might be a man's body, or a woman's; it is
so mutilated that it might, on the other hand, be the body of a pig' (Woolf,
1938/1986: 13). But it could be argued that her concern is with the aftermath
rather than the action of war. In *Three Guineas* Woolf does not want to consider
why it might be necessary to fight a war; her argument is that of a pacifist
aiming to delineate the insanity of patriarchal aggression. Woolf defines the
photographs as 'statements of fact addressed to the eye' (1938/1986: 13), and
their absence might be seen not as an inability to acknowledge this 'fact', but
as a desire to control its reception. As the only one with immediate access to
the image, Woolf can control and manipulate the public memory, thereby
ensuring the pictures' unambiguous support for her polemic.

The violence of war and human aggression remain a constant problematic
within Woolf's work. It resurfaces, and is perhaps more clearly articulated, in
both the form and imagery of her final novel *Between the Acts*. Giles's killing
of the snake and the frog is an unmistakable symbol of arbitrary violence, while
the frequent disruption of the narrative at both a conscious and an unconscious
level powerfully delineates the impact of war. However, in her exploration of

this 'continuing silence about what war actually is', Reid has identified the nebulous but vital distinction between Woolf's war writing and the influence of war upon Woolf's writing, and it is here that the apparent contradictions of Woolf's work have their roots.

The Years and Three Guineas are texts about the near impossibility of change that yet conclude with a vision of hope for change. In the case of The Years, this contradictory tension makes the novel a utopian strategy for survival at the same time as it forms a political indictment and a radical plea for change. The comparative freedom of fictional form also makes The Years an arena in which Woolf can acknowledge the gaps, inconsistencies and contradictions embodied in the prospect of war – contradictions which the formal demands of polemic, irrespective of its cause, must of necessity repress. Thus the structure of The Years, reputedly Woolf's 'most accessible' work,[4] can be seen as only superficially straightforward. Although it presents a coherent challenge to the institutions of history and the family, its narrative is also elliptical and fragmented, a diffuse conglomeration of glimpses into the intensely underwritten story of the Pargiters. In so far as The Years can be said to have a centre, that focus must be Eleanor. Not unlike Orlando, she seems to attain a supra-historical capacity to transcend the individual ages in which she lives. Always retaining a recognisable self, she none the less revels in the change she perceives around her. Eleanor's fluidity, her flexibility and openness, forms in itself a challenge to the tyranny of a patriarchal history which had confined her to the prison of the private house.

However, Eleanor's strength lies not only in her multiplicity – she also represents a force of continuity binding together the disparate members of the family. She is a symbol of stability and constancy within the fragmented narrative. Although she comes to travel, she never becomes an exile in the manner of her brother Martin or her nephew North, and once no longer chained to Abercorn Terrace she realises her potential to blend in anywhere, from an English village to India. Throughout the novel her affections remain constant, as do her social awareness and concern for others. Her long imprisonment (within the enforced childhood of Victorian womanhood) also has the effect of making her vision of the 'outside' world the fresh perspective of the innocent. She remains largely uncontaminated by the patriarchal order, and this gives her observations a desirable critical distance. When she visits Morris, the brother to whom she had once been closest, she finds him stagnating in the country, and enters a world that seems in many respects a precursor of the environment of Between the Acts. Morris's village offers the quiet tranquillity of a secure, undemanding Englishness – a rural idyll that, in her final novel, Woolf would show to be under attack from without and from within. In the context of The Years, however, the environment is presented as almost wholly negative. Meeting again the man she might once have married, she is shocked by his superfluity:

> But are we all like that? she asked herself, looking from the grisled, crumpled red-and-yellow face of the boy she had known – he was almost hairless – at her own brother Morris. He looked bald and thin; but surely he was in the prime of life, as she was herself? Or had they all suddenly become old fogies like Sir William? (Woolf, 1937/1977: 153)

Eleanor's capacity to stand outside the time of the oppressive symbolic order is emphasised here. The clock of her subjective female experience is shown to be at odds with the remorseless process of man's ages. That it is also a kinder time is evident from the juxtaposition of Eleanor's vitality against the men's decay. In her implicit rejection of the linear progression to old age in favour of a cyclical time of renewal and change, Eleanor's 'woman's time' is represented as one of regeneration, rather than the degeneration of a 'masculine' time.[5] Eleanor rejects the stasis of old age, choosing instead a new life of continual change and stimulus: 'Sir William was getting into bed next door, his life was over; hers was beginning' (Woolf, 1937/1977: 164).

As the cohesive force of the novel, Eleanor embodies the courage to accept change – an attitude epitomised by her reaction to Nicholas's homosexuality:

> For a second a sharp shiver of repugnance passed over Eleanor's skin as if a knife had sliced it. Then she realized that it touched nothing of importance. The sharp shiver passed. (1937/1977: 228)[6]

With her loose ego boundaries that de-emphasise the distinction between individual and communal, Eleanor goes some way to understanding the other characters. She sympathises with the unpopular Digby and quickly recognises the reasons for Peggy's resentment of North. Her successful transition from the Victorian to the Modern, and from the private to the public, gives the family a cohesion that holds them back from the brink of complete dispersal.

ALIENATED LIVES: PATTERN AND ITS DISRUPTION IN THE YEARS

Beyond the cohesion of Eleanor, the novel is composed of isolated and alienated characters who interact in accordance with a complex network of pattern and repetition that forms the framework of the novel. The alienation springs from social restrictions based on the construct of respectability. There can be no shared experience for the women of *The Years*, for the stories of their lives must be presented to the new generation in bowdlerised form. Old Aunt Warburton can only give the virginal Ann a 'selection from her memoirs . . . an edition with asterisks; for it was a story that could hardly be told to a girl in white satin' (1937/1977: 199). The isolation of ignorance is supplemented by the divisions of class and age. One generation finds it impossible to identify with the experience of another. Peggy, living in an age of fear and uncertainty, yearns for what she imagines was the security of Eleanor's youth, while Eleanor's perspective focuses on the opportunities and knowledge that were denied her in 1880:

> 'You used to dine . . .' Peggy began. She wished to get her back to her past. It was so interesting; so safe; so unreal – that past of the eighties; and to her, so beautiful in its unreality.
> 'Tell me about your youth . . .' she began.
> 'But your lives are much more interesting than ours were,' said Eleanor. Peggy was silent. (Woolf, 1937/1977: 254)

Peggy's silence here articulates the counter-current of pessimism, embodied by the persistent denial of potential, that acts within the novel to negate the optimism inherent in Eleanor's innocent vision of an exciting new world. As Eleanor is revitalised by her comparative freedom, so Peggy is deadened by the absence of real change. However, Eleanor's violent response to the photograph of Mussolini (1937/1977: 252) is perhaps an indication of the extent to which she realises the precarious and precious nature of her new-found freedom.

Patterns of characterisation within the family are evident in the similarities between Martin and North. Both are ex-army exiles returning after years spent in an alien land, the life of which is scarcely conceivable to those in England. Their outsider's eye becomes a useful device through which Woolf depicts the developments within the family. Similarly a pattern can be seen in the leitmotif developed for Kitty through her belated dramatic entrances in evening dress; while a pattern of common experience reveals Peggy to be in spiritual proximity to Delia through her emotional self-consciousness. Neither woman feels able to experience the appropriate emotion at the appropriate time. Delia was emotionally numb at the death of her mother, and when we see her again fifty years later she has adopted a protective persona of ebullient Irishness. In this guise she enacts a series of larger-than-life emotions which disguise the disappointments of a lost cause and a senile husband. Peggy, watching Eleanor en route for Delia's party, marvels at the older woman's emotional range and tries in an imaginary conversation to describe her aunt:

> And how does one get that right? Peggy thought, trying to add another touch to the portrait. 'Sentimental' was it? Or, on the contrary, was it good to feel like that . . . natural . . . right? She shook her head. (1937/1977: 255)

These patterns of incomprehension, character and situation combine with a high incidence of repeated conversation to infuse the novel with a perpetual sense of *déjà vu,* which Woolf uses to stress the remorseless patterning of history. Brown's insight into the nature of dictators is repeated so often that it becomes a cliché – a warning to which nobody pays any heed. Its third repetition is an ironic piece of reported speech between North and Sara:

> 'Napoleon; the psychology of great men; if we don't know ourselves how can we know other people . . .' He stopped. It was difficult to remember accurately what had been said even one hour ago.
>
> 'And then,' she said, holding out one hand and touching a finger exactly as Brown had done, '. . . how can we make laws, religions, that fit, that fit, when we don't know ourselves?'
>
> 'Yes! Yes!' he exclaimed. She had caught his manner exactly . . .
>
> 'And Eleanor,' Sara continued, 'says . . . "Can we improve – can we improve ourselves?" sitting on the edge of the sofa?'
>
> 'Of the bath,' he laughed, correcting her.
>
> 'You've had that talk before,' he said. That was precisely what he was feeling. They had talked before. (1937/1977: 241; third ellipsis mine)

Later, through Eleanor, Woolf offers the suggestion that there might be security in patterns:

> She knew exactly what he was going to say. He had said it before, in the restaurant . . . As she thought it, he said it. Does everything then come over again a little differently? she thought. If so, is there a pattern; a theme, recurring, like music; half remembered, half foreseen? . . . a gigantic pattern, momentarily perceptible? The thought gave her extreme pleasure: that there was a pattern. But who makes it? Who thinks it? (1937/1977: 282; first ellipsis mine)

It is in the question 'Who makes it?' that Woolf's conception of the fundamental problem facing society lies, and for this reason the whole fragmentary nature of the narrative opposes this easy assumption of patterning. Patterns encourage complacency. They epitomise a patriarchal society's resistance to change and disguise their essentially reactionary nature behind a façade of security; social rituals present themselves as a refuge from disruption, fragmentation and the dislocation of war. 'Business as usual' – it has always been thus and it always will be – even if this means a constant pattern of war and aggression across the centuries.

In *Three Guineas,* anticipating her correspondent's reluctance to abandon the security of tradition, 'Why should we hesitate to do what our fathers and grandfathers have done before us?' (1938/1986: 81), Woolf provides an uncompromising indictment of the pattern of that tradition's power and exclusivity:

> Almost the same daughters ask almost the same brothers for almost the same privileges. Almost the same gentlemen intone the same refusals for almost the same reasons. It seems as if there were no progress in the human race, but only repetition. (Woolf, 1938/1986: 76)

Consequently, above all the other patterns in *The Years*, there rises an anti-pattern of unspoken thoughts, silence and isolation. Woolf demands change – the breaking and disrupting of the traditional. Like Smith and Sayers she responds to the threat of chaos, but by locating this threat in the apocalyptic crescendo of the patriarchal social pattern she makes an unprecedented advance into the possibilities of a feminist alternative. There is an interesting contrast here between Woolf's textual strategy and that of Dorothy L. Sayers. For Sayers the threat of chaos lies in the disruption of the social pattern, and her work attempts to resist this disruption through the rules and regulations of genre fiction. However, for Woolf, the threat of chaos is situated within and because of pattern, and her work attempts to challenge and undermine, rather than preserve, the assumptions of these patterns. Yet, just as absurdity persists in disrupting the logic of Lord Peter Wimsey's tidy investigation, so Woolf's texts resist her attempt to expose the danger of pattern. Eleanor's sense of security in patterns is also Woolf's, and much as she works to disrupt pattern, on another level she also cherishes it as a bonding force of shared experience. This is indicative of the complex borderline that divides the repetitive and destructive pattern of patriarchal history from the rhythmic pattern of a natural 'feminine' cycle of renewal and regeneration.

`A CHORUS, ALONE´: ISOLATION AND THE OUTSIDER

The conflicting ideologies embodied in the distinction between patriarchal patterning and natural regeneration are further examined through the isolated and alienated figure of Kitty Malone. Kitty's affluent background puts severe constraints on her movements and choices. She desires the impossible – to be a farmer – and her class, combined with the physical environment of an Oxford college, makes her a particularly discrete character. We never see her in harmony with people, only with the natural environment, and her real peace lies in the solitude she finds escaping from the city: 'A deep murmur sang in her ears – the land itself, singing to itself, a chorus, alone. She lay there listening. She was happy, completely. Time had ceased' (Woolf 1937/1977: 213). Significantly, Kitty's refuge is found outside the temporal order. In an organic return to the land that prefigures the association of women with a time outside history in *Between the Acts*, Kitty's salvation lies in a parallel non-time. Isolated from the temporal symbolic order, her heightened perceptions also posit a challenge to patriarchal concepts of space and subjectivity. Contained within the paradox of 'a chorus, alone' is Woolf's embodiment of the potential conjunction of self and not-self, the integrity of the individual and its multiplicity; in Gillian Beer's terms, the crucial and frequently blurred distinction between 'I' and 'We':

> The alternation between 'I and 'We' is the living quarrel of Virginia Woolf's art, particularly in her later career. Her subject matter is often isolation, and she excels at recording the repetitive, fickle movements of an individual's thought and feeling at levels beneath self-criticism. But she was fascinated by communities: the family, groups of friends, the nation and history. (Beer, 1987: 85)

'We' must be seen to represent both the mass of communal or national experience and the radical disruption of ego boundaries suggested by Woolf's fluid conception of individual consciousness. Kitty finds her communality with the land. Here she is both alone and yet an integral part of a larger, more significant whole. Within the terms of Woolf's debate in *Three Guineas*, however, she has been placed in a situation of double alienation. As a woman she is an outsider, situated on the periphery of the patriarchal symbolic; yet her position within this order, her role as Lady Lasswade, is the very thing which alienates her from her contemporaries, and from the communality they find in non-conformity. Even Eleanor, the person with whom she most wants to communicate (and perhaps the novel's most flexible communicator) finds herself unable to traverse the arbitrary boundaries of class and wealth that divide her from her cousin Kitty. As a result of this displacement, Kitty must find her communality not with people but with the land, and this politically neutral bonding is indicative of another crucial boundary being negotiated by the text. How can isolation and alienation be transmuted into a force for change? Where does the boundary lie between outsider status and the powerlessness of alienation? Perhaps the distinction is contained within the process of self-determination. The act of defining oneself as an outsider is the act of claiming an identity; yet the potential for empowerment within this action is brought into question by the uncertainty of the status that is claimed. Julia Kristeva asks whether it is possible to refuse the extremes of conformity or madness, suggesting that without the 'moorings of the word . . . life itself can't hang on' (1974: 157), and Woolf seems equally uncertain whether an escape from the law of the Father can effectively be transmuted into a force for change. Within the scope of *The Years* Woolf's outsiders become something of a Greek chorus. Those who break free become prophets of doom or anxious commentators – spared from participation but forced to watch as the drama of war proceeds along its preordained and seemingly unalterable path.

The idea of the outsider is central to *The Years*, and the debate is further focalised through Edward, whose membership of the Pargiter family seems entirely nominal. He is a completely isolated figure who never marries and, with the exception of Delia's party, is never seen in the family group. Spiritually he is the counterpart of Kitty, the novel's other extremely isolated character, and gradually Woolf moves towards a condemnation of both their respective isolations. Such extremity is not constructive and makes no gestures towards co-operation. Significantly, the major intellectual achievement of Edward's academic career is his translation of Sophocles' *Antigone*. His life is inextricably entwined with Sophocles' powerful imaginative world of principle, peopled with characters who refuse to compromise. Antigone's stand was laudable, and her famous words ''Tis not my nature to join in hating, but in loving', form an unwritten epigraph to both *The Years* and *Three Guineas*; but that same heedless courage leads to her death, leaving Creon's pride to lay waste to his country.

The Antigone image is widely used within *Three Guineas*, yet Woolf refuses to appropriate the play as a consistent political parable, aware as was Sophocles, that the ambiguities of fiction have implications far beyond the categorical certainties demanded of polemical prose. Here again is the dilemma of the art/politics divide. Woolf seems uncertain of her ability to control a singular political purpose within the dangerous multiplicity of fiction's metonymic language. The language of connotation is antithetical to interpretative certainty; the subtleties of fiction undermine the bold generalisations of polemic and the text resists the imposition of a totemic restrictive meaning. Discussing *Antigone* in *Three Guineas*, Woolf ostensibly rejects the appropriation of art by politics:

> But though it is easy to squeeze these characters into up-to-date dress, it is impossible to keep them there. They suggest too much; when the curtain falls we sympathize, it may be noted, even with Creon himself. (Woolf 1938/1986: 190)

Yet perhaps Woolf protests too much. This denial of the obviously political must be seen as a screen, deflecting attention from the more insidious political message that saturates her fiction. It is in the very suggestiveness of her fiction, in what Rachel Blau DuPlessis (1985) has called the 'writing beyond the ending', that the politics of Woolf's fiction can be located.[7] By resisting the confines of ostentatious allegory, Woolf creates the possibility of squeezing her characters not merely into up-to-date dress, but into a multiplicity of timeless outfits. Through the denial of politics in her fiction, Woolf's Creon becomes an ambiguous figure potentially evoking not only Mussolini, but also the spectre of the father, the brother, and ultimately even the self.

Thus it is only to be expected that any prospect of creating a consistent interpretative identification between Sophocles' play, Woolf's novel and Woolf's polemic will at some point be sundered. In 1907, when Sara Pargiter opens the virgin copy of Edward's *Antigone*, her reading comprehensively undermines the cohesion of his vision. Ironically juxtaposed against the music of her parents' dance, Sara's reading of the *Antigone* rejects the sterile classicism of Edward's prose and focuses instead on the vivid, nightmare images of the text. Her reading is 'random' and inaccurate, culled from 'the litter of broken words', and clinically detached from the catharsis of tragedy. For Sara, Antigone's fate raises no more than a yawn. Yet this reading is also a vision. It forms the apocalyptic premonition of a generation's future, transcending the clumsy precision of the prose to realise the full horror of the text. Here is the music of war that will obliterate the music of the waltz:

> The unburied body of the murdered man lay on the sand. Then in a yellow cloud came whirling – who? She turned the page quickly. Antigone? She came whirling out of the dust-cloud to where the vultures were reeling and flung white sand over the blackened foot. She stood there letting fall white dust over the blackened foot. Then behold! there were more clouds; dark clouds; the horsemen leapt down; she was seized; her wrists were bound with withies; and they bore her, thus bound – where? (Woolf 1937/1977: 105)

The clouds of war and the horsemen of the Apocalypse – Sara's *Antigone* is a new story for a new generation. It is also a story that seems to offer little in the way of hope to the outsider. Antigone's stand against the might of Creon's patriarchy ended in the silence of the tomb. The individual alone cannot break the strictures of the mould.

Yet despite its centrality, the pessimism of the Antigone myth does not go unchallenged – not least by Woolf's illustration of the multiplicity of interpretative possibility. New readers revitalise old stories, and to create new readers Woolf would break the social and educational moulds that formed the outwardly conformist but inwardly dysfunctional characters of Kitty and Edward. Over the course of *The Years*, Woolf painstakingly anatomises two of the fundamental determinants of subjectivity and power: the discourses of class and gender. Within these explorations lie moments of clarity and revelation, but overall the tone is pessimistic. As the threat of war grew stronger, Woolf seemed increasingly to suggest that while we operate within the framework of patriarchy, we will not see change, but simply endless variations on the theme of oppression.

CLASS CONSCIOUSNESS: A CASE STUDY

The figure of Kitty, utilised as an embodiment of isolation, is also central to the discourse of class within *The Years*. The divisiveness of privilege, of class and education, is explored through Kitty's constrained and difficult visit to the Robsons. In this scene Kitty, the daughter of the Master of St Katherine's College, goes to visit Nell, the daughter of a self-educated, working-class professor who 'had done it all off his own bat'; and there follows an uncomfortable dialogue between the upper and working classes. Woolf makes it abundantly clear that the world of the poor is alien to Kitty, who becomes painfully aware of a literally physical disjuncture that is reminiscent of Alice in the looking-glass world. 'I'm much too large, Kitty thought, as she stood for a moment in the room to which the maid had admitted her . . . And I'm too well dressed she thought, looking at herself in the glass over the fireplace' (1937/1977: 53; ellipsis mine). There is, however, another dimension to this scene, which forms a pessimistic indication of the extent to which Woolf was reacting to the changing political climate.

The visit to the Robsons forms the substance of the fifth chapter of *The Pargiters*, although in this early draft of the scene they are called variously the Hughes and the Brooks. The episode as it appears in *The Years* is considerably shorter than the earlier version, but the changes in emphasis between the two are none the less considerable. In the five years dividing *The Pargiters* from *The Years*, the international situation underwent a sharp decline. Woolf's diary for this period records Hitler's purges (2 July 1934; 1977–84: vol. IV, 223), a succession of Austrian *coups d'état* (18 February 1934; 1977–84: vol. IV, 202) and the stirrings of Fascism in Britain (4 September 1935; 1977–84: vol. IV, 337).[8] These disturbing events undoubtedly influenced Woolf, and her embryonic 'Novel-Essay' of 1932 evolved into an altogether bleaker and more pessimistic vision.

Woolf's editorial decisions are strongly suggestive of the influence of external events and seem a clear affirmation of her increasing anxiety at the turn of world politics. Optimistic ideas, comments which confirm moments of understanding between the two classes are cut, but the uncertainty, fear and division remain. Although Kitty warms to the Robsons in *The Years*, the narrative describes it as 'a sudden rush of self-pity':

> If she had been the daughter of people like the Robsons, she thought; if she had lived in the north – but it was clear they wanted her to go . . . Nobody pressed her to stay. (Woolf, 1937/1977: 57; ellipsis mine)

The accuracy of Kitty's impression that she was not wanted is difficult to ascertain from the information Woolf provides in *The Years*. The few indications given are not optimistic. The only member of the Robson family to whose thoughts we are given access is Jo, and his response is a depressing confirmation of the class divide: 'He cast one quick sulky look at her as she stood in the doorway. She's a stunner, he said to himself, but my word, she gives herself airs!' (1937/1977: 56). The change in emphasis from *The Pargiters* is considerable. The contrast between the portrayal of Mrs Robson and her alter ego Mrs Brooks is typical of this change. There seems little connection between the inscrutable and stately Mrs Robson of *The Years* (1937/1977: 57) and Mrs Brook of *The Pargiters* who 'positively beamed' (Woolf, 1978: 143) on discovering Kitty's Yorkshire connection.

Kitty leaves the Brooks' house with her head full of dreams, and experiences a 'queer sense of changed proportions' (Woolf, 1978: 149) when she reaches her own home:

> She peeped into the drawing room. It looked very large, very stately, very still. [*after the crowded little room in Pinbright Road.*] It looked very dull, very solemn, very pretentious. (Woolf, 1978: 149)

This affirmation of the validity of alternatives never occurs in *The Years*. We see Kitty oppressed by her home environment, but there is never any suggestion that change is possible, and indeed, her faint hopes are denied by the progression of the narrative. She leaves the Robsons on a note of uncertainty: 'Did they know how much she admired them? she wanted to say. Would they accept her in spite of her hat and her gloves?' (Woolf, 1937/1977: 58). That fear is resolved in *The Pargiters*. We are provided with the reassuring responses of the Brooks themselves:

> he had come to the same conclusion as his wife – they often came to the same conclusions – that Kitty Malone was a very nice girl whose parents were going the right way to ruin her by the way they brought her up. (Woolf, 1978: 141)

Not only does this statement suggest an understanding that defies the inadequacy of language – Mr and Mrs Brook sympathise with Kitty despite her inability to communicate – it also reinforces the sense of a relaxed family unity suggested by the use of 'Dad' and 'Mum'. Their unity is seen to be something positive and potentially creative as opposed to the stultifying 'darkness' of both Abercorn Terrace (Woolf, 1937/1977: 65) and the Master's Lodge (1937/1977: 60). Woolf seemed determined in *The Pargiters* to create a positive image of a new family unit that recognises the needs of its individual components and is therefore capable of change:

> she had the odd sensation that she was nobodies [sic]daughter in particular. Accustomed as she was, at the first mention of her name to be asked 'The

daughter of Dr. Malone? And how is your father?' . . . he never asked her
'How is your father?' And thus . . . Kitty began to be aware that there
were a great many things [*sh*] that she could say here, to Sam and Nell,
once she found her tongue. (Woolf, 1978: 139–40; ellipses mine)

This moment is retained in *The Years* (1937/1977: 54), but is not sufficient
to overcome the sense of uncomfortable realism that Woolf's revision has
brought to her original somewhat utopian idea. Kitty never finds 'her tongue'
– language has again defeated communication. Indeed *The Years* contains a
bitter postscript in Kitty's discovery, almost at the end of the novel, that Nell
had died. This information is provided at Delia's party and thereby gives
added emphasis to Woolf's portrayal of a society largely blind to the need
for fundamental social change. Kitty had romanticised the Robsons/Brooks,
denying the evidence of their poverty through the rose-tinted spectacles
of their 'happy family' unity. Similarly, Delia congratulates herself on the
social mix at her party, ironically only drawing attention to the intensely
limited scope of her experience. Martin's perspective, a few pages later,
reinforces our sense of her complacency and reminds us that Delia is only
playing the part of the rebel: 'For all Delia's pride in her promiscuity, he
thought, glancing at the people, there were only Dons and Duchesses'
(1937/1977: 308).

   In abbreviating *The Pargiters* Woolf has created a paratactic picture of
non-communication through the careful removal of any comments that
make explicit the possibility of understanding. Through the connections
with Delia's party she makes evident the complacency of the privileged.
Class divides, and under the current social status quo it will continue
to do so, irrespective of the well-meaning condescension of the mon-
eyed classes.

THE PROFESSIONAL WOMAN: A GENDER DILEMMA

The fragmentary nature of *The Years* is Woolf's illustration of the divided
nation of the private house and the public world. Peggy's alienation forms the
outstanding symbol of just how little progress has been made in the breaking
down of class and gender barriers over the fifty-seven years encompassed
by the novel. As an educated, professional woman she is technically more
powerful than the frustrated daughters and sisters of 'educated men'. But
in qualifying for the ranks of the élite her alienation has been exacerbated
rather than relieved. She is no longer a member of the excluded classes, her
education and 'conspiracy' with the patriarchal establishment has divided her
from these roots. She should be a member of the professional classes, but as
a woman she is denied access to the status and power of the establishment.

Peggy has no illusions about her position; 'I'm the exception; hard; cold; in a groove already; merely a doctor' (1937/1977: 270); a denial of gender which is the price patriarchy demands of the professional woman. Peggy's achievement has not introduced her to the pleasures of androgyny – society defines her not as multiple, but as neuter. Patriarchal society suffers acutely from the disease identified by Woolf in *Three Guineas* as 'infantile fixation'. It will not let women grow up, marry or in any way interact with the enticing suitors, Independence, Education and Politics. A woman cannot 'belong'. She is a member in name only, and even the strength of that name is denied Peggy.

Of all the female characters in *The Years*, Peggy alone is known by a diminutive that totally distorts the shape and sound of her name. This diminutive is the only name by which she is ever addressed and we only learn that she is Miss Margaret Pargiter when she gives her name to the maid at Delia's party. By containing the fact of her serious professionalism within the patronising security of a belittling diminutive, she is effectively neutralised as a force for change. The presence of her teacher, 'her master', at the party seems only to confirm her status as a gifted child – a clever woman – a freak. *Three Guineas* makes explicit what is suggested by *The Years*. A woman can effect change only by remaining outside the established order of power and influence, and by abandoning the narrow concerns of 'our' country for the global concerns of universal change. This is the creed of the outsider:

> as a woman, I have no country. As a woman I want no country. As a woman my country is the whole world. (Woolf, 1938/1986: 125)

An admirable ideal: but it is worth asking whether in the narrator's eventual decision to send a guinea to the treasurers of the compromised funds for education and the professions, there would seem to be a tacit recognition of the impossibility of the outsider's position.

BREAKING THE MOULD OF GENDER

It is the subtleties of *The Years* rather than the certainties of *Three Guineas* that do most to illustrate the crucial distinction between the private brother and the public father that is central to Woolf's understanding of patriarchy. *The Years*, like the pre-war novels of Dorothy L. Sayers and Stevie Smith, depicts a complex reinscription of gender roles. This evolutionary pattern, which depicts a constructive escape from the dictates of biological determinism, is, however, contained within the restrictive framework of an unchallenged patriarchal hegemony. But this limited escape is, as Woolf argues in *Three Guineas*, an essential prerequisite of change. Defeating the dictator in Europe is contingent upon the defeat of the dictator in the house. Only by imagining domestic change can global transformation be envisioned.

The gradual reconstruction of gender demanded by *Three Guineas* is illustrated in *The Years* through the Pargiter family tree, the roots of which are firmly grounded in the Victorian era. The founding couple of Rose and Abel Pargiter together epitomise the traditional polarities of gender differentiation. Rose is positively sick with femininity; before the year is out, she is dead.[9] Abel is the embodiment of 'masculinity', an aging patriarch, with a mistress and a war wound, who intimidates his children and keeps his emotions safely within his 'tightly buttoned frock-coat' (1937/1977: 14). Yet within the lives and the lifetimes of their children, there begins a process of redefinition, a blurring of gender boundaries, which was an essential prerequisite for Woolf's dream of co-operation.

Yet this desire for the creation of 'good wholes' is constantly undermined by the simultaneous articulation of the project's impossibility, embodied in the fragmentation and dislocation of *The Years*. The progressive ideal of 'feminine' men and 'masculine' women seems destined for defeat as these prototype androgynes struggle to conform (or become 'outsiders' through their refusal to conform) to the dictates of a society out of sync with the process of their personal evolution.

The limited options available to women in the late nineteenth century are made abundantly clear in the fates of Delia and Milly. These daughters of the house of Abel Pargiter are connected in rivalry at the beginning of the novel. Initially they compete for their father's affection and for knowledge of the outside world, but while Milly 'always brings the conversation back to marriage' (1937/1977: 26) and ultimately develops into a sordid specimen of the stereotypical female, Delia rebels against 'femininity'. Nursing a confused semi-romantic, semi-political interest in Parnell she eventually becomes the dominant partner in a disappointingly unromantic marriage. Interestingly it is Delia more than any of her brothers who identifies emotionally with Abel Pargiter, recognising a shared sense of emotional numbness. As her mother dies, Delia listens outside:

> Then there was a stir, a shuffle of feet in the bedroom and out came her father, stumbling.
>
> 'Rose!' he cried. 'Rose! Rose!' He held his arms with the fists clenched out in front of him.
>
> You did that very well, Delia told him as he passed her. It was like a scene in a play. She observed quite dispassionately that the raindrops were still falling. (Woolf, 1937/1977: 38)

Rejecting identification with the passivity of her mother, Delia can only assume the guise of 'masculine' anti-emotionalism.

Woolf's development of altered states is, however, most clearly evident in

Martin and Rose, inappropriately named after her frail and feminine mother. Rose is a soldier. She is 'handsome' (1937/1977: 120), 'more like a man than a woman' (1937/1977: 131), 'a military man' (1937/1977: 273) and, the ultimate compliment, 'a fine fellow' (1937/1977: 320). In the 1908 section of *The Years*, Eleanor establishes the incongruities inherent in Martin the soldier and Rose the political activist:

> She ought to have been the soldier, Eleanor thought. She was exactly like old Uncle Pargiter of Pargiter's Horse. Martin, now that he had shaved his moustache off and showed his lips, ought to have been – what? (Woolf 1937/1977: 121)

What indeed? Martin becomes the official soldier to Rose's unofficial warrior before rejecting army life and becoming a dandified observer of Pargiter life. Careful of his appearance, sensitive – he 'never could abide wool next the skin' (1937/1977: 170), and with courage enough to stand up for his individuality and leave the army, he becomes an exile, initially physically, but above all spiritually. In theory he could be seen as an embryonic candidate for the Society of Outsiders, but in practice the boundaries remain insufficiently blurred; the age of co-operation has not yet dawned. The hold of gender stereotypes may be weakening, but it still has Martin in thrall. He is embarrassed by Sara when she speaks in her 'ordinary voice' in the city chop house; 'In deference to him she assumed the manner of a lady lunching with a gentleman in a city restaurant' (1937/1977: 176), and when he struggles to make conversation with the virginal Ann 'he had to reject almost everything that occured to him – she was so young' (1937/1977: 192).

The unconventional Sara is situated beyond the immediate circle of Pargiters, a departure which perhaps suggests that the family must be rejected before it can be reconstituted. She is one of a network of cousins and friends which includes her sister's husband Renny. An outsider by virtue of his nationality, this mispronounced Frenchman is an important part of the redefinition process. The picture North creates at Delia's party presents Renny as a man divided, torn between the opposing polarities of a flawed society: 'A man who made shells; a man who loved peace; a man of science; a man who cried' (Woolf 1937/1977: 265). Not only do Renny's tears set him at a far remove from the 'masculinity' of Abel Pargiter, but he also embodies the contradictions and complexities facing Woolf as the likelihood of war increased. Both Zwerdling (1986: 271–302) and Oldfield (1989) have provided careful studies of Woolf's eventual renunciation of pacifism, and in North's description of Renny she seems to present an early articulation of her own dilemma.

The gender positions of the latest generation, Peggy and North, are even less easy to categorise. Peggy's alienated position, which denies rather than redefines gender, has already been discussed above. Her breakthrough in communication is intimately connected to Woolf's project of gender redefinition, and it is essential that her contemporary, North, be capable of dialogue. Their mutual understanding, if achieved, would symbolise a challenge to the divisive hegemony of patriarchal language, offering a site from which the denial of gender could be constructively reinscribed as androgyny. On the evolutionary scale, North would seem to be a development of Martin, sharing his fastidiousness (1937/1977: 260), his cynicism (1937/1977: 237) and his experience as an exile. Also like Martin, North is presented having dinner with Sara, and it is here that Woolf indicates the progress that has been made.[10] Using the unpredictable, non-conforming Sara as a gauge, the ease of North's response can be compared with the embarrassment and discomfort of Martin. North's conversation with Sara contains the elliptical connections and comfortable laughter of two people communicating a shared experience. The scene is filled both with reminders of the disparity of their experience and with a sense of the potential to bridge that gap:

> a trombone player had struck up in the street below, and as the voice of the woman practising her scales continued, they sounded like two people trying to express completely different views of the world in general at one and the same time. The voice ascended; the trombone wailed. They laughed. (Woolf, 1937/1977: 241)

Here, as later in the novel, in particular at Delia's party, laughter is presented not as the disruption of discourse but as the key to communication. An indication, perhaps, that it is *only* by disrupting discourse that communication can be achieved.

NARRATIVE TENSIONS I: THE FAILURE OF LANGUAGE

The no-woman's-land of the professions is a shared concern of both *The Years* and *Three Guineas*. The two texts condemn the waste inherent in the untapped resources and energy of so many female Pargiters, and Woolf saw this waste of energy and ability as nothing short of criminal. Her concept of a Society of Outsiders was envisaged as a force strong enough to assault the edifice of patriarchal society head on, and it is within the violence of this anger that a reason for dividing the two books lies. In her introduction to the Hogarth edition of *Three Guineas*, Hermione Lee observes:

> That burying of the interchapters [of *The Pargiters*] under the uneasy, evasive, fragmented surface of *The Years* is like the burying of the original titles for *A Room of One's Own* and *Three Guineas*: it is another instance

of her desire to control anger and to separate art from politics. (Woolf
1938/1986: xiii)

Closely related to this anger is the extreme difficulty experienced by Woolf
in the writing of *The Years*. Both Carolyn Heilbrun and Hermione Lee have
described the pain and anxiety of the novel's creation, and Heilbrun observes
that this tension was only resolved when Woolf let her anger flow freely in the
writing of *Three Guineas* (Heilbrun, 1989: 126). Woolf's decision to write two
separate books suggests that she found her anger at the political situation too
powerful to constrain within the carefully crafted boundaries of her fiction.
This anger had the potential to distort the poetic form of her fictional prose,
just as she feared that anger had 'deformed and twisted' the poetic vision
of Charlotte Brontë (Woolf, 1929/1977: 67). Woolf's diary illustrates her
dilemma:

> it would be much wiser not to attempt to sketch a draft of On Being
> Despised, or whatever it is to be called, until the P.s is done with. I
> was vagrant this morning & made a rash attempt, with the interesting
> discovery that one cant propagate at the same time as write fiction. And
> as this fiction is dangerously near propaganda, I must keep my hands
> clear. (Woolf, 14 April 1935; 1977–84: vol: IV, 300)

The roots of the difficulties Woolf experienced in composing *The Years* can perhaps be found in her continued determination to maintain this distinction.

The prose of *The Years* is elegant and elliptical, revealing Woolf's customary
command of what is left unsaid or merely hinted. But even within this precise
format there are signs of an unusual urgency, which may be indicative of
difficulties in composition or of the gravity of the situation in which she was
writing. Woolf makes explicit things that would normally have been left to
the reader's interpretation. A central concern of the novel is the diversity of
individual perception: Woolf is at pains to show that no two people have the
same response to or remembrance of, a particular situation and that therefore
there can be no truly collective experience. An early example is provided by
Eleanor and Martin's diametrically opposed opinions of Eugénie and Digby,
after which Eleanor muses: 'It was odd how different the same person seemed
to two different people, she thought. There was Martin, liking Eugénie; and
she, liking Digby' (Woolf, 1937/1977: 119). Similarly the constant repetition
of themes and patterns in what is, for Woolf, a longer than average novel,
suggests a pressing need to communicate something that she feels unable to
formulate or articulate, in much the same way that her characters are crippled
by their inability to communicate.

Hermione Lee draws attention to Woolf's frequently articulated conviction that the novel had 'failed' and asks 'How could Virginia Woolf write a long, wordy novel about the failure of language? That was the insoluble, near catastrophic predicament she placed herself in, feeling as she did that no other kind of writing would appropriate to the contemporary circumstances' (Lee, 1992: xxv). Lee goes on to explore Woolf's claim that the novel was a 'deliberate failure' and persuasively argues that failure 'fits' the novel, peopled as it is by a cast of doomed Chekhovian misfits. Yet this mood of failure cannot account for the novel's sudden transition from pessimism to optimism – a transition which suggests that Woolf clung to a belief in the possibility of change that was at odds with the grim narrative impetus of her text.[11]

The Years incongruously snatches victory from the jaws of defeat. The transitional movement into optimism occurs when North and Peggy attain a moment of communication despite each other's inarticulacy. Peggy, isolated and resentful of her brother North (a division resulting from the pressures of surviving the First World War) is now frozen with fear in the face of the prospect of another war. Despite her insecurity she is overwhelmed by a need to try and say something she knows to be important. Control of language fails her and instead she makes a stinging attack on her brother:

> She stopped. There was the vision still, but she had not grasped it. She had broken off only a little fragment of what she meant to say, and she had made her brother angry. Yet there it hung before her, the thing she had seen, the thing she had not said. But as she fell back with a jerk against the wall, she felt relieved of some oppression . . . She had not said it, but she had tried to say it. (Woolf, 1937/1977: 298: ellipsis mine)

As befits the complexity of communication within this dislocated narrative, North's response does not appear until some twenty pages later:

> 'What you said was true,' he blurted out, '. . . quite true.' It was what she meant that was true he corrected himself; her feeling, not her words. He felt her feeling now; it was not about him; it was about other people; about another world, a new world. (1937/1977: 322)

The dominant force of the novel is perhaps more accurately described as repression, the deadening weight of the symbolic order, which Peggy's outburst has gratifyingly disrupted. Significantly it is the chaotic force of her uncontrolled laughter that enables her to speak. It had 'relaxed her, enlarged her' and thereby freed her from the self-control that delimits and patrols the jurisdiction of the patriarchy. Thus 'enlarged' she transgresses boundaries and becomes the catalyst for North's outburst, the feelings that he 'blurts out' against the grain of language.

Within the drama of *The Years*, then, the inadequacy of language is clearly established as the villain of the piece. Until our current unsatisfactory language is usurped by a more sensitive form of communication, there can be no hope of attaining a new world. It is therefore significant that the caretaker's children appearing at the end of the novel, the youngest generation represented by Woolf, speak no recognisable language, but a kind of harsh gibberish that only they understand. The sound is 'distorted' to the listeners, and its unintelligibility frightens them: 'There was something horrible in the noise they made. It was so shrill, so discordant, and so meaningless' (1937/1977: 327). Possibly this is a warning against the harsh voices of Fascism, but this seems unlikely coming from the mouths of children. The listeners are afflicted by a fear of change, which they must overcome, because the language those children have 'distorted' is distorted itself – it is the language of the patriarchy, which divides and excludes – and the destruction of this inadequate, man-made language is the prerequisite of the utopian vision contained within both *The Years* and *Three Guineas*:

> But as a result the answer to your question must be that we can best help you to prevent war *not by repeating your words* and following your methods *but by finding new words* and creating new methods. We can best help you to prevent war not by joining your society but by remaining outside your society but in cooperation with its aim. (Woolf, 1938/1986: 164; emphasis mine)

Significantly, both of Brown's attempts to make a speech are destined for failure. His second attempt in particular indicates Woolf's contempt for the empty rhetoric of oratory. The content of Brown's speech is immaterial, what matters is that his intentions are destroyed by the fragmentation of the narrative, which consistently breaks down into the petty squabbles and personal concerns of the Pargiters. He cannot be heard – both because he is an outsider, and because the constant interruptions are appropriate to the ambiguities of a novel that has revealed language to be a totally unreliable medium of communication. A speech would be too cohesive, and nobody would listen. It is a fitting irony that the person keenest to hear the speech is deaf Rose. At Delia's party Martin observes:

> Something's wrong, he thought; there's a gap, a dislocation, between the word and the reality. If they want to reform the world, he thought, why not begin there, at the centre, with themselves? (Woolf, 1937/1977: 309)

A similar divide separates speech and action, and Brown's failure to speak is both an illustration of this social paralysis and an indictment of the establishment's constant marginalisation of non-conformity. On another level, however, that there is no speech can be taken as the central irony of the novel. The speeches will come later, in *Three Guineas*; meanwhile, there are no answers here. *The Years* is rather a novel of symptoms. It reveals the breakdown in communications and the spread of chaos. It is a warning against the cancer of war, but it has no resources to fight that cancer. The medicine might be said to come in *Three Guineas*, where Woolf, for the first time, prescribes a drastic cure instead of surveying the symptoms of decay with the detached and witty eye of the observer.

BREAKING THE MOULD OF THE SELF

There is a tension in Woolf's work that manifests itself as a contradictory desire to both transcend and preserve the integrity of the individual. Woolf's reconstruction of gender roles would seem to be demanding a recognition and acceptance of self above any artificial construct of gender, suggesting that in the political climate of the 1930s such a transition is not merely desirable but an essential prerequisite of survival. With unusual forthrightness Woolf had declared in *A Room of One's Own* that 'it is much more important to be oneself than anything else' (Woolf, 1929/1977: 105), and this declaration raises the question of whether Woolf can be seen to share the faith in individual integrity advocated by Dorothy L. Sayers. When Wimsey writes to Harriet in 1940 that 'the important thing is each man's personal responsibility. They must not look to the State for guidance – they must learn to guide the State' (Sayers, 26 January 1940; 1939–40), Sayers, like Woolf, acknowledges that change cannot come from within the corruption of an old and compromised order. It must come from without, from what both writers conceive to be a society of independent individuals. Yet while Sayers clearly privileges the individual within the social contract, Woolf's priorities are focused elsewhere. In rescuing a concept of the individual from the meaningless and constricting labels of gender, Woolf is not subscribing to the illusion of an homogenous and unified subject. As Makiko Minow-Pinkney has observed, Woolf's concept of the 'unity of the mind' does not refer to 'a single unitary state, but rather a 'wholeness' composed of heterogeneity' (Minow-Pinkney, 1987: 9). The self that Woolf cherishes is a fluid and flexible one, endowed with an enriching multiplicity. It is this multiplicity that enables Woolf's new-found self to live a double existence, to embody the tension between 'I' and 'We' that creates the possibility of a parallel communality. Woolf connects the acknowledgement of interior multiplicity with a nascent capacity for constructive social multiplicity. In the closing peroration of *A Room of One's Own*, Woolf's cry is for a transcendence of individual identity: 'I am talking of the common life which is the real life and not of the little separate lives which we live as individuals' (Woolf, 1929/1977: 108). Yet what Gillian Beer has called the 'living quarrel' of Woolf's art is not resolved in *A Room of One's Own*. It is only later, in the shadow of war, that she attempts a reconciliation between 'I' and 'We' through the arbitrary declaration that both are right. The best hope for a healthy heterogenous social body lies not in the bonding of rigid and exclusive identities, but in the fluid combination of multiple subjectivities. Woolf, then, rejects the alternation of the quarrel and demands instead a state of peaceful co-existence. This duality is fundamental to Woolf's politics and her opposition to the patriarchal status quo. In consequence, given her subscription to what can only be described as a radical feminist position, the question inevitably arises: why in 1938 did Woolf undertake the seemingly contradictory rejection of the word 'feminist'?

PICKING UP THE PIECES: THREE GUINEAS AND RECONSTRUCTION

On page 117 of the Hogarth edition of *Three Guineas* Woolf burns the word 'feminist' and, rising from the ashes, sees a vision of 'men and women working together for the same cause'. This action exemplifies her belief in the destructive power of names, labels and definitions. These must be rejected before a new, more co-operative community can be formed; hence, the gradual demise of rigidly defined gender boundaries in *The Years*. Rose the soldier's right to fight and Martin's right not to fight pave the way for North and Peggy to fight a different kind of battle, on different terms – to identify and build a new world order, to create a powerful new generation unhindered by differential labels of constructed gender. Towards the end of *Three Guineas* Woolf concludes:

> Josephine Butler's label – Justice, Equality, Liberty – is a fine one; but it is only a label, and in our age of innumerable labels, of multi-coloured labels, we have become suspicious of labels; they kill and constrict. (Woolf, 1938/1986: 157)

It is easy to condemn Woolf as premature in declaring feminism 'obsolete'. Indeed she seems to have forgotten her own frustration at the inadequacy of the existing English language and ignored the potential of new names and new words to positively redefine and celebrate the value of a constructive difference, bridging the gulf between the polarities of Victorian gender role prescriptions. But this criticism fails to take into account the catalyst of war. In the face of Fascism the process of change had to be radically accelerated. There was, in Woolf's eyes, no time for an independent feminism. 'New combinations' needed to work together against Fascism now.

Woolf's rejection of the word 'feminism' is also ahead of its time in that it recognises that rigid gender specifications destroy men as well as women. In anticipation of certain strands of contemporary French feminist thought, she deconstructs the binarism that demands a destructive and limiting polarity of thought. She pours scorn on the spiritual, moral and intellectual wasteland that is professional life:

> If people are highly successful in their professions they lose their senses. Sight goes. They have no time to look at pictures. Sound goes. They have no time to listen to music. Speech goes. They have no time for conversation. They lose their sense of proportion – the relations between one thing and another. Humanity goes. (Woolf, 1938/1986: 83)

It is not simply women's lives that must be freed from patriarchy, but men's too. Only when the patriarchal value system is recognised for the worthless, soul-destroying thing that it is can both men and women be freed from its tyranny: 'Can one change sex characteristics? How far is the woman's movement a remarkable experiment in that transformation? Musn't our next task be the emancipation of man?' (Nicholson, 1980: 379) – Woolf's universal vision is undoubtedly revolutionary, but it is still subservient to her overriding concern with the war. These optimistic remarks from a letter to Shena, Lady Simon in January 1940, were prefaced by the essential prerequisite, 'if disarmament comes'.

Thus, in the work of Woolf, as in that of Stevie Smith and Dorothy L. Sayers, there is an awareness of the ambiguity inherent in the terms 'masculine' and 'feminine', and a movement towards a redefinition of these terms, not along the traditional lines of gender, but along the boundary between power and exclusion from power – in the terms of *Three Guineas*: the division between the patriarchy and the outsider, between those whose whole being promotes war and those whose whole being rejects it. Together *Three Guineas* and *The Years* present a radical articulation of the same process of gender redefinition utilised by Dorothy L. Sayers in her development of the relationship between Wimsey and Harriet Vane. Yet although Woolf's vision is radical, it is also fundamentally utopian, and presents an altogether more idealistic vision of human nature than that suggested by Stevie Smith, whose *Over the Frontier* concentrates on a bleak, uncompromising critique of the individual's, rather than society's, implication in the process of war.[12]

Woolf's concern with the guilt of society is not misplaced, but the enormity of its crimes seems, paradoxically, to drive her towards a faith in the ultimate value of individual integrity. Her distinction between the 'private brother' and what Sara Ruddick (1981) has described as the 'public world' is an instance in point:

> Inevitably we look upon societies as conspiracies that sink the private brother, whom many of us have reason to respect, and inflate in his stead a monstrous male, loud of voice, hard of fist. (Woolf, 1938/1986: 121)

It is societies, like the one Woolf has been asked to join, and above all Society itself that transform the private brother into what might be termed the public father. Demanding the assumption of a mental uniform, society creates a schizophrenic male personality that undergoes a Jekyll-into-Hyde transformation when it exchanges the realm of the private for the world of the public.[13] Essentially, then, for Woolf, individual integrity becomes both an article of faith and a spent force. It occupies a contradictory space, an ideological void into which good intentions disappear and are never heard of again, outside the realm of the private. Women's escape from this realm is one of the many narrative strands contained within *The Years*. As the female Pargiters emerge from the private house into the public world, different sisters pursue different strategies to deal with the transition. First steps are tentative, largely consisting of omnibuses and committees, but by Peggy's generation larger steps have been taken, albeit on shaky ground. However, once outside, women must struggle to avoid becoming masculine schizophrenics. They should resist the temptation of 'belonging', struggle to maintain their integrity and learn to be comfortable in the role of outsider.[14] From here women can learn to articulate their position rather than be alienated and intimidated by it – and thereby discover that although they are 'outside', they are not alone.

Although societies, as microcosms of Society, are implicated in the system of patriarchal constructions, Woolf offers hope in the possibility of an alliance, which is only possible due to her redefinition of traditional oppositions. Abandoning the gender divide, Woolf establishes an opposition within the category male, and that opposition is represented by the private brother/public father division, which conforms to the 'feminine'/'masculine' redefinition model. This is reminiscent of Susan Gubar's conception of the 'fascist father' exercising 'sexual mastery over the feminised masses' – an image that is vividly pre-empted by Woolf in *Three Guineas*. As they fought for the vote, women:

> were fighting the tyranny of the patriarchal state as you are fighting the tyranny of the fascist state. Thus we are merely carrying on the same fight that our mothers and grandmothers fought; their words prove it; your words prove it. (Woolf, 1938/1986: 118)

But now the rules have changed and the Tyrant has 'widened his scope':

> He is interfering now with your liberty; he is dictating how you shall live; he is making distinctions not merely between the sexes, but between the races. You are feeling in your own persons what your mothers felt when they were shut out, when they were shut up, because they were women. (1938/1986: 118)

Women, also 'feminised' in the face of war, can form an alliance with the private brother to fight the public father, but this can only be achieved outside the rigid structures of societies and outside the realm of the private house. Woolf demands the creation of this new territory, a no-patriarch's-land, a realm of communication.

Woolf's alternative system of binary oppositions, while initially similar to Sayers's, is in fact a far more complex construction; and this is primarily due to Woolf's recognition of the centrality of difference. By embracing a concept of self that welcomes the constructive contradiction of multiplicity, Woolf establishes the central paradox of *Three Guineas*. The female subject can be part of a co-operative whole working with men against war. The female subject can be different and outside, in the words of Teresa de Lauretis, 'multiple, rather than divided or unified . . . excessive or heteronomous' (1989: x). To strive for unity, for women to join the society of men would be disastrous:

> For by so doing we should merge our identity in yours; follow and repeat and score still deeper the old worn ruts in which society, like a gramo-phone whose needle has stuck, is grinding out with intolerable unanimity 'Three hundred millions spent upon arms.' (Woolf, 1938/1986: 121)

The merging of identities would lead only to the collapse of the female subject; the validity of her difference would be denied by the all-consuming absolutism of the phallocentric society. By acknowledging the revolutionary nature of *Three Guineas*, Woolf's rejection of the label 'feminist' is put into perspective, and her disrupted, fragmented argument, while never making claims to consistency, ironically begins to work as a constructive whole.

NARRATIVE TENSIONS 2: BREAKING THE MOULD OF MODERNISM

If, however, Woolf ultimately fails to fulfil Hélène Cixous's demand that women 'split open the closure of the binary opposition' (Moi, 1985: 108), but like Sayers, settles for the creation of an alternative system of polarities, it must in part be due to the political crisis of the time. In the face of war, Woolf needed to envisage a form, outside the patriarchal order, onto which she could focus her hopes for the subversion of the system that was the cause of war. None the less, working within her structure of constructive opposition she creates a series of what could be termed 'subsets'. It is in these subsets, beneath the rhetorical categories of patriarchy and opposition to patriarchy, that Woolf's most revolutionary ideas of difference and open-endedness can be found.

Toril Moi refuses 'to accept this binary opposition of aesthetics on the one hand and politics on the other', and locates 'the politics of Woolf's writing *precisely in her textual practice*' (1985: 16). This is an important distinction and it opens up an interesting paradox. The revolutionary textual practice of *The Waves* established Woolf at the forefront of experimental modernism – the novel's radicalism lay precisely in its form. Yet *The Years* appears to move away from this position, committing itself neither to the experimental nor the realist. The 'story' of the Pargiters, while initially seeming to anchor the novel firmly in the symbolic realm of the 'grand narratives', paradoxically offers Woolf a wealth of space in which to develop her politics through the artful juxtaposition of elliptical moments and inconsistencies. The complementary vocal diversity of the text, described by DuPlessis as 'a critique both of the hierarchies and authoritarian practice of gender and of the narrative practice that selects and honors only major figures' (1985: 163), forms in itself a political statement. This technique would be expanded in *Between the Acts* to create the intensely ambiguous narrative which Judith L. Johnston has called a 'composite form' – a mixture of 'authorial narration, characters' thoughts, dramatic verse parodies, and dialogue . . . [which] . . . creates alternatives to one tyrannical authorial voice' (1987: 256). *The Years*, largely dominated either by free indirect discourse or the conversation of its characters, does not present the same degree of textual fragmentation as *Between the Acts*. However, Woolf's perennial resistance to the prescriptive forms of Victorian omniscient narration is evident in the almost complete absence of a 'singular' authorial voice within the text. Just as Woolf strives to dispel the illusion of a totalising historical 'truth', so her novel abandons the unifying structure of a single or dominant focaliser. The authorial voice of *The Years*, then, becomes a hybrid – a constantly reformulated mosaic comprised of the countless potential interpretations of her characters' interactions.

Nonetheless, *The Years* is undoubtedly a more immediately accessible fiction than its predecessor *The Waves*, and it is worth considering the implications of this formal transition. The residual traces of Woolf's earlier reputation as an apolitical 'modernist' have perhaps contributed to the element of disappointment that still pervades some responses to *The Years*. Yet to see Woolf's work as a unified modernist progression is misguided. She was a politically engaged writer and she responded to the stimuli of external events. Her diary for 28 July 1934 emphasises the impossibility of consistently theorising her position: 'this needs constant effort, anxiety & risk. Here in H. & N. [*Here & Now* – an earlier title for *The Years*] I am breaking the mould made by *The Waves*' (Woolf, 1977–84: vol. IV, 233). In an ironic transition, the radically deconstructed form of *The Waves* is equally radically reconstructed to form *The Years*.

What, though, of *Three Guineas*: is the text simply another step on the road to reconstruction? Or an acknowledgement of the limits of fictional possibility? Woolf does not seem entirely comfortable writing in a ratiocinative male mode, even when her purpose is to undermine it. There is an omnipresent urge to ridicule and digress – to follow a fluid rather than a strictly logical course –

that in turn threatens to undermine the urgent political plea that motivates the text. There is a sense in which *Three Guineas* strains towards a more flexible form, longing to pursue its ideas further, but sacrificing these desires to the overriding need to engage with the political issues of the threat of war. The textual practice of *Three Guineas* sat uncomfortably on Woolf's politics – or perhaps her politics settled uncomfortably on her textual practice – but seen as a whole, the two texts of the late 1930s prove mutually enlightening. Between them there is a dialogue allowing aesthetics to slip into politics, and politics to hint at aesthetics. The close proximity of fiction and of polemic in these parallel texts, alongside their early conceptual bond in *The Pargiters*, suggests that had it not been for war and the demands it made to be fought at least partially within the terms of the patriarchal discourse which created it, Woolf's polemical texts and essays might have achieved the radical embracement of multiplicity manifested by her novels. In *Arguing with the Past*, Gillian Beer concludes that both Woolf and George Eliot are 'more exploratory in the ordering of their fiction than in polemics', and suggests that this is because 'they work askance from the expected rather than confront it' (1989: 119). Beer's analysis is astute. Although *The Years* and *Three Guineas* represent Woolf's attempt to reconcile fiction with the reality of war, it is perhaps in the way in which *The Years* avoids the issues confronted by *Three Guineas* that we see her most successful political engagement.

NOTES

1. In her introduction to the Oxford edition of *The Years*, Hermione Lee describes the composition of this novel as an 'agonizing story' and concludes that 'The very title which she finally chose for the novel embodies the burden it had become for her: it took her years' (Lee, 1992: xvii).
2. The 'sacred coin' represents the 'bright new sixpence' of an independent income.
3. I am grateful to Su Reid for permission to quote from her unpublished paper (Reid 1991).
4. This claim originates from the back cover of the 1977 Grafton edition of *The Years*, an edition which also attempts to sell its complex contents under the tempting guise of 'a family story from a writer of genius'. *The Years* has since become one of Woolf's least considered works, and it would seem that not even Virginia Woolf can escape the critical death sentence that is encoded in the epithet 'popular'.
5. The idea of a 'woman's time' as articulated by Julia Kristeva in her essay of that name, is more fully the project of *Between the Acts*, where Woolf constantly focuses on the difference between a 'masculine' and a 'feminine' perception of time and space.
6. Laura Moss Gottlieb draws attention to the importance of the conversation in which Nicholas admits his homosexuality to Eleanor (Woolf, 1937/1977: 228), concluding that 'Candour, especially about sex and the emotions, is depicted as the primary way of breaking down individual isolation and of achieving a sense of unity with others' (Gottlieb, 1983: 222). Hermione Lee, however, complains of the novel's lack of candour, drawing attention to the extensive self-censorship exercised by Woolf. Sexual questions and sexual encounters are 'half described' in the book and 'suppression and censorship' reign (Lee, 1992: xxvi–xxvii). 'Half description', or more appropriately displaced description, is however a characteristic device of Woolf's prose. Her writing persistently demands acknowledgement of issues only tangentially occurring in the text, a prime example being the 'Time Passes' section of *To the Lighthouse* (1927). Images of violence and destruction saturate the middle chapters, but direct reference to war is confined to the parenthetical death of Andrew Ramsay.
7. DuPlessis sees Woolf's late novels as transcending both the 'realist sociological novel of 'facts'

and the romance plot of the psychological novel. 'Both late novels' she observes, 'substitute for these discredited narratives the invention of a communal protagonist and a collective language.' The image of the communal protagonist who 'makes the group, not the individual, the central character' is particularly helpful in understanding the singular multiplicity of the individual Pargiters' relationships to the family whole. DuPlessis suggests that: 'Questions of oneness and separation [within *The Years*] ... intimate that the fluid ego boundaries of the preoedipal bond are one source for the communal protagonist' (DuPlessis, 1985: 167; ellipsis mine). Woolf's use of the pre-symbolic as a route to her vision of a new world is discussed in Chapter 7.

8. References to the activities of Hitler and Mussolini are frequent in the diary. Although occasionally flippant, such comments more usually emphasise an overwhelming sense of impotence: 'Then trying, how ineffectively, to express the sensation of sitting her & reading, like an act in play, how Hitler flew to Munich & killed this that & the other man & woman in Germany yesterday' (2 July 1934, 1977–84: vol.IV, 223). The events described formed the so called 'Night of the Long Knives'.

9. According to Hermione Lee, the mother's demise is an essential prerequisite for the daughter's development. Rose Pargiter's spirit is synonymous with the ghost of the 'Angel in the House' – Woolf's symbol of female self-sacrifice that dominates the territory of the private house (Lee, 1992: xiv).

10. That some change has occurred is evident in the fact that for Peggy a career was a possibility, at first hand, rather than indirectly through her brothers; while for North soldiering was a necessity rather than a career. That he should believe it a necessity, however, would seem to imply that there is still a long way to go in the process of gender re-education.

11. In spite of this slightly uncomfortable optimism, I would strongly disagree with Patricia Cramer's claim that the narrative thrust of *The Years* celebrates the coming of a 'postpatriarchal age' (Cramer, 1991: 223). Given the context within which the novel was written and the imminent resurgence of the patriarchal display of war, such a conclusion seems, to say the least, premature.

12. Gottlieb's (1983) conclusion that *The Years* is ultimately pessimistic is, on one level, convincing, but such a position cannot account for the final chapter's attempt to reinscribe a sense of hope within the narrative.

13. There is a potential disjuncture between the benevolent image of the private brother and the spectre of the dictator in the house. It would seem that within the realm of the home, brothers, like sisters, are equally subjugated to the law of the father. The brother's privilege lies in his freedom to escape the paternal home.

14. Accepting the position of the outsider is never easy, and it would seem to be a position that is even harder to maintain during war. Elizabeth Bowen's portrayal in *The Heat of the Day* (1948) of the working-class Louie – an 'involuntary' outsider – illustrates just how desirable the security and comfort of belonging to a conformist ethic can seem to the excluded.

Part Two

A woman has nothing to laugh about when the symbolic order collapses.

Julia Kristeva, 'About Chinese women'

6

Weathering the Storm

Prelude and storm are not seamlessly conjoined. Although war was declared on 3 September 1939, the expected catastrophe was far from immediate. Indeed, the apocalypse that had threatened throughout the 1930s was a long time coming, and expectations of absolute war were confronted by the actuality of absent war. This suspense continued well into 1940 until war's belated appearance was finally heralded by German advances in Europe. Through the spring of 1940, German forces moved inexorably across Norway, Denmark and the Netherlands, culminating in the Dunkirk débâcle and the fall of France. The invasion of Britain was now a real and immediate threat, the magnitude of which was swiftly brought to bear on the British public by the onslaught of the Blitz and the battle for air supremacy that raged overhead. The 'phoney' war was over and Nancy Mitford ruefully reflected on its passing in the preface to *Pigeon Pie*:

> I hope anyone who is kind enough to read it in a second edition will remember that it was written before Christmas 1939. Published on 6 May 1940 it was an early and unimportant casualty of the real war which was then beginning. (Mitford, 1940/1961)

The absence of immediate destruction is, however, somewhat misleading. Even before the 'phoney' war had transformed into the 'authenticity' of the Blitz, an intellectual and emotional economy of war had come into operation, exerting a powerful influence on all aspects of British life. The temporary closure of schools and cinemas, the reservation of hospital beds for as yet non-existent casualties, the blackout and evacuation all served to detach everyday life from its customary contexts and associations. The massive evacuation programme represented an unprecedented degree of dislocation for the urban populations of Britain, while the impact of this migration upon rural communities was similarly disorientating (Allingham, 1941a: 89–118; A. J. P. Taylor, 1965/1992: 454–5). As town met country and middle class met working class, the nation was profoundly and uncomfortably confronted by its differences.

Jenny Hartley's *Hearts Undefeated* bears testimony to the immediate impact the war had on women's lives, and to the difficulty many experienced finding a role in the new climate of war. Jobs for women were at first increasingly scarce (Hartley, 1994: 60–4) and official communications seemed to demand nothing but an unquestioning passivity. Daily life was thrown into confusion – but this domestic fragmentation was not counterbalanced by any active sense of engagement in the business of war. Yet perhaps the most disturbing manifestation of the paradoxical co-existence of change and continuity is found in the work of women for whom active participation was not even a distant possibility. For a generation of women who experienced the First World War, the continuities of 1939 were rooted not in war's absence but in its presence. In the depths of the winter blackout, Vera Brittain wonders whether future historians will regard the peace of 1918 'as anything more than a pause in the long struggle between Western and Central Europe' (1941: 25), while Nella Last's diary records a profound sense of emotional fragmentation stemming not from a fear of the unknown, but from a knowledge of the all too familiar: 'We who remember the long drawn-out agony of the last war feel ourselves crumble somewhere inside at the thoughts of what lies ahead' (Last, 14 September 1939; quoted in Hartley, 1994: 29).

Last's memories indicate from the outset of hostilities the near impossibility of directly confronting the Second World War. Memories of the First World War remained too close and too vivid for the reasoned contemplation of a second large-scale conflict, and in Last's description can be seen the beginnings of what would become a national avoidance of the fact of war. The strategies of normalising that characterised wartime Britain are rooted not only in the destruction of the Blitz, but also in the domestic dislocations that began in the earliest days of the war.

Dislocation, or displacement, can be seen as key terms in an analysis of the physical and emotional economy of war. They are also characteristic features of its literature. I discuss in Chapter 1 the perceived changes in patterns of reading and cinema-going that evolved over the course of the conflict. These actions were integral components of the strategies devised to cope with and survive the ideological imposition of war, and they frequently reflected a need for a temporary temporal displacement, something that would remove the reader/spectator from the moment of war. Dislocated from the regular patterns of everyday life, people sought *re*location in imaginative realms that were found to be infinitely preferable to the constrained spaces of war. The fiction of the war years both reflects and engages with this desire for displacement. Daphne Du Maurier's *Frenchman's Creek* self-consciously acknowledges this function before transporting the reader back to a world of sensual women and daring French pirates:

> The yachtsman dreams – and as the tide surges gently about his ship and the moon shines on the quiet river, soft murmurs come to him, and the past becomes the present.
>
> A forgotten century peers out of dust and cobwebs and he walks in another time . . .
>
> . . . lying on his back asleep he breathes and lives the lovely folly of that lost midsummer which first made the creek a refuge, and a symbol of escape. (Du Maurier, 1941/1976: 11–12; ellipsis mine)

Sue Harper has attested to the wartime popularity of both costume fiction and its filmic counterpart. Arguing that the audience for historical fiction was primarily composed of middle-class women she claims that '[t]he way in which these novels dominated the market until the end of the war suggest they provided a congruence or "fit" with the audience's fears and desires, and permitted them to envisage some pleasures and bury others' (Harper, 1982: 21). 'History' she concludes, 'becomes a country where refugees from common sense may temporarily reside, but it is a place of banishment none the less; and there, gypsy, gentry and female excess is safely placed' (1982: 21). The notion of history as a territory, a spatial alternative to the contemporary moment, is a useful one, but Harper seems to suggests that the consequences of such a displacement are ultimately negative. This conclusion is not always borne out by women's wartime writing. The fiction of Naomi Mitchison, for example, sees history as a potential space in which it becomes possible to explore ideas prohibited by the limited horizons of war. It becomes a site for the articulation of alternative futures, where the possibility of regeneration is considered in the face of war's remorseless destruction. Naomi Mitchison sets her wartime historical novel *The Bull Calves* (1947) in the aftermath of the Jacobite rebellion of 1745. By setting her novel in a period of postwar reconstruction, Mitchison is able to look back to a future that would otherwise be hopelessly uncertain. Mitchison's search for a place or a time that can stand outside, or in opposition to, the moment of war is typical of the texts that comprise the storm section. Although vastly contrasting in their literary strategies, these texts are united by a dominant concern with the concepts of absence and escape. Woolf, Mitchison and Bowen all engage with temporal and spatial explorations in an attempt to absent themselves from the overwhelming reality of war.

The work of Virginia Woolf forms a bridge from the prelude into the storm. *Between the Acts* was completed in 1941, just a few months before Woolf's suicide, and within the text Woolf attempts to escape from the contemporaneity of war into an alternative time and space represented through the idea of *pre*history. As a strategy for surviving war it was, in literal terms, obviously unsuccessful, but *Between the Acts* none the less represents a radical attempt to envisage a challenge to the phallocentric thought that lies at the root of war. The novels of the storm all present some form of challenge to patriarchal thought. They represent women writers' attempts to 'write themselves out' of the trauma of war, and one route of escape is found in this recourse to the past. Alternatively escape may lie in an idea of absence that rejects the *time* of war. This is the strategy of Elizabeth Bowen in both *The Heat of the Day* (1948) and short stories such as 'Mysterious Kôr'. The characters of her fictions create for themselves a timelessness, a space which rejects the temporal order of war, and enables them to spiritually abscond from the physical environment of conflict. These defences against the disruptions and chaos of war leave the characters emotionally isolated and distanced from their environment, but in Bowen's work alienation is frequently presented as an essential prerequisite of survival.

The bleakness that permeates *The Heat of the Day* stems in part from Bowen's refusal to embrace a comfortable alternative to the landscape of war. Her characters adopt and adapt a variety of coping strategies, all of which are dissected and found wanting. Bowen rejects the cyclical model of a 'woman's time' that Woolf attempts to set against the linear time of war, moving instead towards what Julia Kristeva would term a 'monumental' conception of temporality. Yet, although the two writers would seem to have shared diametrically opposed conceptions of women's relation to time, they both reject the time of the father – suggesting that female subjectivity is denied by the linear temporality that structures the patriarchal order. The temporal explorations undertaken here, and in Mitchison's similar desire for a regenerative temporality, all imply a belief shared by these writers, that the time of war is antithetical to the time of women.

The alienation that characterises Bowen's work returns us to the notions of displacement and dislocation. All of these states are connected to a more general wartime concern with powerlessness – and for the writers considered here, questions of power are equally questions of gender. Woolf, Mitchison and Bowen, and the writers of the prelude, all undertake analyses of power that crucially destabilise notions of gender. For Sayers and Smith powerlessness is presented as a state of metaphorical emasculation – it is the male characters within their novels who must come to terms with an understanding of what it means to be excluded from the discourse of power. Lord Peter Wimsey, at the behest of the Foreign Office, is no longer his own master; Tom Satterthwaite in *Over the Frontier* (1938) loses his job to the talented and ambitious Pompey. The process of adjusting to an ever changing, fluctuating power dynamic is equally evident in *Between the Acts*. Giles inwardly rages at his exclusion from the theatre of war, and attempts to resolve his anger and frustration through the violent crushing of the deadlocked snake. Even Black William, Naomi Mitchison's eighteenth-century 'new man', must come to terms with the blow to his highland pride represented by the loss of his sword after defeat in the 'Forty-five rebellion.

Yet although the roots of this discourse are evident in the 1930s, power, or the lack of it, is a particular concern of the wartime texts. The novels of the storm embody both fantasies of agency and dreams of escape into a different world – a world that would somehow avoid the dialectic of oppressor and oppressed that characterises the patriarchal symbolic realm. The fictions present in these texts are creative strategies of imaginative escape. They are methods of repressing or disengaging from the dissolution of the known world's secure, comfortable obsolescence. They are fictions of order that try to provide a framework through which to cope with the actuality of chaos, and they are fictions of disorder – disrupted and problematised by the eruption of the very material they are formulated to repress. The 'reality' of war threatened not only a literal death, but also a metaphorical collapse of the fragile female sense of self. The surface homogeneity of these texts is equally fragile. The story that cannot be told, the story of the 'reality' of war, is also a story that will not be denied.

This paradox exerts a constant and unremitting pressure upon the texts of the period, and this pressure can never be wholly resolved or assimilated. Women writers must somehow reconcile the conflicts of fiction and reality. Their attempts to live in war while existing out of war represent the formulation of a necessary compromise between the merciless 'truth' of destruction and the terrifying freedom of fiction.

The Second World War was not a straightforward war – if such a thing can be said to exist. It was a truly global conflict in a way the First World War had never been. The extent of the war in geographical, spiritual and scientific terms was – and is – beyond our grasp, and its literature is similarly complex. It is impossible to identify a single voice that speaks for women in wartime. For both male and female writers of the 1940s the experience of war is, above all, a catalogue of dislocation. The story of the impact of the Second World War is encoded behind a series of myths, façades and fantasies, and makes its presence felt only through disruption, hiatus and fragmentation. Elizabeth Bowen's distinction between wartime stories and war stories is thus both central and superfluous – all these texts are war stories waiting to be decoded. That we do not recognise them as such is perhaps an indication of how little we understand the Second World War.

7

Violation of a Fiction: Between the Acts and the Myth of 'Our Island History'

Unless we can think peace into existence we – not this one body in this one bed but millions of bodies yet to be born – will lie in the same darkness and hear the same death rattle overhead.

Virginia Woolf, 'Thoughts on peace in an air raid'

[H]er laughter had had some strange effect on her. It had relaxed her, enlarged her. She felt, or rather she saw, not a place, but a state of being, in which there was real laughter, real happiness, and this fractured world was whole; whole and free. But how could she say it?

Virginia Woolf, *The Years*

While *The Years* (1937) and *Three Guineas* (1938) together represented Virginia Woolf's attempt to engage with the threat of the Second World War, *Between the Acts* is her attempt to escape from the terrible reality of that war. *Between the Acts* is a novel beyond the political, written when the question had changed from the 'how . . . are we to prevent war?' of *Three Guineas* (1938/1986: 5) to a bleak unspoken cry of 'How are we to survive war?' Woolf's final novel represents a strategy for survival. It is her search for a fiction that would write her out of the war situation and at the same time destroy the insidious myth that she held responsible for the imminent demise of the world she held dear. In *Between the Acts* Woolf can be seen both as the active destroyer of a propagandist vision of English rural 'innocence', and as the victim of her own failed fiction, or strategy, for survival.

There is a disparity between form and content in *Between the Acts*. It is a beautifully crafted novel that skilfully manipulates the insularity of its feudal village setting into a complex web of ellipsis and ambiguity. Yet it is also a novel of fragmentation and contradiction, filled with violent images of death and destruction completely at odds with the lyrical tone of the writing. The choice of setting is curious. Woolf's distrust of the English country house, the values of insularity and sterility it seemed to encapsulate, had been clearly articulated in *The Years*, where Eleanor's open vitality is vividly contrasted with the stagnation and premature closure represented by Morris and Sir William Whatney. This suffocating image from *The Years* has to be taken into consideration in an examination of *Between the Acts*, and the question asked: why does Woolf situate her final novel – her war novel – in the midst of a defunct rural backwater? The social system prevailing in *Between the Acts* is positively medieval.[1] The opening of the novel seems obsessed with origins: 'The Olivers couldn't trace their descent for more than two or three hundred years. But the Swithins could. The Swithins were there before the Conquest' (Woolf, 1941/1978: 26). Even the delivery boy can trace his name back to the Domesday Book, so it is not entirely surprising to find that a feudal hierarchy reigns in the tea room:

> She [Mrs Manresa] laid hold of a thick china mug. Mrs Sands giving precedence, of course, to one of the gentry, filled it at once. David gave her cake. She was the first to drink, the first to bite. The villagers still hung back. 'It's all my eye about democracy,' she concluded. So did Mrs Parker, taking her mug too. The people looked to them. They led; the rest followed. (Woolf, 1941/1978: 78)

The emphasis on the pedigree of the neighbourhood seems to have a dual purpose; on one level the waves of French influence and the occasional newcomer seem designed to emphasise the novel's concern with the issues of invasion, rape and colonisation; but primarily the absolute Englishness of the community is established to enable Woolf to explode and disrupt the cosy image of a benevolent village England cruelly under siege from external forces. Woolf's demythification and her parody of propagandist visions of national identity was startlingly prescient, as is revealed by the rapidity with which the cinema of the period adopted the idea of village England. The 1941 film *This England* is described by Jeffrey Richards as 'a glorified village pageant' (Richards, 1988: 47), and indeed its symbolic re-enactment of English history in adversity is remarkably (and disturbingly) close to the vision of Miss La Trobe's play. Within *Between the Acts*, however, Woolf reveals 'village England' to be a dangerous, complacent fiction, growing apace under the simple 'them and us' polarities of the war situation. In the new climate of war, the patriarchal system indicted in *Three Guineas* becomes just another blameless victim of somebody else's Fascism, and is acquitted of its share in the responsibility for that fascism.

The patriotic myth is an insidious one. It pervades *Between the Acts* in the cryptic form of 'the view', recurring with alarming frequency. The view is the enemy of the artist, always threatening to catch the audience's attention, seducing them into a complacent vision of unity. This is a false sense of security:

> 'What a view!' she exclaimed . . .
>
>   Nobody answered her. The flat fields glared green yellow, blue yellow, red yellow, then blue again. The repetition was senseless, hideous, stupefying. (Woolf, 1941/1978: 52–3; ellipsis mine)

The stupefying effect of the endlessly repeated view reinforces the potential *double entendre*. The view is also the opinion, the belief, the 'anonymous bray of the infernal megaphone' (1941/1978: 137). Woolf's description of the Mayhews illustrates this tunnel vision, concluding with a sentence that could just as easily read 'They subscribed to the myth':

> 'Why leave out the British Army? What's history without the army, eh?' he mused. Inclining her head, Mrs Mayhew protested after all one mustn't ask too much. Besides, very likely there would be a Grand Ensemble, round the Union Jack, to end with. Meanwhile, there was the view. They looked at the view. (Woolf, 1941/1978: 115)

This possibility is reinforced by the Victorian episode of Miss La Trobe's drama, where Edgar helps Eleanor to stand at 'the top' and look at 'the view' (1941/1978: 120). Throughout the novel Miss La Trobe is engaged in a battle against the forces of history, politics and distraction – a struggle to maintain control of the audience. She fears the weather and the disruption of the interval, but above all her enemy is the myth of complacency – 'She could feel them slipping through her fingers, looking at the view' (1941/1978: 111). That the strength of the view is made so explicit in the Victorian era indicates Woolf's own preoccupation with the 'Victorian view'. Gillian Beer (1989) has illustrated the extent to which Woolf was indebted to her Victorian heritage, both as a context from which to work and as an orthodoxy against which to write. Beer identifies a 'process of resistance, exorcizement, transformation, and a new levelling relationship' between Woolf and her parents in *To the Lighthouse* which she believes 'expresses also Woolf's relations with Victorian culture and writing' (Beer, 1989: 139). Woolf, she concludes, 'jostles Victorian language into new patterns, establishing her separation from them. And that makes it possible for her to acknowledge them as kin' (1989: 156). This seemingly contradictory juxtaposition none the less encapsulates the complex symbiotic relationship between Woolf and her past. The tensions that both bound Woolf to, and drove her from, the Victorians are paralleled in the dialectic that concerns this chapter – Woolf's simultaneous love of her country and loathing of patriotism.

Although Miss La Trobe is undoubtedly in conflict with the view, it is not so easy to discern exactly what she and her pageant represent. She is filled with an obsessional need to make the audience see, but it is part of the essential ambiguity of the novel that that vision is never clearly articulated. Streatfield, who completes the triumvirate of male exclusivity identified by Judith L. Johnston (1987), makes an attempt to contain her vision within a single interpretation.[2] His imposition is ironically severed by the zoom of twelve aeroplanes, mistaken for music but in reality harbingers of war. Whatever value his interpretation might have had, it is rendered meaningless and irrelevant by war. Ultimately the significance of Miss La Trobe lies outside the pageant, in her act of creation and the consequent pain of giving birth. The play is merely a device for Woolf's skilful parody. Woolf's fiction is not situated here, in the hopes and aspirations of La Trobe's ludicrous pageant, but outside – in the space before, between and after the acts – where she attempts to create an alternative to the catalogue of rape that is patriarchal history. The myth that Woolf destroys through La Trobe's play leaves a void, an empty chasm of non-belief. Without the patriotic myth, there is nothing tangible in which to believe – and this complete absence of moral certainty undermines the ratiocinative hegemony, hinting at the prospect of chaos. Outside the play, but within the novel, Woolf attempts to formulate an alternative to fill this void at the heart of Englishness.

How then does Woolf construct this alternative, this fiction? The twin concerns of the novel can be seen as parallel anti-plots that consistently overlap, and are at times inextricably entwined. Like Miss La Trobe's stage and the surrounding scenery, it is hard to distinguish between them. The simultaneous destruction of myth and creation of fiction are linked by a subplot of violence, which infiltrates the narrative at every level. The pageant reveals England in her true colours, presenting its history of colonial rape; while Isa's reading of the newspaper reinforces the conviction that a substratum of violence exists beneath the precarious veneer of civilisation. Throughout the novel Woolf is at pains to stress the illusory nature of the perceived world. The intrusion of reality is shocking and unwelcome. As Lucy and Bart conduct a ritual conversation, Isa's mind is filled with the reported reality of the rape:

> Every year they said, would it be wet or fine; and every year it was – one or the other. The same chime followed the same chime, only this year beneath the chime she heard: 'The girl screamed and hit him about the face with a hammer.' (Woolf, 1941/1978: 20)[3]

Giles is similarly oppressed by the pressure of external reality. He chaffs against the demands of his complacent world after reading 'in the morning paper, in the train, that sixteen men had been shot, others prisoned, just over there' (1941/1978: 38). Violence, and war, are 'just over there', ready to erupt at any moment. The newspaper contributes to their potential for disruption. A lifeline to the real world, yet also described as the book of the current generation (1941/1978: 19), it occupies a curious space on the borderline of fiction and reality. It is with a newspaper, folded into a giant beak, that Bart terrifies the child, George. Looking back on the event at the end of the novel he reflects 'that he had destroyed the little boy's world. He had popped out with his newspaper; the child had cried' (1941/1978: 147). It is not only Bart and the patriarchy he represents who have destroyed the child's security, but also the 'reality' contained within the newspaper – the words and faces of the dictators who reduce even Eleanor in *The Years* to a state of impotent, violent rage.[4] Woolf wants this illusion to be shattered. She wants the reality of war to be brought home to the 'England under glass' – the sterile, blinkered community blind to its share of the responsibility for the rise of Fascism. 'England under glass' was the title of Malcolm Cowley's review of *Between the Acts* in the *New Republic*, 6 October 1941. He sees Woolf's novel as 'her comment on the war, or rather her elegy for the society the war was destroying' and concludes that 'the spirit if not the body of Georgian England survives in her novels' (quoted in Majumdar and McLaurin, 1975: 449) – a conclusion which somewhat depressingly suggests that the very myth that Woolf was at pains to shatter in fact remained intact. However, in the light of Woolf's desire to break the glass of complacency, it is interesting to consider Miss la Trobe's conclusion as she experiments with 'ten mins. of present time':

> 'Reality too strong,' she muttered. 'Curse 'em!' . . . If only she'd a back-cloth to hang between the trees – to shut out cows, swallows, present time! But she had nothing . . . Panic seized her. Blood seemed to pour from her shoes. This is death, death, death, she noted in the margin of her mind; when illusion fails. (Woolf, 1941/1978: 130–1; ellipses mine)

If the failure of illusion is death, the implications for Woolf are considerable. There is a degree of confusion in the text between her desire to destroy the complacent myths of patriotism and a desire to preserve aspects of a world that she cherished. With the loss of the familiar objects of belief, the necessity of formulating an effective alternative becomes imperative. The creation of an alternative fiction is not simply a strategy, but the sole life line of survival.

The pageant, then, throws unwelcome light on to the harsh realities of the past. In the so-called Age of Enlightenment, Reason offers a history where

'*In distant mines the savage sweats; and from the reluctant earth the painted pot is shaped*'(1941/1978: 92), while in the background the progress of man is inscribed through the image of violation and procreation suggested by the villagers' chorus '*digging and delving, ploughing and sowing*' (1941/1978: 92). Things have not improved by the Victorian age, appropriately epitomised by the figure of a policeman:

> *On Thursday it's the natives of Peru require protection and correction; we give 'em what's due. But mark you, our rule don't end there. It's a Christian country, our Empire; under the White Queen Victoria. Over thought and religion; drink; dress; manners; marriage too, I wield my truncheon.* (Woolf, 1941/1978: 119)

Although Woolf's critique of Empire is a hallmark of her political thought, her attack is not simply aimed at a patriotic vision of England. In the much earlier *A Room of One's Own (1929)*, she anticipates the gender dimension which is central to her understanding of imperialism in *Between the Acts*: 'So with Mr Kipling's officers who turn their backs; and his Sowers who sow the Seed; and his Men who are alone with their Work; and the Flag – one blushes at all those capital letters as if one had been caught eavesdropping at some purely masculine orgy' (1929/1977: 97).

Through the litany of conquest and invasion that is English history, Woolf aims to illustrate that national history is synonymous with patriarchal history. Thus in the opening section of the novel, 'before' the acts, an opposition is established between what can conveniently be termed 'male' time and 'female' time – although significantly the categories are not mutually exclusive. A female eternity is juxtaposed against a male absolute, and the extremes of this opposition are epitomised by Bart and Lucy. Bart demands focus; Lucy's thought processes are fluid: 'She would have been, he thought, a very clever woman, had she fixed her gaze. But this led to that; that to the other' (Woolf, 1941/1978: 22). Similarly a conversation between Isa, whose thought processes are remarkably similar to those of Lucy, and Bart emphasises the distinctions:

> 'Are we really,' she said, turning round, 'a hundred miles from the sea?'
>
> 'Thirty-five only,' her father-in-law said, as if he had whipped a tape measure from his pocket and measured it exactly.
>
> 'It seems more,' said Isa. 'It seems from the terrace as if the land went on for ever and ever.' (Woolf, 1941/1978: 25–6)

In *Between the Acts* Woolf develops the opposition of time and space into a juxtaposition of 'male' history against a hypothetical alternative 'female' history, and it is here that Woolf's fiction is situated. She attempts to encode and take refuge in a vision constructed around a mythical sense of a female continuum. This continuum, which is both an alternative concept of time and an ongoing cycle of birth and rebirth, is an attempt to radically re-envisage the process of history, indeed to reinscribe history as a continual process or pattern rather than a linear progression. This is an issue that frequently recurs in Woolf's writing. *The Years* is famous for its refusal to acknowledge the accepted 'highlights' of European history, concentrating instead on familial patterns of power and exclusion; while Rachel Bowlby (1988: 129) has illustrated *Orlando*'s concern to 'show up the illusory position of the history-writer as a reliable reconstructor of a past "world"'.

In her last novel Woolf experiments with a model that again denies the certainties of male precision and focus, but which, going a stage further, also posits the replacement of the sterile old structures with a female other. Bart Oliver acknowledges the fragility and the temporality of his existence, in his old age seeing Isa as his only connection to the ongoing process of life. It is surely ironic that Isa is only his daughter-in-law, an outsider, but none the less essential not only to Bart's continuation but also to that of his son, Giles:

> he was grateful to her, watching her as she strolled about the room, for continuing.
>   Many old men had only their India – old men in clubs, old men in rooms off Jermyn Street. She in her striped dress continued him. (Woolf, 1941/1978: 17)

In this sense of continuity through the female there is an echo of Woolf's earlier injunction to 'think back through our mothers' (Woolf, 1929/1977: 72). It is through the rediscovery of the female line that regeneration becomes a possibility. The regenerative potential of a female inheritance is fleetingly suggested by *The Years* (Woolf, 1937/1977: 55). It is the Yorkshire legacy of Kitty's mother's family that briefly creates the possibility of a shared past from the restrictions of an alienated present. To think back through our mothers is to reinscribe a history of communality and co-operation that transcends the sterility of the imperialist legacy.

The scope of Woolf's vision in *Between the Acts* can be usefully illustrated and analysed through the ideas of Julia Kristeva (1974; 1979). Kristeva distinguishes between the symbolic, the dominant order of language that constructs our identity, and the semiotic, the elements that must be repressed in order to maintain or enter that order. Here the term 'semiotic' refers to the pre-Oedipal stage of child development, the period in which the child knows no boundaries and has no sense of itself as an independent social (or gendered) being. She also theorises a revolutionary potential within this 'chora' of repressed drives. These constantly fluctuating forces never leave the symbolic order, but exist in parallel, or beneath the surface, to return as irruptions and dislocations that have the power to destabilise and disrupt that order. These theories have considerable implications for a reading of Woolf's wartime work. In 'About Chinese women' (1974: 153) Kristeva goes on to posit an 'underlying causality', defined as 'the social contradictions that a given society can provisionally subdue in order to constitute itself as such', and in *Between the Acts* Woolf can be seen to present a social order constituted on the subjection of the contradictory female. The patriarchal order encloses the fluidity of the female other and utilises it to ensure its own continuation, as it is only through the woman that the man can be continued. This Woolf establishes as the status quo; but throughout *Between the Acts* the strength of the female continuity perpetually threatens to undermine patriarchal authority. Rachel Bowlby draws attention to the point where Woolf 'brings family history downstairs to a succession of cooks' reigns, replacing the father's name with a different kind of nominal shift' (Bowlby 1988: 149; Woolf, 1941/1978: 29). The status of the patriarch as head of the family is ridiculed and challenged when the era that should by rights be his, is instead remembered as the time of his cook.

This revisioning is evident from Woolf's earliest work. In her manuscript '[The journal of Mistress Joan Martyn]' (Woolf, 1906), Woolf depicts a pivotal role for women as both a centre of stability and the force of continuation. The fictional journal dates from the fifteenth century and through it Woolf attributes considerable power to the position of the respectably married woman. Joan envisages a clear line of female descent – 'It is a great thing to be the daughter of such a woman, and to hope that one day the same power may be mine. She rules us all' (Woolf, 1906: 46). Even more emphatically, Joan's mother tells her daughter:

> If you marry such a man as Sir Amyas you become not only the head of his household, and that is much, but the head of his race for ever and ever, and that is more. (Woolf, 1906: 50)

Continuity is always seen to lie with the female. In *Between the Acts* Lucy is not only possessed of the oldest name, it is also she who performs the proprietary act of showing Dodge the house, remembering the bed in which she was born and drawing attention to the morning room where, 'my mother received her guests' (Woolf, 1941/1978: 54).

In Woolf's final novel then, the rules and boundaries of time and space undergo a radical reinterpretation. Lucy Swithin lives mentally in a time of no divisions, her imagination shows no regard for the demands of reason or logic and she easily collapses millions of years of history into a primeval image that excites her:

'Once there was no sea,' said Mrs Swithin. 'No sea at all between us and the continent. I was reading that in a book this morning. There were rhododendrons in the Strand; and mammoths in Picadilly.' (Woolf, 1941/1978: 26)

Her fertile imagination is closely related to the poetry that Isa secretly writes. Together these two women can be seen to represent a form of choric space into which Bart and Giles impose themselves and their patriarchal civilisation in a manner consistent with Kristeva's theorising of the thetic phase. These women's lives and their histories form a continuum pulled into shape by the patriarchal social order in much the same way as Miss La Trobe struggles to impose order on her unruly play. Miss La Trobe is able to exercise this symbolic power on account of her position as director of the pageant; she, like Mrs Manresa, has chosen to derive her identity through identification with the father. Kristeva's model sees two options for women: to identify with the mother, remaining true to the pre-Oedipal semiotic elements of the self, a course which can ultimately only confirm her marginality; or to identify with the father and thereby be implicated in the very symbolic order that oppresses her. The dilemma thus created for woman is articulated in 'About Chinese women':

We cannot gain access to the temporal scene, that is, to the political and historical affairs of our society, except by identifying with the values considered to be masculine (mastery, superego, the sanctioning communicative word that institutes stable social exchange). (Kristeva, 1974: 155)

This dilemma focuses the questions with which Woolf grappled in *Three Guineas*. How can a woman have power enough to prevent war, when access to that power is in the gift of the corrupt and will inevitably compromise those who engage with it? However, Woolf's position in *Between the Acts*, as in *Three Guineas*, continues to resist a straightforward categorisation. The issue is complicated when we consider that whether Miss La Trobe identifies with the paternal or the maternal, she is still not a 'powerful' character. As a lesbian and a newcomer to the village, she remains an outsider:

At the corner she ran into old Mrs Chalmers returning from the grave. The old woman looked down at the dead flowers she was carrying and cut her . . . She was an outcast. Nature had somehow set her apart from her kind. (Woolf, 1941/1978: 153; ellipsis mine)

The 'kind' is ambiguous, referring possibly to humankind in general, the community of the village or the (unnamed) community from whence she came, or to other women – presumably alienated by her ambiguous position in the symbolic hierarchy. A similar fear of the unknown, of uncertainty and ambiguity is evident in Giles's instinctive and faintly ludicrous response to the homosexual William Dodge: 'At this word, which he could not speak in public, he pursed his lips; and the signet-ring on his little finger looked redder, for the flesh next it whitened as he gripped the arm of his chair' (Woolf, 1941/1978: 48). Unlike Eleanor's easy assimilation of Brown's homosexuality in *The Years*, Giles's response situates him firmly under the glass of the symbolic order. Miss La Trobe, then, is not part of the patriarchal order, and exactly where she belongs is further complicated by her role as writer and creator. She gives birth to her play among images of pain, sweat and tears – she is involved in the agony of trying to 'bring a common meaning to birth' (1941/1978: 112) – and almost before it is over she has conceived, in an astonishingly primeval image of fertile mud, of the first words of another creation (1941/1978: 153–4). La Trobe and Dodge may both derive their identity from the same symbolic order, but they ultimately remain excluded from the power structure that enshrines that order, that is, the patriarchy.

The positioning of La Trobe and Dodge indicates that Woolf is not satisfied by a simple male/female division in her indictment of patriarchy and its history. Her anti-biologistic imagining of the division between 'masculinity' and 'femininity' is again indicative of an affinity between her work and the much later theories of Julia Kristeva. Kristeva's position is articulated in 'Women's time', where she identifies and rejects two earlier forms of feminism: the egalitarian variety, demanding equality in all areas, and the radical variety, separate from and opposing every aspect of the symbolic order. Her solution is a third position:

> In this third attitude, which I strongly advocate – which I imagine? – the very dichotomy man/woman as an opposition between two rival entities may be understood as belonging to *metaphysics*. What can 'identity', even 'sexual identity', mean in a new theoretical and scientific space where the very notion of identity is challenged? (Kristeva, 1979: 209)

For Woolf, I believe, war provokes just such a breakdown of identity, and can be seen to represent a not-so-new 'theoretical and scientific space' which challenges the very notion of existence.

In order to escape the destructive patterning of gender, Woolf envisions an alternative binary opposition between the patriarchal order and a loosely-knit Society of Outsiders. This is similar to the gradual disruption of gendered identities she undertook in *The Years*, but in *Between the Acts* the opposition is explored through the juxtaposition of an historical critique against the unchanging continuity of contemporary society. The rigid forms of the stock male characters uphold the symbolic order and impose it upon the fluid continuum of the more complex women. They persist in an historical pattern that renders woman nothing more than the biological servant of the colonial master. Yet once again masculinity and femininity are largely superficial; Woolf's prototype chora underpins all, regardless of gender, and her alternative history or female continuum continually resurfaces not as a conflict, but as an attempt to envisage a non-history, a space outside the linear temporality of historical narrative.

How successful is Woolf's imagining of this primordial time? Daniel Ferrer (1990) suggests that the conclusion of *Between the Acts* with its 'strangely Lawrentian tone' is highly problematic. This raises the question of whether Woolf herself is unconvinced by the strategy she had attempted to create. Is there a lack of faith in her vision of primitive life forces that will, through the feminine continuum, regenerate life after war? The problem is perhaps not with the vision itself, although there is something incongruous in Woolf's exploration of a violent prehistory[5], but with the actual idea of an alternative fiction. Woolf's work had always struggled to challenge the notion of a single unified vision. She was, in a sense, the last person to believe in the possibility of a consistent, effective strategy, and it is therefore not surprising that she should undermine the one she hoped to create for herself. Ferrer, emphasising the complexity and uncertainty of the novel's narrative voices, concludes:

> This absence in the place of the ultimate subject guaranteeing the enunciation reactivates all the gashes which the text opened up but *immediately pretended to mend*, in order to carry on, *in order to exist*. (Ferrer, 1990: 140; emphasis mine)

Ultimately Woolf's fiction is closer to a façade. It was a hopeless situation – a vision she could not write herself into, and a war she could not write herself out of. In the end absenting herself from life would be the only certain way to absent herself from war.

The place of madness and suicide in Woolf's final novel has been much debated. The extent of the fragmentation suggested by Ferrer makes the novel exceptionally slippery, and a reading of his analysis would seem to suggest that Woolf's real vision is one of death. He speaks of the pressure throughout the novel of 'something . . . which is not really expressed by articulate rational language, but is trying to inscribe itself through that language by disrupting it' (Ferrer, 1990: 122), and suggests that 'this plethora of voices pushing behind every word ends with a kind of cacophony, and even with "white noise" equivalent to a silence' (1990: 119). His linguistic analysis returns us to the space of the Kristevan chora, the pre-Oedipal semiotic that in its unbroken state is the site of silence, madness and death. In order to engage with language

Woolf has to engage with the symbolic, and in so doing she distances herself from her fiction, and her death. There is still abundant evidence of Woolf's meticulous craftsmanship within the text: the symmetry of the build-up to and descent from the focal point 'between the acts'; for example. This is achieved not only by balancing the quantities of text, but also by the careful repetition of key phrases and images, such as M. Daladier's pegging down of the franc (Woolf, 1941/1978: 14, 156), and the disturbing report of the girl raped by the soldiers (1941/1978: 19, 157). Situating this combination of control and disruption, order and chaos, within the context of European war indicates the possibility of reading the novel as a last will and testament; or, more appropriately, a last will and hope. *Between the Acts* can be seen as a semi-ironic bequeathing of a 'woman's time' to future generations, accompanied by a 'last (act of) will' through her assault on the patriarchal myth of benevolent Englishness. I say semi-ironic because although Woolf was always aware of the difficulties inherent in the envisaging of an alternative time or history in the midst of a cataclysmic, but paradoxically necessary war, I believe she had still made a considerable emotional investment in her alternative fiction.

Between the Acts, then, is a novel of wishful thinking. On the level of individual characterisation, male impotence and female frustration combine in a climate of repression. Giles's impotent rage simmers throughout the novel:

> Giles nicked his chair into position with a jerk. Thus only could he show his irritation, his rage with old fogies who sat and looked at views over coffee and cream when the whole of Europe – over there – was bristling like . . . He had no command of metaphor. Only the ineffective word 'hedgehog' illustrated his vision of Europe, bristling with guns, poised with planes. (Woolf, 1941/1978: 43)

Not only is he politically impotent, he is also defeated by language. By comparison Isa inhabits a world rich with metaphors, but her poetry is kept in a secret book. Lucy, who could have been 'a very clever woman', has repressed her vivid life of the imagination into the symbolic order of organised religion, convincing all around her that her moments of absence are meditations on an appropriate theme: 'She was thinking, he supposed, God is peace. God is love. For she belonged to the unifiers; he to the separatists' (Woolf, 1941/1978: 88).

Exactly what Lucy is thinking is, unknown. Here and elsewhere her piety is imposed on her by others who seek to give structure to the potentially threatening expanse of her day-dreaming. It is not until the final moments of the novel that Lucy's religious allegiance is seen to be a superficial comfort, protecting her from the harsh intrusions of the patriarchal symbolic, and disguising her true allegiance to the fluid realm of the imagination:

> She stood between two fluidities, caressing her cross. Faith required hours of kneeling in the early morning. Often the delight of the roaming eye seduced her – a sunbeam, a shadow. (Woolf, 1941/1978: 148)

On a second level the wishful thinking belongs to Woolf herself, and in *Between the Acts* she explores the possibility explicitly developed by Elizabeth Bowen in the short story 'Mysterious Kôr' (1945) of thinking or writing oneself out of one place or time and into the possibility of an other. In Bowen's story Pepita has created a fantasy which enables her both to rationalise and to opt out of the fact of war. She takes the immensity of war's destructive power and uses it as a logic on which to base the possibility of escape into the fantastical city of Kôr: 'This war shows we've by no means come to the end. If you can blow whole places out of existence, you can blow whole places into it. I don't see why not' (Bowen, 1983: 730). Bowen's idea suggests an intimate connection between the forces of destruction and creation. Their proximity is reinforced in Woolf's dialectic, where the demand that England wake up to the realities of the Second World War is inextricably linked to the fiction that would take Woolf out of that war. In order to write herself out of time Woolf attempts to envisage a *pre* history – a space outside the symbolic order of the father's history. Ultimately she is looking to a place *beyond* the acts; beyond the illusions, beyond the protocols and beyond the negative actions that characterise the past and are destined for the future. The oft-quoted moment in which Giles, confronted by the impasse of the snake choking on the frog, resolves the situation and relieves his frustration by the act of killing them both, typifies the arbitrary violence of an impotent patriarchy. At the heart of war lies the instinctive resort to force that is characteristic of a society in which status and self-respect are based on the capacity of an individual to take action. Beyond the acts Woolf imagines a space from which the outsiders of *The Years* and *Three Guineas* can subvert this realm of patriarchal signification.

But the final stages of *Between the Acts* were completed as the Blitz decimated Virginia Woolf's world, and ultimately her vision reaches the same impasse of action/inaction that concludes Kristeva's theorising. Kristeva calls for a 'constant alternation between time and its "truth", identity and its loss', situated 'outside the sign, beyond time'; but her resolution of what she terms the 'impossible dialectic' remains problematic:

> But how can we do this? By listening; by recognising the unspoken in all discourse, however Revolutionary, by emphasizing at each point what-ever remains unsatisfied, repressed, new, eccentric, incomprehensible,

that which disturbs the mutual understanding of the established powers. (Kristeva, 1974: 156)

Kristeva's provisional answer is listening – a solution not far from Stevie Smith's 'watching brief' – but a watching brief failed to prevent the rise of dictators, so how can it defeat their triumph in war? If, as Kristeva fears and as Woolf's death would seem to confirm, this strategy is untenable, does not listening then effectively become silence, and how far is silence from death?[6]

NOTES

1. Woolf maintained a considerable interest in the fourteenth and fifteenth centuries, seeing them as a crucial transitional point in the formation of the modern world. Her essay 'The Pastons and Chaucer' (1925) illustrates her beliefs and portrays Sir John Paston as one of the first to escape into a book from a life that was 'rough, cheerless and disappointing'. The Middle Ages are a beginning for Woolf, representing the birth of the popular printed word, and she envies Chaucer for the freedom of his time: 'Chaucer could write frankly where we must either say nothing or say it slyly. He could sound every note in the language instead of finding a great many of the best gone dumb from disuse' (Woolf, 1967: 11).

   Woolf also envies a certain animal simplicity that she finds in the period. Men and women unite in a basic struggle for survival in a hostile environment. This is an image vividly created in '[The journal of Mistress Joan Martyn]' (1906) the implications of which I discuss below.

2. Johnston observes that the three men in the novel, Bart, Giles and Streatfield, represent the three exclusively male professions of the army, the City and the ministry. She does not mention William Dodge, who in this context it seems does not count as male. The omission, however, can be supported in terms of the subject's relationship to the symbolic order. William's homosexuality and his domination by Mrs Manresa render him effectively marginal to the structures of power represented by the other biologically male characters. Johnston also makes the interesting observation that Lucy and Isa have much closer ties to the Saxon heritage than the men with their distinctly Norman names; a situation which suggests that 'The conquest of Anglo-Saxon England by the Normans is mirrored in the domination of Lucy and Isa by Bart and Giles' (Johnston, 1987: 261).

3. The tension between fiction and reality is more complex here than is at first perceptible. In her introduction to the Penguin edition of *Between the Acts*, Gillian Beer relates the details of the contemporary rape case which impinged on Woolf's fiction, and concludes: 'The identification Isa makes with the victim is altered, I would assert, by the knowledge that the bodies and persons in the case existed, just as the coming war was a "real" war, communally experienced' (Beer, 1992: xxiii). Throughout *Between the Acts*, external reality exerts a constant pressure on the form and content of the text.

4. Eleanor's vehement response to a picture of Mussolini in the evening paper shocks her niece Peggy who has become inured to the 'reality' represented by the faces in the news:

   > As far as Peggy could see, but she was short-sighted, it was the usual evening paper's blurred picture of a fat man gesticulating.
   >
   > 'Damned–' Eleanor shot out suddenly, 'bully!' She tore the paper across with one sweep of her hand and flung it on the floor. Peggy was shocked . . . For when Eleanor, who used English so reticently, said 'damned' and then 'bully', it meant much more than the words she and her friends used. (Woolf, 1937/1977: 252; ellipsis mine)

   For Peggy 'reality' has become 'blurred' and Eleanor's words, like Woolf's novel, demand a sharpening of the observer's focus.

5. The underlying scepticism that creates the disjuncture between Woolf's vision and her capacity to believe in it is grotesquely anticipated in a scene from *The Years*. North's description of Milly and Hugh Gibbs situates prehistory not in the sublime, but in the ridiculous. Imagining Milly reproducing like an amoeba, the animal imagery used here is in stark contrast to the visionary aura that concludes *Between the Acts*:

   > That was what it came to – thirty years of being husband and wife – tut-tut-tut and chew-chew-chew. It sounded like the half-inarticulate munchings of animals in a stall.

> Tut-tut-tut, and chew-chew-chew – as they trod out the soft steamy straw in the stable; as they wallowed in the primeval swamp, prolific, profuse, half-conscious. (1937/1977: 186)

If this is the conception of the primitive life forces from which society must regenerate that lurked at the back of Woolf's mind, the future must indeed have looked bleak.

6. Perhaps the area where Woolf and Kristeva most diverge is the political. Kristeva has certainly been criticised for her political naivety. Gayatri Chakravorty Spivak finds many problematic areas in 'About Chinese women', in particular criticising Kristeva's assumption of a homogeneous form of woman which takes no account of the differences of class, religion and culture that subdivide the category (Spivak, 1981). In 'Women's time', however, Kristeva shows an increased awareness of these difficulties and is careful to distinguish the voice of 'European' women, and even to question the homogeneity of this group. Toril Moi, while concerned by Kristeva's 'grossly exaggerated confidence in the political importance of the *avant-garde*' (1985: 172), sees political differences as no reason to dismiss the theories which have 'opened up new perspectives for further feminist enquiry'. Discussing the three generations of feminism identified by Kristeva, she concludes:

> The relationship between the second and third positions here requires some comment. If the defence of the third position implies a total rejection of stage two (which I do not think it does), this would be a grievous political error . . . But an 'undeconstructed' form of 'stage two' feminism, unaware of the metaphysical nature of gender identities, runs the risk of becoming an inverted form of sexism. It does so by uncritically taking over the very metaphysical categories set up by patriarchy in order to keep women in their places, despite attempts to attach new feminist values to these old categories. (Moi, 1985: 13)

The political position of the outsider advocated by Woolf in *Three Guineas* suggests that her vision attempted to incorporate the paradoxical co-existence of stages two and three of the Kristevan model. The radicalism of the outsider's position is none the less one which is able to acknowledge that the patriarchal order, for all its intrinsic misogyny, is essentially indiscriminate in its discrimination.

8

Constructing the Future Through the Past: Naomi Mitchison's Brave New World

He of course feels that there will be a future; he's full of hope underneath. I feel I must carry on, but the underneath hope isn't there; I see endurance but no happiness. I try and tell people that it will be a world full of building and excitement and new things: but not for me.

Naomi Mitchison, *Among You Taking Notes . . . The Wartime Diary of Naomi Mitchison,* 9 July 1940

[W]riting is precisely *the very possibility of change,* the space that can serve as a springboard for subversive thought, the precursory movement of a transformation of social and cultural structures.

Hélène Cixous, 'The laugh of the Medusa'

Naomi Mitchison was a believer – not in a strictly religious sense, for she rejected all ideas of a paternal God – but rather in a socio-political sense. She believed in the abstractions of politics, ethics, morality and justice, and consequently it might have been very significant that in 1943, halfway through the writing of her immense historical novel *The Bull Calves,* she discovered Carl Gustav Jung. Reading *The Integration of the Personality* (1940) had a powerful effect on her, as she recorded in her diary:

Almost at once I came on the clue which showed me where my book was to go next, the moral plot, I mean, Kirstie and William as animus and anima, the projection by intelligent people who half know what they're doing. I went half to sleep, getting this into images of a kind, then had cider for lunch, felt drunk and elated and talked, I think, with considerable brilliance and semantic quality, to the others, very largely about the difference it would make if there were not four airts or compass points but five, and so no complete opposite to anything. (29 August 1943; Mitchison, 1986a: 252–3)

Jung's work seemed to crystallise important aspects of Mitchison's own thought, in particular her vision of 'the saving of a soul' which she equated with Jung's process of individuation.[1] However, although Jung's ideas excited and stimulated Mitchison intellectually, they failed to provide a system of thought or ethics that could satisfy her desire for belief. The notes to *The Bull Calves* explain why ultimately she found Jung an unsatisfactory guru:

> This re-reading [1945] confirms me in an earlier opinion that the whole thing is (perhaps inevitably) written so much from the male point of view that it is sometimes quite disconcertingly difficult for a woman to follow it sympathetically. The man is the individual; women are a lump. It is not very pleasant to read a book in which you are considered as part of a lump. It is deplorable that, so far as I know, no woman of genius has written on the psychology of the unconscious from the female point of view: or that it has not been possible for any psychologist to overcome his or her limitations and write about it from a bi-sexual point of view which would be even more valuable. (Mitchison, 1947: 512)

The unthinking misogyny of Jung's theories struck at an element of Mitchison that was a prerequisite to all her other ethical and political concerns – her feminism. As her wartime diary reveals, the desire to question the founding principle of binary oppositions was part of a wider anxiety about the rationale of socio-political organisation that she found little scope to express within the context of pre-war socialism or wartime survival. Beneath the superficial conformity of her political loyalties and her non-experimental grand narratives, Mitchison explored a series of sophisticated feminist possibilities, which emerge as suggestive subtexts within her public writing. It is perhaps not surprising that her most explicit feminist statements are either contained within the distancing privacy of her Mass-Observation diary, or buried within the dense undergrowth of notes that accompany her wartime novel. Yet, although she appeared to experience some difficulty in its articulation, feminism was fundamental to Mitchison. Her diary makes this clear when, following a quarrel with her close friend Denny, she observes:

> I don't think he sees my point very much, however it will no doubt clear itself up. I think it all means that my feminism is deeper in me than, say, nationalism or socialism: it is more irrational, harder to argue about, nearer the hurting core. (22 December 1941; Mitchison, 1986a: 172)

'The hurting core' is a telling expression, suggesting something vital, yet vulnerable, something always present, but often disguised or suppressed. I believe this phrase is crucial to an understanding of Mitchison's work, offering a key to open up the dynamics of her rather reluctant texts and their relation to the historical moment of war.

Mitchison was a prolific writer, but the decade surrounding the Second World War was perhaps the quietest of her publishing history. In the period 1938 to 1948, alongside short stories, articles and a Mass-Observation diary running to a million words, Mitchison produced two major novels and two book–length polemical essays. Crammed into the brief, but intense, space of 1938–9 were the polemical works *The Kingdom of Heaven* (1939) and *The Moral Basis of Politics* (1938), and a highly allegorical historical novel, *The Blood of the Martyrs* (1939). Mitchison's fears of Fascism and European conflict receive a thorough and essentially pessimistic airing in this novel about a group of early Christians in the reign of the Emperor Nero. To cut a very long story short, the Christians are persecuted for Nero's political convenience, imprisoned, tortured and fed to the lions. The climax of the novel, however, lies not in the death of the Christians, but in the impact of their deaths upon the spectators. The conflicts articulated here remain central to Mitchison's intellectual outlook throughout the war, and I return to them later. Yet in the eight years following *The Blood of the Martyrs* there are no major publications. This is the period of war: for Mitchison a time spent in the west of Scotland, involved in a constant grind of farming, fishing and organisation, during which she worked on the novel that primarily concerns this chapter. *The Bull Calves* was finally published in 1947, and although it is couched in the comparatively safe metaphoricity of history, this novel encodes a complex and, at times, contradictory response to the moment of war. Mitchison, like her contemporaries, found the moral, social, political and physical demands of the Second World War to be almost overwhelming. Unlike Virginia Woolf, however, she survived – and on a superficial level it might seem that there is very little to connect these two women writers' responses to the fact of war.

As writers Woolf and Mitchison have little in common. Stylistically they are about as far removed as it is possible for two writers to be. To put it crudely, Woolf is in the vanguard of modernism, while Mitchison, for all her fascination with the supernatural, is in the rearguard of an almost Lukácsian realism. Yet as feminists they share a fundamental agenda which permeates the very fabric of their works – although it seems unlikely that either Mitchison or Woolf was aware of this common ground. Interestingly, when explaining her decision to write *The Bull Calves* in dialect, Mitchison contrasts her writing with Woolf, whom she describes as an exponent of the English 'literary tradition' (Mitchison, 1947: 411). Woolf, on the other hand, is simply disparaging about Mitchison, describing her as 'the rather sordid fat . . . greyfaced intense Naomi' (21 November 1935; Woolf, 1977–84: vol. IV: 354) However, exploring Mitchison in conjunction with Woolf can prove surprisingly liberating. The contemporary feminist ideas that have been used to constructive effect in the analysis of Woolf can equally be applied to Mitchison, making it possible to discern and examine the 'hurting core' of her fiction. In the case of Woolf, many critics have turned to the work of Julia Kristeva to illustrate the conflicts and tensions beneath the smooth façade of modernism; and although Mitchison's façade is the seemingly very different one of ostentatious social and political concerns, Kristevan ideas can none the less be used to explore both the radical feminism and the unreconcilable contradictions that underpin her apparently orthodox socialist realism.[2] Yet there is also another dimension to Mitchison's wartime text. As I suggested above, *The Bull Calves* operates on a multiplicity of levels, and one of the most complex and contradictory aspects of the text is its fascination with the inexplicable and the excessive. The novel considers the definitions of 'civilised' behaviour and depicts the dangerous but powerful allure of something beyond the rigid codes of the patriarchal symbolic – a power that is outside the boundaries of the rational, and yet is capable of destabilising and disrupting that order. Men and women succumb to this fascination with what could be described as the semiotic, and at key points within the text Mitchison situates this power within the realm of the female imagination through the transgressive figure of the witch/hysteric. This dangerous and potentially destructive female body is juxtaposed against a recurring motif of the pregnant woman, whose body is seen to be a symbol not only of regeneration but also of reinscription. Throughout *The Bull Calves*, then, body and text are linked in a symbiosis more readily associated with the utopian writings of Hélène Cixous than the deconstructive theories of Julia Kristeva.

The Bull Calves can be seen to represent the maintenance of Mitchison's 'hurting core' against the constant demands and the threatened intellectual, and bodily, dispersal of wartime. The demand of Hélène Cixous that 'woman must write herself: must write about women and bring women to writing, from which they have been driven away as violently as from their bodies' (Cixous, 1980: 245) is perhaps singularly appropriate to both the literal and metaphorical project of this text. At a time when almost all writing can in some sense be seen as a strategy for survival, *The Bull Calves* represents a reinscription of the feminine in a world consumed by a cataclysmic masculinity. The novel is a multi-faceted creation: historical novel, war novel, coming-of-age drama, romance, mystery and, I argue, a feminist utopia.

In early July 1940, at the age of 42, Naomi Mitchison gave birth to a baby that died after only a few hours. In more ways than one, Mitchison had invested a considerable amount of emotional energy in the baby, in particular hoping that it would create a bond between herself and the Carradale community. The Mitchisons had moved to Carradale before the outbreak of war, but as mistress of the 'big house', Naomi still felt herself essentially to be an outsider:

> Here I have to be good. And it's difficult, especially with no supernatural sanction . . . all round there are men and women waiting to catch me out. Sometimes I could scream. How can a writer work in these conditions? (16 March 1940; Mitchison, 1986a: 58; ellipsis mine)

The poem 'Clemency Ealasaid', which prefaces *The Bull Calves*, emphasises this sense of exclusion and gives expression to her frustrated hopes and sense of alienation:

> This was to have been a binding between me and Carradale.
> Weeper of Carradale Glen, fairy hare, cleft rock, did none of you speak?
> How shall I stay here, how go on with the little things,
> How not hate Carradale, the flowery betrayer,
> Dagger in fist?

The image of the 'flowery betrayer' is symbolic of the tension that underlay Mitchison's wartime relationship with Carradale, while the objects of her appeal reveal her sense of a natural alliance between women and the inexplicable. Mitchison was strongly attached to the community, its values and its socialist potential; but the village could not fulfil a utopian role. It was not ready to become the site of her 'brave new world', and the disparity between its real and ideal sides were to prove a frequent source of frustration and disappointment. These small betrayals, springing from inescapable divisions of class and education, and from an often fundamentally different sense of priority, were perpetually undermining the fiction of equality that Mitchison sought to enact within the 'real' world.

Mitchison's attempts to create a constructive community were more successful within the realm of fiction. After the death of her baby, Mitchison's Mass Observation diary records the processes that combine to make her wartime novel both a strategy for survival and a dream of reconciliation. *The Bull Calves* enables Mitchison to write herself out of the war situation and into an abstract future postwar that is imagined through the past of her historical novel. The diary makes explicit the ties which bind the baby to the as yet unwritten book, and explores the connection between these two acts of creation and the act of destruction that is war:

> I dread going about again and facing people; they will be extremely sympathetic, but damn their sympathy. I feel I shall get landed with

agricultural work which would have been tolerable and even delightful
with a background of baby – of creation. But intolerable with one's mind
empty and groping. To some extent, too, I had used this as an excuse to
be out of the war, out of destruction, still on the side of creation; now
that's over. (4–7 July 1940; Mitchison, 1986a: 72)

The following day, after being advised by her doctor to think of writing as a
means of overcoming her grief, she concluded:

I must consider it, even if nothing comes of it . . . If only I had my baby
I wouldn't need to write a book that probably nobody wants to read'.
(8 July 1940; Mitchison, 1986a: 73)

Mitchison was surrounded by a war that contravened her deepest social and
political convictions, yet the evil implications of a Nazi Europe left her on the
horns of what she termed a 'complete dilemma of the worst possible sort' (4
August 1940; 1986a: 78). Political engagement seemed impossible: the time
for polemic was past and for the sake of national unity most internal debate was
suspended. Jill Benton's biography makes the situation abundantly clear. Even
before the outbreak of war, a backlash against feminist thought was gathering
momentum, culminating in the atmosphere of sex antagonism that would fuel
Virginia Woolf's *Three Guineas* (1938), and which prompted Mitchison's friend
Stevie Smith to conclude 'they can't see what anybody means unless it's said in
the accepted voice' (quoted in Benton, 1990: 113–14). Mitchison, like Woolf,
was forced to look for an imaginative solution to the problem of intellectual
and emotional survival. The baby, and afterwards the book, represented her
strategy, and *The Bull Calves* can be seen as a fiction of reconstruction; a dream
of community, reconciliation and above all understanding which would enable
her to escape from the present into a time beyond the war, when once again it
would be safe to forgive (but not forget), to plan and to rebuild.

The Bull Calves is a long and detailed narrative woven around the events
of two days in the summer of 1747. It opens with an initially overwhelming
deluge of characters about whom we know little more than their relation to
the prosperous lowland Scottish family of the Haldanes. It seems like a cast
of thousands, until you work out that every character has at least three names
(Christian, family, estate), and devise a method for matching them correctly.
This complexity, however, is not gratuitous. The stress on a multiplicity
of names, by taking away the single authority of the patronym, serves to
emphasise the novel's concern with issues of inheritance. Here the father's
name is undermined, as later the value of his inheritance will be challenged.
Most of the initial necessary information is imparted through dialogue, and
Mitchison uses the eyes of an innocent observer of a younger generation to

hint at the unarticulated tensions beneath the surface of family unity. As the initial confusion of identities begins to clear, these tensions become increasingly evident. New puzzles are thrown up by the text and various characters take on the role of storyteller, each offering fragments of a jigsaw puzzle for the reader to assemble. The central characters, Kirstie Haldane and her Highland second husband Black William, have pasts wracked by difficult secrets that need to be spoken and forgiven, but the security of their relationship and the stability of the whole family is threatened by the influence of evil represented by their cousin Kyllachy. The book has a quasi-dramatic four-part structure, of which the fourth has all the characteristics of a theatrical denouement. The skeletons have emerged from their closets and all the players are assembled, powerless to decide their own fates and dependent for their futures on the wisdom of a new character, the figure of the detective – or judge – played in this instance by the lord president, Duncan Forbes of Culloden. Justice is seen to be done and the conclusion is an optimistic one which seems to affirm the possibility of reconciliation.[3]

This, then, constitutes the surface text of *The Bull Calves*, just as the ideal of reconstruction forms its ostentatious project: but the disruptions of wartime are perhaps not as easily contained as these narratives might suggest. Mitchison's diaries direct us to a link between the female body and the body of the text, but the nature of this connection is far from clear. We are offered several archetypal possibilities: the witch is present, as are the virgin and the mother. The pregnant woman in particular becomes a recurrent motif, and given the context of its creation, this becomes perhaps the text's most multi-faceted and redolent signifier. *The Bull Calves* functions not only as a surrogate child but also as a surrogate mother. There is a transition over the course of composition: the surrogate child is transformed into the figure of the mother, pregnant not with individual life, but with the life of the community. The text becomes an active producer, writing becomes 'precisely *the very possibility of change*' (Cixous, 1980: 249; emphasis in the original), and throughout the narrative, patriarchal values and figures are challenged or destroyed through the transgression of the very laws that on the surface, at least, would appear to be upheld.

What, then, is the nature of this mothering motif? Naomi Segal, discussing the Old Testament Book of Ruth, explores the story of Naomi in terms of patrilineal and matrilineal genealogy (Segal, 1990). In contrast to other biblical mothers, excluded from the bond between father, son and God, Segal suggests Naomi to be the originator of a matrilinear inheritance. The death of all her menfolk situates Naomi in an unusually autonomous position, and the absence of these men enables her to form a significant bond with her daughter-in-law, Ruth, that disrupts the norms of both inheritance and mothering. There are echoes of this move towards a matrilinear genealogy in Kirstie's story. The deaths of her two boy children, and eventually of her first husband and oppressor, Andrew, leave her alone and open to the possibility of an active subjectivity. Yet there can be no place within a patriarchal society for such a woman, and Kirstie finds her communality not within society, but without in the coven of witches:

> Yet times I had a feeling that we were near to understanding in the heart of things that could have been turned to good, yet not good of a kind that would be recognised by the respectable and the members of the congregation. Least of all, maybe, by the men. (Mitchison, 1947: 166)

The text never makes clear to what extent this body of women, their moonlight dances, fearful apparitions and inexplicable powers exist as figments of Kirstie's imagination, and to what extent they have some reality as social outlaws and outcasts. The 'reality' of Kirstie's experience remains unresolved, and Mitchison draws back from this rejection of society. Kirstie is restored to a place within the boundaries of the social through the return of the man she desires, the Highlander William Macintosh of Borlum. This is not, however, a straightforward marriage. The Lowlands' historical position as the base of Enlightenment rationality is defined in opposition to the perceived 'untamed' and irrational nature of the Highlands. This juxtaposition suggests that the Highlands could potentially be theorised as a 'feminine' space – but such a binary is comprehensively destabilised by the traditional association of the Highlands with an aggressive masculinity, while the Lowlands are seen to represent the 'soft' life of the city, their national identity diluted through contact with the English south. Through uniting Kirstie with William, Mitchison is in effect creating a compromise. After marrying William, Kirstie's fertility returns, and in producing a daughter she challenges the patrilineal norm – but her transgressive potential is contained within submission to William, who, although other to the conformity of the Lowlands, is none the less her master. When Kirstie dreams of the coven, the balance of power is made abundantly clear in William's reply: 'they just canna have you, Kirstie, not ever any more, for you belong to me now and for all eternity' (Mitchison, 1947: 162). There is, as Cixous observes, 'no place for the hysteric; she cannot be placed or take place' (Cixous and Clement, 1991: 129) and Kirstie as hysteric is recuperated by the discourses of religious conformity that her longing for the devil had enabled her to abandon. Mitchison's novel, then, weaves an unsteady line between historical verisimilitude and imaginative desire: Kirstie's rebellion must be contained within the bounds of a constrained possibility.

Yet this conformity to the historical record does not preclude the possibility of utopia. Cixous continues to observe that hysteria 'is necessarily an element that disturbs arrangements' (Cixous and Clement, 1991: 129), and in the bonding of these two relative outsiders there lies the possibility of disrupting the stability and complacency that surrounds them. This is evident from the very first pages of the novel where Kirstie's happiness alone is enough to cause anxiety among her brothers. Her laughter disrupts Captain Robert's expectations of female propriety, and as he tries both physically and verbally to restrain her, she easily eludes his grasp with another laugh and a 'dancing step' (Mitchison, 1947: 21–2). The marriage of William and Kirstie, then, departs from essentialist notions of matriarchal superiority, moving instead to promote the constructive interplay of cultural difference. The acknowledgement of the Outsider becomes a metaphor for the possibility of change.

The border crossing symbolised by Kirstie and William's disruption of the Highland/Lowland divide is repeated and renegotiated in a variety of forms throughout the novel. Maggie Humm has observed that '[p]assing across the borders of languages is a way of making the arbitrariness of national cultures very visible' (1991: 22), and Mitchison's wartime border crossing aims to do just that. The book is intended to be provocative, disrupting our complacent patterns of reading with the unfamiliarity of its language, and demanding that we think again about the 'rational' and the 'inevitable'. In the notes to *The Bull Calves*, Mitchison suggests that some readers might have found the rhythm of the text to be 'slightly unfamiliar, perhaps slightly irritating' (1947: 407), and goes on to explain that the language used is a border hybrid, combining Gaelic grammatical structures with familiar English phrases and the vocabulary of Lowland Scots. Mitchison claims a political purpose for her choice (1947: 411), but the impact of her 'irritating' rhythms goes far beyond the specific debates around 'proper' speech. The notion of an official language, the language of the Law, is displaced and destabilised by this novel. As readers we are forced into a change of focus; an otherwise readerly narrative is transformed into a writerly text that demands we pay attention, not only to the structures of its language, but also to the border-crossing debates that this language engenders.

Historically and philosophically the scope of the novel is considerable, and complex enough to merit 130 pages of immensely detailed notes; while the main narrative itself is interspersed with anecdotes, stories within stories, that form parables assisting in the presentation of Mitchison's central concerns. Mini-utopias, projections of an ideal future world, are juxtaposed against mini-dystopias characteristic of the past (1947: 92, 98). In the midst of providing her niece Catherine with the narrative of her own life, Kirstie breaks off to tell the story of Isobel of Ardsheal. Isobel's husband was on the losing side at Culloden and after the burning of her home by the English, the pregnant Isobel was forced to run into hiding, giving birth to her baby in a hut before being helped by Kirstie, who observes that 'wars will take no count of the reasonable things of life, such as the getting and bearing of bairns' (1947: 57). Catherine is shocked by her aunt's disregard for the letter of the law, but Kirstie's response makes it plain that there is a higher moral law, associated in this instance with the bodily law of reproduction, whose dictates are more pressing than the demands of a vengeful penal code. Mitchison is keen to emphasise the dangers of over-literal interpretations, and this fear is most comprehensively explored in relation to the ur-text of patriarchal domination, the Bible.

These anxieties are first explored in *The Blood of the Martyrs* where Mitchison offers a reinterpretation of the troublesome epistles of Paul, based not on a rereading of his words, but on an imaginative rewriting of the context in which they were written. Lalage, one of the Christian women, warns Paul:

> 'Take care, Paul . . . or you'll write once too often. I'll tell you how it'll be. You write a letter for some particular Church that's got it's own difficulties, but that letter's going to get kept just because it was you that wrote it, and some day someone's bound to find it and say you've left directions for how all Churches are to be, always, everywhere!'
>
> 'Nonsense!' said Paul, 'people aren't such fools as that.' (Mitchison, 1939b/1988: 285)

This idea is revisited in *The Bull Calves* (1947: 120) as part of Mitchison's concern to illustrate the arbitrariness of what becomes law, and the novel constantly returns to an emphasis upon the instability of 'justice'. This is not something fixed and eternal, but a state of flux that demands constant reassessment and moral choices. Her awareness of this uncertainty extends to a concern with the instability of language itself.

In his usefully detailed article on *The Bull Calves*, Douglas Gifford draws attention to the number of lies told by Black William in the course of the narrative and distinguishes these 'white' lies from the power-motivated lies of Kyllachy (Gifford, 1990). The fate of these two characters articulates Mitchison's concern with the deceptiveness of language. She stresses the necessity of looking beneath words, beyond the familiar unthinking usage to an awareness of language's essential inadequacy and concludes that it is not the words that matter but the intent behind. Mitchison remains confident that intent can exist outside the structures of language. She recognises the relative nature and problematic uncertainty of signifying systems, but does not develop her ideas beyond the notion of language as a descriptive medium: something that can be manipulated to obscure an essential 'truth'. Yet, in this conflict between the spiritual and the verbal, between William's good intentions and Kyllachy's command of language, it is the spirit – something Mitchison suggests can never be adequately articulated – which is optimistically seen to triumph. When Forbes must judge between the claims of the two, both of whom have been distinctly economical with the truth, he is criticised for his leniency by the puritanical young Captain John. Forbes's response is a categorical statement of Mitchison's philosophy: 'Captain Haldane, I am looking beyond the action at the motive behind it' (Mitchison, 1947: 386).

Mitchison, then, sees language as a mask which disguises the true nature of acts and emotions, and a prime example of this deceit is the word 'principle'. For Mitchison, as it did for Dorothy L. Sayers, 'principle' has become a dirty word,[4] which can be directly juxtaposed against the moral world of love (a sphere that transcends the rational rules of principle). William's description of the Pretender establishes this contrast in the opening chapters of the novel: 'If only King James had been a different man, with fewer principles and a better heart, he might have carried all before him' (Mitchison, 1947: 73). The idea that principles kill is constantly reiterated throughout *The Bull Calves*. It is Captain John's fanatical belief in principles that gives Kyllachy his opportunity to destroy William and Kirstie: they had acted in an unorthodox manner, exceeding the boundaries of an arbitrary law, and principles leave no room for such unorthodoxy.

Mitchison is keen to illustrate the instability of a social order constructed on the unreliable foundations of a constantly shifting language. In her notes to *The Bull Calves* she concludes that 'sometimes we forget that this moral structure of society is temporal in history, above all in economic history, and held together by words' (1947: 457). There are no boundaries to interpretative possibility:

> for indeed the Old Testament is gey and full of texts about the down-setting of enemies . . . and it wasna till I was far, far older, Catherine, that I ever jaloused that the same set of texts would do for the other side, gin ourselves were the enemies! (Mitchison, 1947: 65; ellipsis mine)

Ultimately, however, Mitchison's concern with language is secondary. Although verging on an acknowledgement of society's linguistic constitution, she chooses to reject the philosophical for the pragmatic, needing to believe that there is some graspable socio-political reality that transcends linguistic uncertainty. This action creates a recurrent tension in her work which manifests itself as a conflict between the supernatural and the rational – a recognition of the semiotic, combined with a sense of obligation to the symbolic. The 'hurting core' of her feminism notwithstanding, on a day-to-day basis Mitchison believed it was her duty to participate in the masculine political world. Feminism represented a refuge; socialism, a 'realistic' strategy for political change. Although she conceived of utopias, she believed in compromise. Change could be accomplished piecemeal if necessary. Mitchison had little choice but to make such a pragmatic decision. Jill Benton describes the intellectual climate:

> Literary women, at least those who wrote for *Time and Tide* throughout the mid-1930s – women such as Lady Rhondda and Naomi – continued to speak out against patriarchal values. But a flow against thinking women was becoming floodwater; feminist issues became associated in the public mind with communism, a dangerous association in the polarised political situation in England during the 1930s, especially since official socialism in the Labour Party and official communism had both disavowed interest in women's issues. No conventional political organisation backed feminism.
>
> Nevertheless, Naomi studiously practised her socialism, still believing that some version of it was women's best political hope. (Benton, 1990: 83–4)

Benton's image is apposite, depicting socialism as a difficult social form that must be learnt – a marked contrast to the 'hurting core' of Mitchison's integral and 'natural' feminism. None the less, within the climate of war it would seem that for feminism to retain any hope of articulation, its only option was to take refuge in the strategies of fiction.

Within *The Bull Calves*, Mitchison's desire to engage with the discourses of religion is introduced through the story of Kirstie's first marriage, in a phase of self-sacrificial depression, to a hell-fire minister. This marriage represents the apotheosis of patriarchal domination. Kirstie is driven from her body, her barren state symbolising a physical negation that coincides with Andrew's remorseless attack on her voice. As the minister's wife she is distanced from the community by her perceived relation to authority (1947: 87), and increasingly her presence becomes superfluous. The gradual erasure of her signification culminates in her brother Mungo's refusal to hear her words after listening to Andrew's accusations of betrayal (1947: 130), and in Andrew's own fantasy of her biological redundancy. Frustrated by Kirstie's inability to bear him sons, 'he began to have a notion towards raising himself up a spiritual son . . . a son not born of woman' (1947: 126). The body of the Church becomes the missing link in the archetypal androcentric grouping of father, son and God.

Andrew Shaw's religion is an exclusive and vicious one, founded on a debased interpretation of righteousness. His assaults on Kirstie are verbal ones, but none the less destructive for that, and his conception of religion as a holy war against the forces of sin, situates him clearly in what Mitchison would term an unchristian position. For all its proclaimed rationality, his religion collaborates with the forces of unreason and war. Although separated by millennia, the philosophical debates of both *The Blood of the Martyrs* and

The Bull Calves suggest that Mitchison is attempting to rewrite, or recover, nothing less than Christianity itself. Mitchison's fantasy is ambitious. Through changing the narrative of society's master text she hopes to lay a foundation that will facilitate real social change. Society is based on Christianity, but traditional Christianity is a patriarchal religion used to oppress women. In an archaeological spirit Mitchison strives to remove the surface of accumulated misogynist debris that has obscured the original narrative, and to indicate the possibility of selecting a new story and of reinscribing religion. Mitchison's revised narrative is set out in her essay *The Kingdom of Heaven*, a text that combines her ethical interest in religion with her political and social concerns. The essay formulates no consistent theoretical structure, but it attempts to convey an idea of community that is central to Mitchison's *Weltanschauung*. Mitchison desperately wanted to believe in a future, but in the insecurity of war, and without a strong sense of place or belonging, the future seemed a distant, intangible dream. By using her family – her own history – as the foundation of *The Bull Calves*, Mitchison was able to write herself into a Scotland from which she largely felt excluded. Once there she could attempt to create, textually, a fiction of rebuilding, of growth – a vision of what might be possible if only we can attain community, or the Kingdom of Heaven.

Mitchison's dream of community was one she lived both physically and spiritually. In coming to Carradale and engaging with the politics of village life she was attempting to put into practice her own vision of a reorganised political and social structure. Increasingly she had come to doubt the value of large political units, fearing their proximity to totalitarianism, and espoused a return to a loose federation of small self-governing communities that typified her idea of true democracy. Many of her short stories are based on examples of such communities and explore the tensions within them (Mitchison, 1986b), while her doubts about large political units are also evident in her ambiguous response to the Soviet experiment. These concerns are articulated in her 1935 novel *We have been Warned*. Although the protagonist Dione is impressed by what she sees in communist Russia, she remains worried by the persistence of 'that public-school spirit which all sensible women are up against' (1935: 295). However Mitchison's community is more than just a method of social organisation. Primarily it is a state of mind, and this idea is symbolised by the concept of the Kingdom of Heaven. Thus Mitchison's idea of community and her rewriting of Christianity combine to create a 'rational religion', the founding principle of which is the concept of 'love':

> the Kingdom of Heaven is not either a reward for good conduct or a consolation for the poor. It is not in the scales at all. It is not a thing but a relationship. (Mitchison, 1939a/1988: 69)

The Kingdom has to be attained by a re-birth or catharsis, by a change
of focus . . .

At present there is a considerable split between those who interpret
this re-birth in terms of community or at-one-ment with other men and
women, expressed in general in action together, and those who interpret
it in terms of community with Jesus or with God and only incidentally
with other people. (1939a/1988: 75; ellipsis mine)

The notion of the Kingdom and its unselfish 'love' are anticipated and
imagined as a principle of government in *We have been Warned*:

Good will, that curious product of consciousness, of leisure and energy
to spare and share. That thing we put out against the forces of interest.
That extra thing. Religions and nations and political parties have taken
it and used it as coinage, have said you must only give it in exchange
for value. (Mitchison, 1935: 482)

The point, as far as both Mitchison's Kingdom and her earlier concept of
good will are concerned, is that they stand outside the corrupt bargaining
ethos of capitalist society. They cannot be bought, they can only be given.
As such they form a potentially radical excess, transgressing the boundaries of
exchange. Hélène Cixous has distinguished between a masculine concept of
the 'gift-that-takes', and the 'openhanded' giving of woman (Cixous, 1980:
259; 1994: 44). The concept of the Kingdom of Heaven can be related to this
distinction in its transcendence of the 'terrible mechanisms of gift and debt,
of exchange and gratitude' (Cixous, 1991: 162–3). This 'feminine' form of
giving thus assumes a subversive nature similar to the subversive excess of the
female body. It cannot be regulated, and therefore constitutes a threat to the
carefully preserved boundaries of the symbolic.

Cixous's distinction between the gift and the proper (*propre*) casts an
interesting light on *The Bull Calves*. Betsy Wing translates the proper as
'Selfsame: ownself' (Cixous and Clement, 1986: 167), and observes that
these terms carry overtones of property and appropriation. The realm of the
proper is the realm of the masculine subject, from which women as other are
effectively debarred. Yet, the very instability of female subjectivity, the lack of
an ownself in which to garner possessions or power, gives woman a flexibility
that makes her giving an ongoing journey rather than an act of recuperation.
This is the realm of the gift:

Unlike man, who holds so dearly to his title and his titles, his pouches
of value, his cap, crown, and everything connected with his head,
woman couldn't care less about the fear of decapitation (or castration),
adventuring, without the masculine temerity, into anonymity, which

she can merge with, without annihilating herself: because she's a giver. (Cixous, 1980: 259)

This distinction is seen by Toril Moi as evidence of Cixous's 'slippage away from Derridean anti-essentialism' (Moi, 1985: 110), but within the context of Mitchison's novel, with its emphasis on boundary crossing and the deconstruction of binary oppositions, it is difficult to find a specifically biologistic distinction between the two realms. William provides perhaps the best example. Returning from America, already symbolically decapitated by the loss of his lands, his gift of love to Kirstie is an open-handed one, stemming not from the economy of capitalism, but from the economy of desire.

There is a further dimension to Mitchison's reinscription of religion. Her engagement with biblical doctrine is also a part of her revisioning of the past, through which she hopes to challenge the shape of the future. Religion has been corrupted by the 'Pauline system of rewards and punishments' (Mitchison, 1939a/1988: 135) into a potentially evil superstition, devoid of spiritual generosity, and this has made possible the development of the 'exclusively masculine' (1939a/1988: 143) and totally irrational Nazi world: 'In a Totalitarian State superstition is not diffused, but is condensed into an official body of unreason' (Mitchison, 1939a/1988: 144).

In 1939 'unreason' was Mitchison's major fear, and seeing its pernicious influence on the Church and its triumph in Germany, she clung desperately to a belief in rationality as the only hope for the future. It is important to note the difference between 'unreason' and the supernatural. Mitchison's faith in rationalism is based on her belief that patriarchy is *not* rational – an assumption that is evident throughout her work, as the story of Isobel of Ardsheal reveals. In this faith in the possibility of a reformed rationality she was distinctly more optimistic than her contemporary Virginia Woolf. Woolf saw no significant difference between the totalitarian state of Nazi Germany and the patriarchal state of England, both being totalitarian in their oppression of significant sections of the population, and irrational in their ludicrous ceremonials and beliefs. For Woolf, all patriarchal societies were Fascist societies. Perhaps Mitchison's continued faith in the possibility of a just society was the vision which enabled her to survive the war which destroyed Virginia Woolf. Such faith, however, demanded sacrifices, and this conscious choice would seem to have entailed as its price the repression of aspects of her feminism. This is supported by the evident personal cost of her survival. The strain of attempting to be both farmer and writer; the machinations of 'rational', patriarchal politics and the continued tensions within the village community left her shattered and exhausted at end of the war:

> Even if I want to join in a conversation I feel impelled to distract myself,
> not to give full concentration, to read a book at the same time. I *can't*
> now think in a pointed way about *anything*. I can rather more easily
> concentrate when writing. But it is rare to have an hour undistracted.
> Because of this I know I can never be first class at anything. (12 August
> 1945; Mitchison, 1986a: 337)

Yet in their attitudes to war, the difference between Mitchison and Woolf
is only one of degree; and it is in the two writers' approach to history that
their shared feminist concerns can be identified.

The historical novel is in some respects the ideal form for the feminist
writer. Woolf's *The Years* is an outstanding example of a novel which
questions the assumptions of patriarchal history and consciously changes the
focus of the historical gaze. In his work on the historical novel, Georg Lukács
continually emphasises the necessity of situating the 'great events' of history
within the context of their everyday reality (1962: 33). Both Mitchison and
Woolf display a Lukácsian tendency to use changes in popular life as symbols
of a wider historical transformation, but the primary focus of their historical
concern moves beyond the scope of Lukács's enquiry. Their novels ask: what
are the 'great historical events', and what have they to do with women? For
Mitchison, Woolf and Bowen there exists a troubling discontinuity between
women and *his*tory that is not easily overcome.

Perhaps, then, the great advantage of the historical novel for the feminist
writer is simply that it is a *novel* — it is not history. It owes only the scantest
of allegiance to the 'facts' and it has the potential to resist or question the
'truths' of the symbolic order, its only technical duty being the attempted
re-creation of the characteristics of a particular age. The historical novel offers
the opportunity to revise, even to rewrite, the past; to imagine and include
what has been excluded by the chroniclers of patriarchal history. It can change
the focus — question the assumptions, values and priorities of both the age it
depicts and that from which it is written — and engage with the implications
of its interrogations. This is the philosophy behind *The Bull Calves*, a novel
that avoids the critical, dynamic incidents of war and rebellion, concerning
itself instead with the aftermath of conflict. However, this refocusing of
the historical gaze was also to have been the explicit project of Mitchison's
never-completed book on feminism. The draft of its opening chapter begins
with a lucid analysis of the limitations of an exclusively masculine view:

> If one is in this curious position of being a woman, one cannot
> unquestioningly accept the ordinary historical point of view about the
> values of civilisation. Why not? Because up to the last few years all historians
> have been men. In some branches of knowledge it does not appear to make

any difference whether men or women practise the search for truth . . . But the nearer we get to the human side of truth and especially to art . . . the more we find that the sex of the seeker or researcher or writer makes a great difference to the result. (quoted in Benton, 1990: 74; ellipses mine)

Yet despite the centrality of its concerns to Mitchison's intellectual and artistic development, this work remained unfinished. It is interesting to note Jill Benton's comment on this failure:

The project of analysing all culture from a woman's point of view seemed to overwhelm Naomi and in some of its implications to frighten her . . . The time was not ripe; as the complicated politics of the 1930s took hold, the time was blighting to the spirit of feminism. (Benton, 1990: 74)

Mitchison, like Woolf, found the novel an infinitely more suitable arena for the development of feminist thought than the compromised masculine form of socio-scientific analysis. Although she would return to essay form for the development of ideas less close to her heart, it would seem that an undisguised discourse on feminism represented too dangerous a self-exposure for Mitchison to continue. The two writers also shared a domestic approach to history. Mitchison's work is concerned less with the highlights of history than with the impact of these arbitrary actions on the 'ordinary' people. In a comment that is remarkably similar to the reinscription of hierarchies in *Between the Acts*, her diary observes:

I am beginning to wonder whether the tangled affairs of the Scottish nobles in the middle ages and after, aren't perhaps equally explicable in terms of Carradale – in terms of Hugh and Bella and the kitchen balance of power. (Mitchison, 1986a: 76)

Mitchison's concern was with the smaller family units and communities from which society must attempt to regenerate itself in the aftermath of war. Yet the possibility of regeneration is perpetually under threat from what could be termed the dark side of the past.

The sense of the past as a perpetually threatening entity is embodied by Kyllachy, whose blood relation to the Haldanes, and clan relation to William, also makes him an all-purpose shadow-self. A devil's advocate figure, he appears from nowhere on what appears to be a mission to disrupt the comfortable complacency of his Haldane cousins. He is a constant reminder that the past never dies, and that it has the potential to become a dangerous weapon. His divisive influence, which exacerbates the tensions beneath the surface of the family, illustrates the difference between using the past to think of the future and using the past as an instrument of revenge. In the defeat of Kyllachy's schemes *The Bull Calves* suggests that the ghosts of the past can be laid to rest through an aspect of the gift, namely, forgiveness. This conclusion is supported by the patterns of confession, assimilation and reconciliation that recur throughout the novel.

Many characters undergo this process of absolution, but the most important revelations pass, in a neatly cyclical fashion, between Kirstie and William and their closest friend within the Haldane family, the unconventional sceptical lawyer, Patrick. Each must undertake both to speak and to listen, and the series of interactions portrayed reveals Mitchison's underlying interest in psychoanalytic theories. Kirstie confesses to William who confesses to Patrick who confesses to Kirstie. Each must listen without the expectation of being listened to in return. It is not the subject of the confession that matters (indeed William has heard Kirstie's tale of witchcraft before), but the act of confessing itself. The process of working out old griefs and guilts is essential to a healthy relationship. Left inside, Kirstie's worries would fester and destroy her, and although he finds it difficult to listen, William realises that 'she must speak or she would turn it over and over in her mind until it became solid and dangerous, a malignant growth' (Mitchison, 1947: 163). When Kirstie finishes speaking, and falls into a healing sleep, he longs to feel the same release. But to demand this return would be to transform his gift into the gift-that-takes. None the less, the act of listening is seen to be a beneficial one. In Catherine's case, assimilating the knowledge of Kirstie's 'witchcraft' brings about positive personal growth:

> So there was the truth of it, thought Catherine Duncan, and I am not caring. It is neither here nor there between my auntie and myself. And who would have thought of me feeling this way, it is most surprising and yet it is most natural and it has given me a new insight altogether into the nature of good and evil. (Mitchison, 1947: 256)

Catherine learns much from Kirstie in the course of the novel. She learns to find the courage of her convictions and in so doing becomes a symbol of the continuity between past and present, between Kirstie Haldane and Naomi Mitchison. This line of female descent, reminiscent of Woolf's ideas in '[The journal of Mistress Joan Martyn]' and *Between the Acts*, possesses a rich inheritance of tolerance and understanding which far exceeds that of its sterile male counterpart. Within the text, Kirstie's gift to Catherine, a gift of speech, narrative and knowledge, is paralleled by the childless Captain Robert's gift of land to James. James and Catherine will marry, and Mitchison makes it plain that his inheritance is worthless without the complement of hers.

Mitchison has a strong belief in the potential of a constructive partnership between a man and a woman, but in her perception it is women who bear the responsibilities – largely due to the incapacity of men. Kirstie suggests this in her vision of an ideal world:

'If a' the governing of the world were left to the women of it, they would never do the daft-like things the men do, throwing away their own lives, aye and others'. The world could surely be managed the way a household is, cannily. Aye, a good household under a good and careful woman. And the men and the bairns would be free to dream and to have their adventures.' (Mitchison, 1947: 38)[5]

This matriarchal conception echoes the dreams of other women writers of the period. There was a sense among female intellectuals that men, while still holding the reins of authority, had effectively lost control of their power. However, with the effective repression of feminism, women were obliged to support in practice what they disavowed in theory. The Christian feminist Wrenne Jarman expressed her very similar ideas in a long poem to a friend grieving over the loss of her son. *Letter to Claudia* condemns the false ideal of 'progress' and suggests that all the factions of the male political order, whether they profess communism or Fascism, are essentially grounded in the same corrupt structure of power. The mistake, she concludes has been 'female indolence':

> Our easy confluence to the natural bent,
> > We have laid safety at the shrine of sense
> > > Entrusting government to the dominant male,
> > > Who, albeit charming, is incapable.
> > > > . . .
> > > Of what use glory, since it cannot heal?
> > > Men are but dreamers: only we are real.

Jarman's conclusion is that after all these years of patriarchy, 'The millennia could spare / One fleeting age to compensate our pains' (Bax and Stewart, 1949: 133–6) – a matriarchy could hardly do any worse!

Matriarchal ideas seem to have tempted Mitchison, and her writing repeatedly returns to images of matrilinearity, but there is no doubt that they remained a fantasy – a dream even within the realm of her fictions. Her ideas of a parallel or 'superior' female inheritance can be interpreted as part of a more general, anti-essentialist privileging of the 'feminine' over the 'masculine' that is articulated in *The Bull Calves* through the juxtaposition of agriculture and war. The novel sets an ideal cyclical time of natural seasonal growth and regeneration against man's artificial linear time. Linear time strives constantly for some form of progress, defined in terms of unnatural (*man*made) boundaries and borders, and its end product is war. It represents a scheme of constant acquisition instead of the organic process of give and take according to the rhythm of the land.

This pattern dominates *The Bull Calves*. Those associated with the actual working of the land enjoy an increased emotional awareness, which, combined with the imperative of survival, frees them from the narrow patterns of thought that lead to conflict. Thus William and Kirstie's Highland poverty forces them to abandon rigid hierarchies of class, and drives them closer to this seasonal time:

> Another thing came into Catherine Duncan's mind now and she asked, 'Do you yourself go out into the fields, Aunt Kirstie? And in winter? I am sure I should never be able to bear it for a day! There can be nothing more tedious than sowing turnips!'
>
> 'It is away worse, thinning them!' said Kirstie, laughing, 'but indeed I am scarcely ever working in the fields, Catherine, except maybe at har'st. It is only that I go there with my William, and times two heads can be better than one . . . We would go to the turnip field, wherever it would be most days; this is the first year we have dared to leave Borlum for a wee while in the growing season.' (Mitchison, 1947: 91–2; ellipsis mine)

The political division of the Highlands and the Lowlands is used to symbolise the divergence of agrarian and capitalist cultures. This is Kirstie speaking again:

> you will never get a right Highlander to live in an orderly way in a town and take his wages year by year and do as he is bid by a master. The Highlanders will do best when they are sharing, the way the fishermen mostly do, and it was the same with their farming, even; they do best with everything held in common, the old way. Indeed they are altogether against progress, as we see it in the Lowlands. (Mitchison, 1947: 55)

The Lowlanders of the novel are seen to be distanced from the land, either through wealth or occupation. For Mungo Haldane of Gleneagles, land is an investment; while for his brother, Captain Robert, a roving military existence has resulted in his conception of land not as a living thing with which we interact to survive, but as something sterile that is simply passed from generation to generation. The Lowland conception of the land sees it as currency or commodity, a short-sighted policy that pays no heed to the necessity of giving back to the land.

Such a framework is very much in sympathy with Julia Kristeva's project in the first part of 'About Chinese women', where she examines the establishment of patriarchal monotheism and its implications for the 'feminine':

> Let us note that by establishing itself as the principle of a symbolic, paternal community in the grip of the superego, beyond all ethnic considerations, beliefs or social loyalties, monotheism represses, along with paganism, the greater part of agrarian civilizations and their ideologies, women and mothers. (Kristeva, 1974: 141)

The juxtaposition of maternal and linear time is more fully the subject of Kristeva's essay 'Women's time'. Moving beyond the opposition of incompatible positions, she hopes for a future based on a third stage of feminist development. From the failure of equality feminism and the dangers of a separatist feminism's collapse into religion, Kristeva plots the emergence of a feminism that:

> will be able to break free of its belief in Woman, Her power, Her writing, so as to channel this demand for difference into each and every element of the female whole, and, finally, to bring out the singularity of each woman, and beyond this, her multiplicities, her plural languages, beyond the horizon, beyond sight, beyond faith itself? (Kristeva, 1979: 208)

It would be satisfying to think that this might form the territory of Mitchison's 'brave new world', but I do not believe such a conclusion to be possible. *The Bull Calves* suggests instead that Mitchison, like Cixous, still requires the concept of woman as a creative force. This concrete essence of woman as writer or mother provides a reassuring metaphysics of presence to set against war's threat of annihilation. Both *The Bull Calves* itself and the process of its production demand a recognition of the perceived opposition between motherhood and war that tended to dominate the period – although it should also be noted that images of motherhood are almost as likely to be appropriated by war, as set against it. In her analysis of First World War propaganda, Sandra Gilbert has commented on the curious ambiguity of poster images such as 'The Greatest Mother in the World' (a giant Red Cross nurse cradling a child-sized wounded man). This is perhaps a typical projection of masculine fears regarding the wartime empowerment of women. However, the casting of the mother in a quasi-religious role ensures that she does not exceed the customary parameters of female representation. As the virginal mother of God, she has only a temporary custodianship over the man born to be king. Her power is finite – it is the child she cradles who will ultimately inherit (Gilbert, 1987: 211–12).

Although the role of women had changed by the Second World War, the thinly disguised doctrine of separate spheres was still very strongly in evidence. Susan Gubar's delineation of a hierarchical distinction between the laws of peace and the laws of war indicates the symbolic order's need to keep a firm grip on the potential ascendency of women in a war situation (Gubar, 1987: 246). Within this framework, the figure of the mother becomes a powerless symbol of a creativity designed both to represent the ultimate end of the war, and to fuel its remorseless procession. To a certain extent *The Bull Calves* replicates this pattern. The many mothers it depicts remain marginal to the ordering of events, unable to directly influence the process of change. Yet there is none the less a comfort in the continuity they represent, which can also be seen as resilience. The mothers in this text are symbols of survival, passing wisdom and understanding to a new generation. In contrast, Elizabeth Bowen's engagement with the motif of the mother presents a more cynical picture. In the world of *The Heat of the Day*, Louie Louis is presented as a force of unthinking, almost animal, reproduction – an unlikely cornerstone on which to build a brave new world.

Mitchison's own analysis of her creative process – baby and book as a bulwark against war – is constantly reinforced by the content of the novel. This ongoing dialectic of creativity versus destruction also has implications for Mitchison's religious concerns. As an historical novel, the puritan content is essential, representing an integral part of the social fabric of the time. But Kirstie and William's agrarian lifestyle dilutes the intensely symbolic nature of their puritan consciousness, and opens them to a more organic mother-orientated religion, intimately connected with natural cycles of fertility. Although loosely disguised as Episcopalian, their religion is essentially that of Mitchison's Kingdom of Heaven. In contrast, Kirstie's marriage to the preacher, Andrew, is 'unnatural' in its oppression of Kirstie. His treatment of her represents patriarchy's unnatural repression of the fertile, maternal woman world that Mitchison sets in opposition to the symbolic order. Consequently the two male children that Kirstie bears to Andrew die at an early age, after which Kirstie becomes infertile. In contrast, the child she bears to William is a girl, and at the time of the novel, alive, well and safely at home in the Highlands. The health of this child symbolises a regeneration, the same regeneration that Mitchison desires in a postwar world, and, appropriately, it continues the line of William and Kirstie through a female inheritance. Kirstie's fertility is rekindled by a return to the organic pulsions of an agrarian, cyclical time, the brave new world that is also an old world, a 'woman's time' that can only be conceived of outside the time of war.

But, this is not without its problems. Although Kirstie's fertility may have been rekindled, she, and women in general, remain marginal and endangered by their position as a threat to the symbolic order. In the isolation of their home at Borlum, Kirstie and William can live out their agrarian utopia, but in the social sphere of the Lowlands, the seat of the symbolic order, they are powerless. They cannot ignore the law of the symbolic, because it is the arbiter of war and peace. It holds sway over the arbitrary destructiveness of war, a factor from which not even outsiders can escape. *The Bull Calves* articulates this powerlessness through Kyllachy's attempts to destroy Kirstie with the accusation of witchcraft, and concludes optimistically enough with the defeat of Kyllachy. Yet it is not William and Kirstie who defeat Kyllachy, it is the symbolic order itself. Their position as outsiders does not empower them, and Kyllachy's downfall is the product of internal wrangling on the terms of the patriarchy. His defeat comes not through the establishment of a new order, but through collusion with the old.

The generational conflict within *The Bull Calves* is indicative of a patriarchal system in transition. Forbes of Culloden, who must adjudicate the quarrel, symbolises an old and dying order. In the aftermath of war, a younger generation, epitomised by the inflexible Captain John, is preparing to impose a newly revitalised patriarchy. It is a progression from an outmoded and sentimental paternalism to a proto-capitalist puritan business ethic, and in his desire to cultivate the younger generation (Mitchison, 1947: 387), Kyllachy is under no illusions as to where the power of the future lies. However, Kyllachy's mistake is in an overeager anticipation of this new order, and in an underestimation of the unwritten laws which accompany the official codes of patriarchal government. Although his earlier actions had conformed strictly to the laws of the land, in betraying William's father, Kyllachy had transgressed the code of propriety. He had not behaved as a gentleman – a dying species maybe, but in *The Bull Calves*, not yet extinct. None the less, Culloden's lenient judgement is in keeping with the novel's emphasis on the healing of old wounds. This instance of a principle compromised enables the continuance of regeneration rather than a return to division and strife.

The impasse of Kirstie and William's powerlessness, however, foregrounds the dilemma that also confronts Woolf's attempt to theorise the Outsider in *Three Guineas*. Her proposed solution to the problem of how to prevent war is effectively a boycott of the patriarchal order and all associated with it: but in a society that depends upon the operation of hierarchical binary oppositions, such a solution is inevitably confronted by the threat of disempowerment. Active power lies only in the realm of the symbolic. To be outside is to risk powerlessness, passivity and silence. Woolf is faced with the problem that also concerns Kristeva – from where can women speak? Preventing war, changing society, demands the discovery of a site from which to articulate women's experience; a place that needs must be neither the corrupt realm of the patriarchal symbolic, not the choric site of madness and death.

Mitchison too engages with this dilemma. Her texts work on a multiplicity of levels. Beneath a surface philosophy comprising an almost desperate belief in reason, there lies a contradictory fascination with the very magic and superstition she ostensibly rejects. This tension is intimately connected with Kristeva's model of the symbolic and the semiotic: Mitchison's texts articulate her struggle to identify a site from which to speak, but her recognition of the impossibility of this task co-exists with her ongoing utopian desires. In contrast to Kristeva, Cixous believes that women *can* negotiate the border between patriarchal complicity and choric exclusion. 'Just because there's a risk of identification doesn't mean that we'll succumb' she proclaims, and demands a female invasion of patriarchal discourse that would cause it to explode from within (Cixous, 1980: 257). The difference is perhaps only one of degree; Kristeva's uncontrollable semiotic irruptions become Cixous's mode of assault on the patriarchal edifice. Mitchison's texts, meanwhile, continue their fluctuation between the affirmation of an alternative rationality and the celebration of a spiritual transformation that exceeds the boundaries of definition. This textual instability is particularly evident in *The Blood of the Martyrs*. On the one hand Mitchison rejects Paul's concept of immortality through Gallio the Stoic:

> The curious thing is, Paul, that a good many of your people are certainly not thinking of any other and separate world. They are thinking of your Kingdom, and all that it implies, in this world. Which is a sufficiently subversive idea, in all conscience, but at least a rational one. (1939b/1988: 347)

At this point, immediate practical, political and social change is valued above the promise of spiritual development. However, sixty pages later her focus shifts to conceive of an internal moment of spiritual change, a transfiguration through love, which involves an acknowledgement and acceptance of the irrationality of that love. At the end of the novel, the cynical Felicio undergoes this transformation:

> Common life and necessary actions might also be beautiful, given love. The possibility of love. He hadn't wanted love before; he had been content to be alone and intelligent and ironic, taking lightly what pleasures were to be had. Then he had loved Beric and that had been taken from him. And then? Was this feeling in his breast and head now love of mankind, or was it rather the urgent necessity for something obviously reasonable which was pressing on him? – which was pressing them together, breaking down barriers, making them feel towards one another in an unreasonable and irrational way. You might call it love. (1939b/1988: 407)

The formulation of 'love' as something which elevates and validates the common and necessary could perhaps be read as a determining force – a binding tie of duty that legitimises patriotic discourse. Love of country or home has been extensively manipulated over the course of the twentieth century and cannot easily be read as a liberating strategy. However, Felicio comes to his ambiguously defined conception of love through the transgression of homosexual desire, a factor that detaches him from, rather than binds him to, the codes of the symbolic order. His love is also one that expects no return. It is part of the 'feminine' realm of the gift, and it deconstructs the hierarchies of Roman society.

Mitchison's idea of love refuses to be contained within geographical or legal boundaries. It symbolises instead a sort of joint currency, valid in both the patriarchal symbolic and the realm of the outsider. It shares this cosmopolitan attribute with its opposing quality – fear – which transcends all boundaries, upholding the status quo through a paralysis that dreads the unknown factor of change. Love has the power to defeat fear, and it represents the individual's only ammunition in the battle against chaos and irrationality. This is the dynamic enacted in Kirstie Haldane's struggle against the shadow side of her self, articulated in the text through the juxtaposition of Jungian archetypes. Kirstie embodies the absolute goodness of an archetypal mother figure, but through her bewitchment she reaches the very brink of her shadow-self. She has within her the potential to become the opposing archetype – the destructive goddess or witch – as indeed she believes she has become after the sudden death of her hated husband. William too succumbs to his dark side, which emerges when he is 'bewitched' by the Indian queen, Ohnawiyo, and participates in scenes of sickening violence. It is not the marriage that is his dark secret, but the fact that he succumbed to the fascination of the Indians' brutal rituals. Here Mitchison shares the concerns of her friend Stevie Smith – everyone has a dark side, it is an integral part of the personality, and it is essential that we acknowledge it. The contradictory forces operating on Mitchison's text are very much in evidence here. The 'bewitching' of her central characters, while superficially condemned and rejected, is also seen to be the additional dimension that enables their rejuvenation and restoration. This self-recognition is of fundamental importance, and is strikingly absent from the characters of the complacent Haldanes. Through simple observations, such as Mungo's comfortable reading of a book of 'pleasantly controversial sermons' (1947: 156), Mitchison illustrates the extent to which the Haldanes are divorced from self-knowledge. Their insularity is further illustrated in an image typical of her use of symbolism. As the family gathers to hear the judgement of Duncan Forbes, Kirstie compares William to her brothers:

> It seemed to her that there was a great beauty about him; even the plainness of the plum coloured coat that he had on – and she minded him asking her was it good enough to take to Gleneagles – showed the shape of him through, where the heavy braid and gilt on her brothers' had no meaning at all. (Mitchison, 1947: 384)

In *The Bull Calves*'s juxtaposition of love and fear, Mitchison echoes Stevie Smith's suggestion that the seeds of Fascism lie dormant within every individual. Her solution to this latent threat, however, is a reiteration of

Dorothy L. Sayers's advocation of individual responsibility as the bottom line of defence against mass totalitarian movements. Kirstie, confronted by the originator of her fears, concludes that 'if she did not fear it, she could not be ruled by it' (1947: 404) This self-reliance is not a betrayal of Mitchison's communal ethos, however, as her understanding of community emphasises rather than negates the role of the individual. *The Bull Calves* demands that every individual come to terms with fear, and through this action, change becomes a possibility.

The concept of love, then, exceeds and challenges the boundaries of patriarchal government, and with this challenge comes the threat of a complete marginalisation. Mitchison, however, recognises the dangers inherent in the passivity of exclusion, and uses love to try and overcome the problem of silence and inaction. Love's position, as discovered by Felicio, is on the border between reason and emotion, sanity and madness; and this effectively situates it as an arbiter of the boundary between the semiotic and the symbolic. The provisional articulation of this quasi-spiritual love is proposed by Mitchison as a site from which the excluded, the marginalised, and in particular, women, can speak. The Christians in *The Blood of the Martyrs* act out this search for a site of articulation. Their creed is presented not as a religious heresy, but as a political revolution, and it is their position on the margins that makes it so.

But what sort of revolution is this? The Christians cannot kill. They cannot take direct action, and if they do (as Beric does), this only escalates the scale of the violence, drags in the innocent (Argas, the man he loves), and taints the Christians themselves with the corruption of the law they deny. So what can their passivity and moral superiority achieve? What differentiates Christian inaction from the intellectual and Stoic inaction that the text condemns as morally useless? The answer would seem to be the site of their inaction. Stoics and intellectuals speak from within the establishment. Christians speak from outside the law of the symbolic order, and crucially, they speak a different language, which is the 'language of love'. This language is dangerous and revolutionary, because it incorporates the element of the irrational – epitomised by the action of forgiveness.

Thus the crux of Mitchison's argument brings us back to the nature of rationality. Within her texts the terms rational and irrational are in a constant state of flux which demands that we enter a looking-glass world that inverts our understanding of reality and illusion, reason and unreason. That which is termed rational by patriarchal society – the cult of progress, the necessity of war – must be redefined as irrational. While the irrationality marginalised by the symbolic – forgiveness, love, motherhood – can be reclaimed as rational, and forms the body of 'reason' that underpins Mitchison's utopian vision of a brave new world.

This, then, is Mitchison's fantasy; but how can such a vision be translated into contemporary terms? The answer would seem to be that it cannot. Mitchison represses her vision under a strategic 'rationalism' that is ideologically at odds with her feminist beliefs. The implications of Fascism cannot be directly articulated, and the 'hurting core' of Mitchison's feminism must be relegated to the realm of fiction. The fictional arena thus becomes a sustaining fantasy of absence from the conflagration of war, while yet remaining subordinate to Mitchison's overriding fantasy of belonging to a political world that would exclude her. The two fantasies are irreconcilable: but they comfortably co-exist as enabling strategies that facilitate the process of surviving war. Ultimately, then, Mitchison's brave new world is also a pragmatic old world. She evades the impossibility of an unspeakable present and proposes a site of female articulation within a reinscribed and revitalised past.[6] In so doing she negotiates a compromise – but none the less ensures that her concept of a newly 'reasonable' utopia will survive and perhaps even thrive in the air of an unknowable future.

NOTES

1. Mitchison's understanding of individuation incorporated a common theme of her early fiction – the idea of doubling. Individuation required the acknowledgement and recognition of the shadow side of the self. Once acknowledged it becomes possible to attain separation from the shadow, and this process frees us from its potentially damaging control.

2. Mitchison's biographer, Jill Benton, describing the conflict between feminism and socialism in the early 1930s, offers the following estimation of Mitchison's concerns: 'She sought a middle road between communism and individualism, a route for individuals to act within community' (Benton, 1990: 81). Here is a political articulation of the spiritual dilemma explored by Woolf: the integration, without loss of self, of 'I' and 'We', the individual and the community. See Gillian Beer's analysis in Chapter 5.

3. Mitchison's essentially constructive and optimistic philosophy is emphasised by the comments of her friend and correspondent, the writer Stella Benson: 'You couldn't write in my style fortunately for you because you are not cold-hearted like me. Everything you write must be positive and everything I write is negative' (quoted in Mitchison, 1979/1986: 132).

4. See above, Chapter 3: 'the first thing a principle does – if it really is a principle – is to kill somebody' (Sayers 1935/1990: 317). In Mitchison's 1935 novel *We have been Warned* the dangerous baggage of outmoded or overprincipled attitudes (more usually resembling an albatross) is metaphorically transformed into an elephant. An integral part of the hero Dione's quest is to rid herself of the elephants that oppress her.

5. In response, Catherine enquires about the dubious example of Mary Stuart. Kirstie's answer 'maybe she was half a bairn and half a man, for a Queen can never be a right woman' (1947: 38) emphasises the problem of the isolated woman in the midst of a male power structure. All too easily they become corrupted, a part of the symbolic order.

6. Mitchison wrote only one contemporary novel (*We have been Warned*), and its hostile reception drove her swiftly back to the safe metaphoricity of history. It is perhaps also significant that in a monumental publishing history spanning seventy years, one book of Mitchison's that was never completed was the book on feminism she planned in the early 1930s.

9

From Alienation to Absence:
Avoiding the War in The Heat of the Day

Hearing a clock strike, one morning, with more meaning than usual,
I stopped half way up a grandstand to realise that time held war. The
hour was more than my hour; within it people were fighting.

Elizabeth Bowen, *Seven Winters*

He attached himself to the story as to something nothing to do with
him; and did so with the intensity of a person who must think lest
he should begin to feel

Elizabeth Bowen, 'Ivy gripped the steps'

Elizabeth Bowen's *The Heat of the Day* is more obviously and wholeheartedly
a war novel than *The Bull Calves* (1947) or *Between the Acts* (1941). Although
not published until 1948 its genesis lay in conflict, and on a superficial level at
least, war would seem to be its primary concern. The novel is set in 1942; its
principal characters are engaged in war work, and the dynamic of plot focuses
on the question of treachery. Yet for all its contextual engagement with war,
on every other level *The Heat of the Day* strives to shut the conflict firmly
out of its complex examination of interpersonal relationships. The specific
instance of treachery serves as a catalyst for a far wider examination of the
structures of deceit in everyday life. The novel is a text of many paradoxes.
Beneath its surface control, *The Heat of the Day* presents a set of deeply encoded
anxieties about the value of tradition, the disruptions of war and the paralysis
of gender.

The Heat of the Day is not about war, it is about surviving war. Elizabeth
Bowen was concerned neither with the realism of the chronicler nor with
the fictional creation of utopias – her concern was rather with the perceived

experience of the individual. Her fiction depicts the impact of war in emotional terms and engages with the dominant moods of alienation and dislocation. Above all she contemplated the difficulties not simply of somatic but also of psychic survival. In *The Heat of the Day* she talks of the 'curious animal psychic oneness' (Bowen, 1948/1962: 275) created by the circumstances of war, but none of her characters gives evidence of a consistent participation in such a state. It seems to be a togetherness that happens elsewhere, outside their private isolation.[1] In a sense then, we have come full circle from the inward concerns of Stevie Smith, with her fears of the Fascist within us all, to Elizabeth Bowen's vivid but curiously dispassionate depiction of the void at the heart of human existence. Her war novel is preoccupied with issues of existence and reality, yet focuses most often upon the contradictory presence of a terrifying nothingness. This concern is not confined to *The Heat of the Day*. Absence and nothingness also form dominant motifs within the collection of stories published in 1945 as *The Demon Lover*. The collection features absent fathers, absent lovers and stories whose surface chatter only serves to emphasise the void beneath. This is a world in which silence is 'intense' (Bowen, 1983: 666), darkness is 'solid' (1983: 632) and absence attains the presence of ostentation (1983: 642). *The Heat of the Day*, however, remains Bowen's monument to absence. The perception of lack transcends boundaries of class and gender, assailing almost all the novel's disparate characters. The factory girl Louie, lying on her back and staring at nothing, discovers 'it was oppressive, though, how much of nothing there was' (1948/1962: 247). While Roderick visiting Stella, his mother, fantasises that her sofa is a boat:

> The reality of the fancy was better than the unreality of the room. In a boat you were happy to be suspended in nothing but light, air, water, opposite another face. On a sofa you could be surrounded by what was lacking. (Bowen, 1948/1962: 54–5)

Yet this sense of negation is not entirely shared by the narrative voice. The free indirect discourse of Roderick's mental image is usurped by the cool, detached and critical tone of narrative description, which analyses and shapes the perceptions of the characters. This dilution of the characters' isolation through authoritative commentary restrains the novel from its potential extremes of nihilism and melodrama, and forces it instead into the shape of a parable play. *The Heat of the Day* can be seen as a tragedy in the Brechtian sense – it both demands and repulses our sympathies, while at the same time undercutting them with a dark grotesque comedy.[2]

The analogy with Brechtian drama illustrates how techniques used by Bowen create a moral framework for the novel.[3] In some senses it even returns to the terms of Brecht's more consciously didactic theatre – there is something of the *Lehrstück* in the construction of the plot. At first sight the official dialectic of war is apparent, and it forms a simple polarity: good and evil, us and them; but as in Brecht's dramas we are asked to recognise that it is not so straightforward. Stella Rodney, a divorcee in her early forties, meets Robert Kelway in the 'heady autumn of the first London air raids' (Bowen, 1948/1962: 90). They fall in love, and for two years possess a 'hermetic world' which for Stella is abruptly challenged by the appearance of the enigmatic Harrison, who informs her that Robert is a traitor. Harrison has the power temporarily to save Robert, in return he demands that Stella transfer her affections to him. The novel is also the story of Stella's son Roderick and the old Irish house that is his inheritance; and the story of Louie, a working-class girl who inadvertently encounters and becomes fascinated by Harrison. The three plots are connected through Harrison and it is he who undermines and calls into question the structures of language and meaning on which the novel ostensibly stands. At their first meeting Stella refers to Harrison as an enemy, yet he is there to tell her that her lover Robert is an enemy of the country. By the end of the novel, the two men have become indistinguishable – 'It seemed to her it was Robert who had been the Harrison' (1948/1962: 275). The difference in their causes has been subsumed by the mutual corruption of their practices. The final ironic revelation that Harrison's first name is also Robert only confirms this distressing interchangeability. Individuality, the novel threatens to suggest, becomes meaningless in the moral climate of war. For Stella her suitors represent war's dilemma between the private and the public that patriotism demands we resolve in the community's favour. Alongside the question of Stella's choice, Bowen's text raises the conterminous question of whether it is possible, or even desirable, to withdraw from the world.

Through an examination of *The Heat of the Day* in Brechtian terms, it becomes possible to reconsider the problems of plausibility identified by earlier critics. Hermione Lee recounts Bowen's work for the Ministry of Information, and wonders why, with her considerable knowledge of the world of espionage, Bowen did not write a more convincing narrative? As a spy story, Lee suggests *The Heat of the Day* is 'obviously risible' and describes the novel instead as 'a woman's view of the male world of "Intelligence"' (1981: 175). However, from this criticism, Lee draws the apposite conclusion that Bowen's interest was less in the actuality of treason than in the psychological 'climate' of betrayal (Lee, 1981: 176–8). This idea is taken a stage further by Phyllis Lassner, who describes the novel as a subversion of the traditional spy novel. Lassner suggests a fictional strategy reminiscent of Dorothy L. Sayers's refocusing of the detective novel around the figure of Harriet Vane:

As personal history and political history are woven into mystifying stories, Kelway's betrayal and the roles played by Harrison and Stella become interdependant. The texture of their relationship shatters conventional definitions of loyalty and guilt. It does so by situating female character at the centre of a spy story, reversing our expectations of a conventional genre which usually places female characters on the periphery. (Lassner, 1990a: 129)

Both of these approaches are helpful, but neither of them take account of the moral subtext involved. Lee quotes Rosamund Lehmann's complaint about Bowen's choice of Fascism as Robert's treachery: 'What bothers me a little is that I cannot see why he shouldn't have been a Communist and therefore pro-Russian, pro-Ally, rather than pro-enemy' (Lee, 1981: 178). This qualm was shared it would seem, by many readers; but to desire a more acceptable treachery for Robert is to miss the point. For there to be anything admirable about Robert's political loyalties would be to create a romantic figure whose death would be closer to martyrdom than ignominy. For the moral dilemmas of the otherwise creaky plot to be effective, Robert's choice must not be misguided but evil. Only then can the chasm of deceit which has been the subtext of their love affair destroy the hermetic world and make Stella's choice a real choice of evils.[4] The narrative thus emphasises the impossibility of defining or controlling such powerful, and essentially meaningless, terms as 'love', 'loyalty' and 'betrayal'. When one man's treason is another's loyalty, and when language is revealed to be a fundamentally inadequate medium of communication, the possibility of security and certainty is comprehensively destroyed. The intricate dance of the novel's protagonists exposes the gaps and inconsistencies upon which false structures of unity are built, and in so doing rejects the obligation of conformity to values that are ultimately metaphysical.

The difficulties of Bowen's plot, then, can be reassessed if the novel is rescued from the critical demand of realism. The occupations of Robert and Harrison are more important metaphorically than literally. Bowen may base her novels in contemporary realism, but the poetic intensity of her language ensures that they exceed any such limits. Bowen flirts constantly with the supernatural, a tendency which makes even her famously evocative descriptions of blitzed London border on the surreal:

Most of all the dead, from mortuaries, from under cataracts of rubble, made their anonymous presence – not as today's dead but as yesterday's living – felt through London. Uncounted, they continued to move in shoals through the city day, pervading everything to be seen or heard or felt with their torn-off senses, drawing on this tomorrow they had expected – for death cannot be so sudden as all that. (Bowen, 1948/1962: 91)

There is perhaps the influence of Dickens in her carefully controlled social parodies and her skilful deployment of grotesques. Robert's sister Ernestine is one such caricature, whose first sign of human emotion comes in response to the memory of her dog; 'I often think if Hitler could have looked into that dog's eyes, the story might have been very different' (1948/1962: 124); while the 'unflickering velocity' (1948/1962: 252) of Mrs Kelway's knitting, a ludicrous and appropriate symbol of her ruthless cruelty, is logically connected by Lassner to Madame De Farge (Lassner1990a: 128). Bowen's voyages into the absurd give rise to an environment of doubtful and shifting reality in which characters struggle with a powerful sense of dislocation:

> More loss had not seemed possible after that fall of France. On through the rest of that summer in which she had not rallied from that psychological blow, and forward into this autumn of the attack on London, she had been the onlooker with nothing more to lose – out of feeling as one can be out of breath. She had had the sensation of being on furlough from her own life. (Bowen, 1948/1962: 94)

This sense of dislocation is augmented by a considerable degree of almost postmodern self-consciousness which blends into a constant metaphor of performance. Stella's rented Weymouth Street flat bears no imprint of her personality and offers no recognisable points of reference to her returning son Roderick. His response is the first of the novel's many playful references to its own fictionality: 'This did not look like home; but it looked like something – possibly a story' (1948/1962: 47). This sense of uncertain reality is all-pervasive. Stella, awakening to the realisation of her love for Robert, 'felt herself to be going to a rendezvous inside the pages of a book' and asks with unconscious irony 'was, indeed, Robert himself fictitious?' (1948/1962: 97). Perhaps even more disturbingly, this uncertainty is shared by Robert, who tells Stella that '[e]ach time I come back into it [his old bedroom] I'm hit in the face by the feeling that I don't exist – that I not only am not but never have been' (1948/1962: 117). Yet the motif of insubstantiality is at its strongest in the presence of the spy Harrison, a character so shady as to be intangible. In some respects more of an essence than an entity, he not only distorts but contaminates his environment. At one point Stella observes that exposure to Harrison has turned her into a spy (1948/1962: 38) – while the restaurant to which he takes her 'had no air of having existed before tonight' (1948/1962: 225). This restaurant is the setting for the climactic encounter between Harrison and Stella, and the 'aching' brightness of its lighting and its population of 'born extras' turn it into the ultimate unreality of the film set.

The presence of Harrison creates an open-endedness in the narrative. His lack of origins, his lack of place and his role as a spectator, or indeed a voyeur (1948/1962: 43), situates him both nowhere and everywhere. Omnipresent, it is his perspective, the archetypal male gaze, that dominates the narrative. Stella's life has been watched like a movie – she is constantly subject to male scrutiny – even at the end of the novel when Harrison seems no longer part of her life, the surveillance is not relaxed. When Harrison reappears in the final pages he gives the impression of knowing all her plans (1948/1962: 322). As the originator of the gaze, Harrison is situated outside the story of Stella at the same time as he forms an integral part of the narrative. The mystery of his curious presence at Mount Morris is never explained, and in Stella's drawing attention to her appearance 'in two different stories' the impression is created of there being another text running parallel to *The Heat of the Day*, connected only by the ghostly presence of Harrison. As the plots of the novel develop, this sense of a second narrative increases, presenting a constant threat of marginalisation to Stella.

Bowen, then, relishes the 'impossibility' of her characters, distorting and inverting the relation of fiction and reality, and favouring persistently the hegemony of the unreal over the narrow terrain of the real. Stella having asked Harrison where he keeps his razor (a mundane symbol of attachment) is rebuffed by the reply 'I have two or three razors' (1948/1962: 140). This emphasis on Harrison's dubious plurality forces Stella to consider the bizarre inequality of their situation:

> His concentration on her was made more oppressive by his failure to have or let her give him any possible place in the human scene. By the rules of fiction, with which life to be credible must comply, he was as a character 'impossible' – each time they met, for instance, *he showed no shred or trace of having been continuous since they last met* . . . [T]he uninterestingly right state of what he wore seemed less to argue care – brushing, pressing, changes of linen – than *a physical going into abeyance*, just as he was, with everything he had on him, between appearances. 'Appearance', in the sense used for *a ghost or actor*, had, indeed, been each of these times the word. (Bowen, 1948/1962: 140–41; ellipsis and emphasis mine)

Harrison is a 'ghost or actor', identities that embody two of the novel's dominant motifs. These identities also symbolise states of being that disrupt 'normal' temporal and physical relations. Ghosts move freely through time and space, while the actor, spatially confined, moves through the text across the boundaries of 'real' time and enters an arena in which radical transgressions of 'normal' temporal relations become a possibility. Theatrical imagery, however, is not confined to Harrison. Lee observes that Robert's grotesque family home, Holme Dene, is filled with 'touring scenery', and goes on to identify dramatic counterparts for the novel's characters (Lee, 1981: 182). Robert is certainly the consummate actor, and around the quality of his performance hangs the mystery of the plot. His skill, we are told, is a product of his environment; the 'private hours' of the Kelway family were spent 'in working on to their faces the required expression of having nothing to hide' (1948/1962: 256). The novel can be seen to juxtapose two acting techniques, which are appropriate to the narrative tones of melodrama and detachment that accompany the appearances of Robert and Harrison respectively. The two characters never meet, but their techniques are uncomfortably united when Stella must perform in a last ditch attempt to save Robert. The motivation of the act is entirely on the terms of Robert's romantic code, but her performance has the distance of Harrison's cold rationality. Speaking in 'the light, rather high voice which had in the last few minutes become her own', Stella 'was at a desirable distance from her soul' (1948/1962: 233). Robert, then, performs a tragic role in the Aristotelian tradition of empathy. He is a puppet of the theatre, and Stella his audience, bound to his fate in the process of catharsis. Harrison, in contrast, occupies an uncomfortable boundary between actor and spectator, which in the light of his control over Robert's fate could even be extended to that of creator or writer. His position is analogous to the actor of Brecht's epic theatre. His purpose is not to engage the sympathy of the audience, but to make them think. Harrison sets the dilemma and stands back – yet for all his control he is not omnipotent, he even claims he is suffering – a contradiction that is fundamental to the Oedipal plot, the dynamic of which also permeates the novel.[5]

Bowen's writing, then, occupies a border territory between the naturalistic and the artificial, and she manipulates this boundary to emphasise the constant difficulty of discerning between appearance and reality – the impossibility of making judgements or, even in wartime, taking sides. The contradictions and paradoxes of war are everywhere apparent, from the plot's conflict of the public and the personal to Donovan's unconsciously ambivalent cry of 'A terrible victory!' (1948/1962: 178) in response to Alamein. This conflict in Bowen's work also establishes a significant debate about power, and about access to the symbolic order, creating a contradiction which is never satisfactorily resolved within the text.

The novel contains a gender-based opposition between passivity and action which reveals the equality suggested by Stella's independence to be a fiction. Although Harrison, Robert and Stella are all described as being engaged in secret, 'not unimportant' government work, in actuality Stella remains powerless. Her economic independence represents only a superficial emancipation and she is manipulated by Harrison in a manner that blatantly acknowledges the supremacy of male truth. When Harrison first proposes his sexual blackmail, her immediate response is to threaten to report him. His response is, in effect, a statement of female powerlessness:

> No, to put me out wouldn't close the case against him: in point of fact it would have the reverse effect. You're not only the most charming woman, if I may say so; you're also officially known to have quite a heart . . . If you hadn't gone round by Robert's to drop the word to him, it would none the less be assumed you had – a woman's always a woman, and so on. (Bowen, 1948/1962: 40–41; ellipsis mine)

Harrison exploits a head versus heart version of the traditional male/female binary opposition. He is asking Stella for a passive acceptance of a sexual trade-in – one spy for another. There is something blackly comic about the interchangeability of Harrison and Robert, perhaps suggesting that the illusive nature of their characters is more a case of two-dimensionality.[6] Their shared first names suggest two generations of the same basic model, although to decide which is the father and which the son is perhaps more complex. Yet in the terms of the novel, the power they share is far from two-dimensional. Harrison demands that Stella play the customary role of the passive woman and thereby removes her from the potential position of equality created by the exigencies of wartime employment. Within the scope of the novel, the two spies are more actively concerned with the possession of Stella than with the intricacies of international espionage.

A similar demand of conformity to a state of stereotypical passivity has been placed on the more peripheral character of Cousin Nettie. Her story is the product of a previous generation, and her 'madness' the result of being pressured into the role of wife to Cousin Francis. Francis is a traditional patriarch; he is the head of a house in search of an heir, which Nettie could not provide. This is the patriarchal order which gave birth to Harrison. He may be something of an illegitimate offspring, but the rules are the same, and the result for women is the same. Women must exist within a severely constrained environment. Nettie's answer is an escape into madness which leaves Cousin Francis short of a successor. The only available option is Stella's son Roderick, and it is in the story of Roderick's inheritance that Bowen identifies the contradictions inherent in patriarchal ideas of tradition and continuity.

There is an opposition in the text between a desire for the preservation of tradition (representing the security of the known) and a depiction of the exclusivity of that tradition. This dynamic is similar to Woolf's dilemma in *Between the Acts*. Love of England co-exists and conflicts with a loathing of its patriarchal imperial legacy. Bowen clearly wants to disrupt the complacent surface of patriotism, and attempts to debunk the structures that uphold its edifice. Phyllis Lassner observes that 'the myth of the ancestral home, which was demystified in [Bowen's] earlier works, now burns more widely: as the mother-nation-England' (Lassner, 1990a: 121). Women are marginalised by the mores of the past, and no matter how much Bowen's plot suggests a desire for tradition and the potential regenerative power of the past, it also suggests that same tradition is flawed, not least because its side-effects are the isolation and silencing of women. Standing in the drawing room at Mount Morris, a room decorated by Cousin Nettie's framed photograph of the sinking Titanic, Stella stares into a mirror and sees herself briefly as the lady of the house:

> There was something inexorable in the judgement: she turned away from it. After all, was it not chiefly here in this room and under this illusion that Cousin Nettie Morris — and who now knew how many more before her? — had been pressed back, hour by hour, *by the hours themselves*, into cloudland? Ladies had gone not quite mad, *not quite even that*, from in vain *listening for meaning in the loudening ticking of the clock.* (Bowen, 1948/1962: 174; emphasis mine)

'Not quite even that' — Bowen suggests in this phrase the complete negation of women's being. This is the realm of a specifically female madness suggested by Luce Irigaray: 'An absolutely immense bodily suffering . . . which finds expression in depressive collapses. But that is not even the blaze of madness' (Irigaray, 1991: 48). Irigaray is not certain that women 'even have the right to madness', and indeed Stella's predecessors in that room achieve neither the concreteness of sanity nor madness, they simply fade away.

Here, as elsewhere in the novel, the symbol of patriarchal oppression is time. Its remorseless continuation, evident in the above quotation, relates it to the inexorable demands of masculine succession. Indeed the madness of Cousin Nettie also seems to be bound up in a failure of motherhood. She has not provided an heir, she has failed in her biological function, and in consequence has no place or sense of self within the terms of patriarchal definitions. The ideal of female continuance, which Woolf attempted to reclaim as a woman's time to set against the patriarchy's sterile legacy, is rejected by Bowen as a function compromised by patriarchal appropriation. Cousin Nettie's reproductive lack sets her in a state of symbolic non-existence. This depiction of the non-mother is part of a large and complex examination of mothering in the novel, which is most straightforwardly manifested in the juxtaposition of Stella, the comparatively 'good' mother against the grotesque 'bad' mother, Mrs Kelway.

For women, however, the ultimate futility is to look for meaning in the 'ticking of the clock'. The capacity of clock time to destroy the equilibrium of women is emphasised by Bowen's short story 'The inherited clock'. A skeleton clock which Paul desires is loathed and feared by Clara, who even before inheriting the object is oppressed by its remorseless presence: 'if she did not yet feel she could anticipate feeling her sanity being demolished, by one degree more, as every sixtieth second brought round this unheard click' (Bowen, 1983: 627–8). The story concludes with a new generation's rebellion against the clock's meaningless continuity. Stopping the clock, stopping time, frees Clara from the poisoned legacy of the past. As Julia Kristeva has emphasised, clock time is the time of the symbolic order.[7] It rules men and oppresses or alienates women. Harrison is described as 'punctual, wheeling in on the quiver of the appointed hour as though attached to the very works of the clock' (1948/1962: 22), whereas Stella seems distanced from the regiment of time (1948/1962: 41, 56, 277). This symbolism is closely related to Virginia Woolf's juxtaposition of a female eternity against a male absolute in *Between the Acts* and suggests a similar concern with the concept of 'male' and 'female' time. Bowen does not share Woolf's interest in the reinscription of history, but instead of time past she considers the idea of time lost, challenging patriarchal order through the absence of one of its founding principles. While Woolf can be seen to anticipate Kristeva's association of women with a cyclical time of repetition, Bowen's conception is closer to the monumental or eternal time that Kristeva suggests is 'all-encompassing and infinite like imaginary space' (1979: 191). This monumental time is described in the essay 'Women's time' as a 'massive presence . . . [that] has so little to do with linear time (which passes) that the very word "temporality" hardly fits' (1979: 191). This contrast highlights the distinction between the stasis which seems to characterise Bowen's parallel or private time, and the linear temporality of war. 'Time held war' she concludes in a crucial transitional moment from her memoir of childhood, *Seven Winters*. This moment encapsulates the loss of innocence and the awareness of the social that marks the end of the Oedipal phase: 'The hour was more than my hour; within it people were fighting' (Bowen, 1943: 25).

Time and war are, thus, inextricably linked and in *The Heat of the Day* Bowen's portrait of war is a catalogue of stopped clocks and disrupted time. When Stella and Robert meet, the clock in the restaurant has been 'shock-stopped' (1948/1962: 99) and at the climax of their final encounter 'the room had the look of no hour' (1948/1962: 277). Holme Dene is similarly afflicted. We are told that time had 'clogged' (1948/1962: 108) the ticking of the grandfather clock in Mrs Kelway's sitting room – an image of congestion and atrophy that aptly suggests a social order on the verge of a deserved extinction. Kristeva states that 'there is no time without the father' (1974: 153), and within Bowen's text it would seem that there are no fathers in this disrupted time. Yet this is not entirely the case; the general absence of fathers within the plot only serves to emphasise the presence of a different father – war.

None the less, the two arenas of disrupted time represented by Robert and Stella's relationship and life at Holme Dene are highly significant. In Stella's flashbacks to the early days of her romance, time does not exist. The clocks that are 'shock-stopped' represent a denial of time that situates the relationship in the realm of the pre-symbolic. Together Robert and Stella forge a pre-Oedipal dyad, an out-of-time unity that protects them against the time of war. To acknowledge time would be to re-enter the symbolic order, and expose themselves again to the burden of social responsibility. In sharp contrast to Robert and Stella's 'absence' from time is the sense that life at Holme Dene has exceeded its allotted span. This is the realm of the old order, appropriately presided over by a grandfather clock. A patriarchy without a patriarch, this is the stagnant and outmoded world that will be destroyed by war. However, the apocalypse of war encompasses not only the death of the old, but also the birth of the new, and Bowen presents the infant patriarchy struggling to be born through the figure of Roderick, the inheritor.

There is a certain irony that in *The Heat of the Day*'s world of absent fathers, the mantle of authority must fall on to, in Stella's words, 'a bad mother's fatherless son' (1948/1962: 71). Nonetheless, Roderick takes his inheritance seriously:

> Possessorship of Mount Morris affected Roderick strongly. It established for him, and was adding to day by day, what might be called a historic future. The house came out to meet his growing capacity for attachment; all the more, perhaps, in that by geographically standing outside war it appeared also to be standing outside the present. (Bowen, 1948/1962: 50)

The past can offer a salvation to Roderick that it denies to Stella and the women who preceded her.[8] The past, though, is only a springboard into the future, and war, rather than representing a force of arbitrary destruction, becomes for Roderick a facilitator of change. War replaces the absent father, freeing Roderick from the dyadic mother/child bond, and preparing him for his masculine responsibilities in the social sphere. Stella's fear 'that the army was out to obliterate Roderick' (1948/1962: 49) is the fear that her son will be destroyed in an Oedipal struggle with the omnipotent father. Yet there is also comedy in the war's fathering of Roderick. The enigmatic Fred, whose name and opinions dominate Roderick's discourse can be seen as a comic surrogate, preparing the mother's boy for the role he must assume: 'Fred's sure the whole thing ought to be simpler' (1948/1962: 57), 'In fact, as Fred says, it comes to seem fishy when one *is* told anything'

(1948/1962: 64), 'Fred took an if anything still more dim view than I did' (1948/1962: 201).

Within the multi-faceted legacy of Mount Morris (female marginalisation, the decline of the old and the regeneration of the new), Bowen presents a patriarchy that is paradoxically threatened and threatening; but there still remains a contradiction within the text that stands outside the deliberate juxtapositions of the plot and which is integral to the issue of survival within the text. This contradiction lies in the undoubted value that Bowen attaches to the ideas of continuity and inheritance represented by Mount Morris. Irrespective of the dangers that tradition holds for women, Bowen seems drawn towards the comfort of a lost world. That circumstances have placed a different premium on the past is perhaps best revealed in the character of Colonel Pole who can be read as a reincarnation of *The Death of the Heart*'s Major Brutt. In *The Death of the Heart* (1938) the Major is a creature on the verge of extinction, a defunct model:

> Makes of men date, like makes of cars; Major Brutt was a 1914–18 model: there was now no market for that make. In fact, only his steadfast persistence in living made it a pity he could not be scrapped . . . (Bowen, 1938/1962: 90)

In 1938 Brutt was a dinosaur, but ten years later he is permitted an unexpected comeback. His return and promotion to the rank of Colonel Pole represent not so much a rebirth as a rehabilitation. The new model is no more streamlined than the old, and its survival in the modern world is equally uncertain; but, in the context of a second war, its value would seem to have increased.

Roderick may represent the new world, but in the resuscitation of Colonel Pole, Bowen seems reluctant to let go of the old. Consequently, the colonel and the major have much in common. They both exist at a remove from the dynamic of modern life. Indeed they are so out of touch that the twenty years between youth and middle age have become a hazy indeterminate blur – only the golden memories of the past and the uncomfortable realities of the present are in focus. The connections between the two that reveal the chain of cause and effect have been conveniently repressed, allowing the myth of a golden time to stand unchallenged. Major Brutt recalls '[t]he picture of that great evening together – Anna, Himself, Pidgeon – was framed in his mind, and could not be taken down – it was the dear possession of someone with few possessions, carried from place to place' (1938/1962: 91); so vast and incomprehensible are the changes of the intervening years that Brutt's logic is defeated – 'For hospitality, and that little girl on the rug, he began to abandon Pidgeon already' (1938/1962: 92). Colonel Pole suffers from a similar incapacity to comprehend the preceding twenty years, and as he crosses the frozen wastes of family disapproval to talk to Stella at the funeral, he makes a similar transfer of allegiance:

> He dared not decide whether her eyes, with their misted askance look, were those of the victim or of the *femme fatale*. He did not know the whole of that story and did not want to . . .
>
> Colonel Pole, however, still could not but think it gallant of her to have come . . . She was better than gallant, she was feeling; she brought grace to this sparse ignoble burying of poor old Frankie far from his own land. (Bowen, 1948/1962: 84–5; ellipses mine)

Colonel Pole's limited list of potential roles for Stella serve as a timely reminder of the illusory nature of the good old days, but none the less his appearance and his mock-heroic rescue of Stella like a damsel in distress, are indicative of Bowen's wishful thinking – as well as the double bind of patriarchal regeneration. She sets Pole as a bulwark of tradition against the shifty modernity of Harrison. For a brief moment the reliable force of the colonel's existence seems capable of negating Harrison's corruption. A moment of fantasy to which can be added the irony of the patriotic Pole's unwitting defence of Stella against the knowledge of Robert's treachery. Yet the colonel himself is not a joke. His time may be past, but at least he has a past, and next to the rootless interloper Harrison that makes him, like cousin Francis, one of the fragile upholders of an endangered tradition. Indeed Bowen, like Mitchison in her juxtaposition of Forbes and Kyllachy, almost seems to be establishing two competing lines of patriarchal descent – a legitimate, nostalgic old guard and a dubious, bastardised new order.

The insecurity of war gives an added premium to the past, attributing a potentially dangerous sentimental value to its symbols of security, be they houses, families or stray colonels. Yet Bowen's work has always been critical of the middle classes, as indeed was illustrated by the sacrifice of Major Brutt in *The Death of the Heart*, and *The Heat of the Day* is no exception. The attitude to the past epitomised by the creation of Colonel Pole is undercut by the novel's concern with tradition's 'fatal flaw' – its oppression of women. Thus Roderick's inheritance is an ambivalent one, situated on the borders of two narratives. This returns us to the idea of a double narrative in *The Heat of the Day*. There is something highly appropriate yet ironic in Lee's dubbing the novel 'a woman's view'. Throughout the exposition of Stella's story, there is the sense of another plot encroaching. This is the master narrative, usurped by Bowen's change of focus, but carrying the full weight of the symbolic order embodied in the restoration of Mount Morris, which, we are bluntly told by Stella, 'was not her story' (1948/1962: 194).

Alongside its multiple narratives, the novel also embraces more than one

Oedipal plot. The out-of-time dyadic utopia that Stella, the mother figure, has established with Robert, the child, is challenged by the disruptive appearance of Harrison. Yet Harrison is an ambiguous figure, representing both the law of the father and a state of unlawful excess – nothing is quite what it seems. His entry into the mother/child dyad can therefore be seen as an ironic inversion of the traditional Oedipal process. In *The Heat of the Day* a progression into the realm of the symbolic is rejected in favour of a regression into the fantastical security of the pre-symbolic bond. In a calculated resistance to the tyranny of time, the established order is reversed. The son does not challenge the father for access to the mother in the symbolic, instead Harrison, the father, challenges Robert, the child, for the enviable timeless unity of his relationship with Stella. The process of socialisation moves backwards, and in a retreat from the 'sign and time' of the father, the social order is not acknowledged but rejected. Throughout the rituals of male combat, however, Stella remains powerless. Although Lassner (1990a) is right to say that all must bring their stories to Stella, she cannot actively interpret the texts. She remains the unchanging mother around whom her suitors are fixated.

The Oedipal conflict also forms a constructive metaphor for the process of patriarchal regeneration inscribed by war. War is not a straightforward destruction of the existing order, it is rather the visible manifestation of the patriarchy's internal struggle between the old and the new. The generational conflict is resolved through identification, not destruction. If war is to be understood as the regeneration of patriarchal government, then the circumstances of women will also need reassessment. As Mount Morris reveals, for women the security of the past is illusory. Yet this does not mean, as Lassner suggests, that they are better off in the disruption and dislocation of wartime: 'only disturbances in cultural stability can provide opportunities for a way out of conventional fictions and imagined fates for female characters' (Lassner, 1990a: 139). Such an escape is equally illusory. The historical record may reveal war's offer of increased mobility to women, but the history of the postwar period records its repeal. This is generosity born of necessity. The employment opportunities of war are an integral part of the myth of patriarchal breakdown encoded in conflict. The 'freedom' represented by women's labour is short-lived and conditional. The wartime emancipation of women can more accurately be seen as a mother's breast from which the infant patriarchy must feed, and which, as the infant grows older and stronger, it will inevitably reject.

This is the pessimistic scenario that emerges from the contradictions of Bowen's narrative. What, in the face of this paradoxical confluence of flux and stasis, can Bowen propose as a woman's strategy for survival? Virginia Woolf and Naomi Mitchison both engage with a similar dilemma – how to subvert or rewrite an ostentatiously male tradition. Woolf revels briefly in the resilience of female continuity, changing the focus of history from the political to the domestic. Mitchison celebrates the vitality of a female inheritance of tolerance and understanding which she contrasts with the sterility of a materialistic male legacy. Bowen's vision of the past is less optimistic, and does not permit such a reading. In *The Heat of the Day* she seems to resign herself to an acknowledgement of the necessary evil of a tradition that is not a woman's story. Is the nation's salvation inevitably bought at such a cost? Perhaps Bowen is simply more of a realist than Woolf whose fictions ultimately collapse in *Between the Acts*, or less utopian than Naomi Mitchison, who wrote of a female tradition, but none the less had to work for what seemed the best available alternative – the Labour Party. Bowen was a sophisticated commentator on the impact of war on the civilian population, but her wartime novel persistently resists the imposition of a coherent message. Indeed, as I have indicated in Chapter 1, her concern was not to chronicle the events of war, but rather to study 'war-climate, and . . . the strange growths it raised' (Bowen, 1950: 48). The roots of Bowen's conception of a parallel time can be discerned in this distinction between the 'history' and the 'territory' of war. Yet this formulation does not present itself as an optimistic or a straightforward strategy of escape. Bowen's biographer, Victoria Glendinning, finds in her fiction a pessimism so powerful that it borders on nihilism. Suggesting that Bowen behaves like the 'God of Genesis' in her novels, Glendinning continues:

> There is no remaining in Eden, but little hope outside it. There is no virtue in remaining within stifling conventions, but only trouble awaits the delinquent. Her women are so often stultified or trapped, but when they take steps to free themselves they open Pandora's box. It's a can't-win situation. (Glendinning, 1977: 97)

For women, war is an equally impossible situation, and their narratives must struggle to articulate their experience against the remorseless logic of war. Perhaps the hallucinations Bowen describes in the Preface to the American edition of *The Demon Lover* form in part the unconscious delineation of women's escape: 'Dreams by night, and the fantasies – these often childishly innocent – with which formerly matter-of-fact people consoled themselves by day were compensations' (Bowen, 1950: 49). Dreams and fantasies – the random relief of 'an unconscious, instinctive, saving resort' – rather than the structures of history or the search for a *her*story, represent the arena of Bowen's strategies for survival.

Thus, the evidence of *The Heat of the Day* indicates that ultimately Bowen rejected the past as a resource for women's survival. Here women cannot retreat into the past, it holds nothing for them and the future is not in their hands. Bowen's short stories are equally pessimistic. 'The happy autumn fields' seems initially to depict the past as an escape, but as the story progresses, this is seen to be an illusion. Mary attempts to free herself from the war, and from war's dessication of human experience, by returning to the past through a box of letters. The Victorian past is portrayed as a world of vivid intense colours in contrast to the grey and dusty present, but Mary's strategy cannot ultimately empower her. Her vision concludes with a premonition of disaster and a sharp sense of the paralysis of her alter ego Sarah: 'The others, in the dark on the chairs and sofas, could be felt to turn their judging eyes upon Sarah, who, as once before, could not speak' (Bowen, 1983: 683).

With the past rejected, Bowen's fictions focus instead on alternative imaginative routes out of the time of war. The fantasy of survival that pervades both *The Heat of the Day* and the stories of *The Demon Lover* is one of absence. This is not a displacement or escape into an earlier or primeval time, but is instead a movement into what can be described as a parallel non-time: another dimension. Bowen's characters survive by means of an absence that is spatial rather than temporal.

On one level this is a fantasy of hibernation – as evinced by Robert and Stella's 'hermetic' world. This idea is commensurate with the 'sealing off' described by Linda M. Shires as characteristic of the artistic response to the Second World War (Shires, 1985: 3). Yet it is also a fantasy of escape – a freeing of inhibitions and an opening out of imaginative space in the face of the narrowed horizon of wartime 'reality'. This is certainly the case in the short story 'Mysterious Kôr' where the logic of destruction is inverted and thought alone has the power not only to rebuild what war has destroyed, but to create whole cities anew (Bowen, 1983: 730). Pepita's fantasy is a deliberate strategy of detachment, and when this 'inhumanity' is questioned she acknowledges that its purpose is self-preservation:

> 'Don't be cross about Kôr; please don't, Arthur,' she said.
> 'I thought girls thought about people.'
> 'What, these days?' she said. 'Think about people? How can anyone think about people if they've got any heart? I don't know how other girls manage: I always think about Kôr.' (Bowen, 1983: 730)

The Heat of the Day is peopled by 'absent' characters. At its centre are the absent fathers – Stella's husband, Louie's husband, and Robert's father, while on the periphery of the novel lie Cousin Francis and Cousin Nettie. Francis – the ultimate absent presence – has expired while attempting to reintegrate himself into wartime England, in spite of which, and through the power of the law embodied in wills, he remains a central presence in the novel. His estranged wife, Cousin Nettie, is a self-proclaimed madwoman who implies she has chosen her isolation in Wystaria Lodge, 'a powerhouse of nothingness' (1948/1962: 203), in preference to the demands of a patriarchal society. Significantly, the nothingness that Roderick finds so oppressive is a comfort to Cousin Nettie:

> One could argue, she had chosen well. Here in this room her own existence could be felt condensing around her in pure drops . . . *Here* was nothing to trouble her but the possibility of being within reach: seated on the sofa with her back to what she had ascertained to be nothing, Cousin Nettie was well placed. (Bowen, 1948/1962: 215; ellipsis mine)

Stella, on the other hand, builds a self-imposed absence from the dislocation forced upon her by war. War has intervened forcefully into her relationship with Roderick, and when he visits her on leave from the army, they are each coping initially with the presence of a stranger:

> And he traced his way back by these attitudes, one by one, as though each could act as a clue or signpost to the Roderick his mother remembered, the Roderick he could feel her hoping to see. He searched in Stella for some identity left by him in her keeping. It was a search undertaken principally for her sake: only she made him conscious of loss or change. (Bowen, 1948/1962: 48)

Roderick works hard to overcome the alienating effects of uniform, understanding to some extent Stella's need to recognise some part of him from the past. But he too is isolated – and by choice: 'he could see, not feel, war's cruelty to a world to which he had so far given no hostage; with which, warned, he had never engaged himself' (Bowen, 1948/1962: 49). Stella's sterile rented rooms both protect her from further loss and serve to emphasise 'what was lacking'. But in self-sufficiency there also comes a danger – 'from hesitating to feel came the moment when you no longer could' (1948/1962: 55).

Stella's love for Robert has resulted in a two-handed absence. They have formed a bond in which '[h]is experiences and hers became harder and harder to tell apart; everything gathered behind them into a common memory' (1948/1962: 99). Prior to their meeting she had lived a timeless and self-contained existence, and it is not until she wakes up to an 'apprehension of loss' (1948/1962: 97) that she realises her armour of isolation has been pierced – she has allowed herself to care about Robert. To care is to be vulnerable, and her waking conviction that something has happened to Robert is accompanied by a new and terrifying awareness of time. Her usual defensive avoidance of the real world turns in on her and begins to eat away at even her tangible surroundings (1948/1962: 97). To care for Robert is to engage with the symbolic, and to be subject once again to the tyranny of time:

> Nothing she saw or touched gave token of even its own reality: her wrist watch seemed to belie time; she fancied it had lost hours during the night, that this might be midday, the afternoon – her first act as she hurried into the street, was to look in vain for a public clock. (Bowen, 1948/1962: 97)

Stella's self-protection, like Pepita's, can only function through emotional isolation, and Robert has invaded this territory. Quickly, however, the lovers are seen to unite in a contract of absence from the world. There is a conscious abandoning of other acquaintances, 'a first and last wave, across widening water, from a liner' (1948/1962: 95) and the deliberate submergence of two individuals into a carefully constructed 'us'. Stella's precious equilibrium, her self-protection, was nearly destroyed, but together she and Robert forge a new fantasy of absence in which, as Robert tells his mother, 'you would not notice the war' (1948/1962: 113).

Absence, however, is not only portrayed as a strategy. In the case of Louie it is rather a condition, imposed by the arbitrary whim of war. Louie's absence is situated in her extreme isolation. War has deprived her of her parents (via a bomb) and her husband (via the army). She wanders the streets and parks of London looking for company so as not to go home alone and face 'the fact of her being of meaning only to an absent person, absent most appallingly from this double room' (1948/1962: 146). Her fantasy is initially one of belonging. She desires the ratification of her existence through the presence of another – she is still, in effect, searching for her parents. In her desperation Louie latches on to Harrison who looks to her to be another sufferer (ironically, in terms of his desire for Stella, he is), and in the weeks after their first meeting she even fantasises belonging to Harrison: 'It had begun to appear to her, looking back, that Harrison had fathered and understood her' (1948/1962: 144). Although Louie's attentions are constantly rejected by Harrison, her belief that they have something in common is more accurate than either of them realise. Harrison is the embodiment of Louie's fear – his ghostly presence and his 'going into abeyance' emphasise that in isolation he becomes, as Louie dreads she will become, meaningless. After the failure of this attempt to verify her existence through attachment to Harrison, Louie turns instead to newspapers. These prove far more satisfactory, and Bowen wittily presents a character constituting herself through the language and images of the media:

> Louie, after a week or two on the diet, discovered that she *had* got a point of view, and not only *a* point of view but the right one. Not only did she bask in warmth and inclusion but every morning and evening she was praised . . . Dark and rare were the days when she failed to find on the inside page of her paper an address to or else account of herself.

Was she not a worker, a soldier's wife, a war orphan, a pedestrian, a Londoner, a home- and animal-lover, a thinking democrat, a movie-goer, a woman of Britain, a letter writer, a fuel-saver, and a housewife? (Bowen, 1948/1962: 152)

Louie's relations with the media form a ruthless parody of wartime propaganda, and they also indicate that Louie represents an archetypal blank page. Each day she reconstitutes herself anew according to the dictates of her newspaper. This honeymoon only ends when Louie comes into contact with Stella. A real person impinges on her consciousness, and when the newspaper later records Stella's dubious activities, the fall of Louie's idol creates a disenchantment with 'virtue' that extends to her newspapers and their prescriptions. The connections between Louie and Stella are important. Louie is constructed as the other; heavy, clumsy and foolish she stands in sharp contrast to Stella's almost etherial qualities. Harrison finds the physicality of Louie repulsive and he, like Louie, places Stella on a pedestal. From the first meeting of the two misfits, Harrison shows his discomfort in the presence of the animal sexuality of Louie and longs to escape to the shrine of his perfect woman, Stella. When the narrative finally unites the two women, the effect on Harrison is startling. His desire is only for the idealised figure of Stella alone. The presence of Louie 'debases' her, he is repulsed by the conjunction of these two extremes, and he rejects both women as if they were one:

'You must congratulate me before you go,' said Stella, her hand still on Louie's arm. 'I've good news, I think.'
'You have?'
Stella nodded. 'A friend is out of danger.'
Harrison's unfolding of his arms, on which he had been leaning heavily, let the table restore itself to equilibrium with a bump and a flash of cutlery . . . He scrubbed at this eye, the left, with a finger-tip, raising and lowering his eyebrows. 'Why not you two both go along together?' he said, looking at the finger when it had done. 'Don't you hear what I say?' he asked in a louder, less absent voice. 'You two had better both be getting along.' (Bowen, 1948/1962: 240–41; ellipsis mine)

The casting of woman as virgin or whore is also the subject of the myth of Stella's infidelity. Patriarchal language is insufficiently flexible to be able to express an accurate account of the relationship between Victor and Stella. Stella, however, through inertia chooses to propagate the image of herself as whore in preference to being forced into the opposite category of victim.

When Louie hears that Stella is not conventionally virtuous, she feels herself released from the social injunctions that oppress her (these are the laws of

Connie, a surrogate husband figure, and the newspapers). This release frees her from her inhibitions and enables her to commit the betrayal that will become her salvation. Ultimately Louie's salvation comes through pregnancy. Hers is a literal manifestation of the dyadic bonds that characterise the novel. The life within her enables her to feel with unconscious irony that she is finally 'one of many' (1948/1962: 323). This sense of belonging rescues her from her unwanted isolation, but otherwise it is clear that the child has not effected a serious change in Louie's relations with reality, but has rather moved her from an absence with which she could not cope, to a manageable and even welcome one in which she, like Stella, feels self-contained and secure.[9] As soon as possible she takes the child to the site of her parents' bomb-flattened home, resolving the search for her parents through the displacement of becoming a parent. This necessary act performed, she has established the boundaries of her new existence: 'Reeds grew out into the still water; ahead, there was distance as far as the eye could see – a thoughtless extension of her *now complete life*' (Bowen, 1948/1962: 329; emphasis mine). Paradoxically the novel concludes with Louie, who desired to belong, achieving a semi-mystical self-sufficiency; while Stella, self-contained in her detached secure fantasy, is on the verge of belonging, through marriage, to a brigadier. Yet both attempt to resolve their quests in the security of a dyad, suggesting that the strategies of absence and belonging might perhaps be one and the same.

Thus the optimism of Louie's achievement is illusory. As Lee observes, her fertility is 'haphazard' – accident rather than design has brought her to this point. It is an achievement that she creates a satisfactory existence from her position of alienation, and there is a pleasant irony in the creation of a fictional father for her child.[10] None the less, Louie's empowering takes place within the most limited of spheres. She had few choices and made none. Ultimately, like Stella, she is a commodity, constrained into one of the few stories available to her under the existing patriarchal order.

Thus it is that the difficulties of Phyllis Lassner's interpretation of the novel become apparent. Lassner suggests that:

> Each man brings his plot to Stella for interpretation, all the while fearing that she will either withhold its meaning or that the meaning she holds within her may cause their dissolution. (Lassner, 1990a: 125)

This interpretation of Stella as a 'key', as the 'guardian of knowledge', is highly problematic. Stella is asked to choose between Harrison and Robert, but instead she vacillates. Lassner, in her desire to situate Stella as the unchallenged centre of the novel, sees this as a strategy of empowerment. Yet how can it be? Stella does not choose to vacillate, she vacillates because she cannot choose. Stella may be ostentatiously situated at the centre of the novel, but her position is continually under threat. Roderick's story, and the other plots of Harrison, threaten to encroach on her limited hegemony. Indeed, she is more of a figure-head than a ruler. Robert and Harrison certainly seem to negate each other, and on one level they can be seen as competing suitors – but Stella is not free to choose. She has been set up by Harrison as a laboratory experiment, and the only way in which she can challenge the moral dilemma confronting her is through the traditional woman's role of passivity. Is this to suggest a Kristevan position of revolutionary silence? An absence from speech that challenges the contradictions of male discourse? In the work of Bowen, as in that of Woolf, I think it is impossible to define a revolutionary strategy in the passivity of listening. While Stella remains the object of masculine desire, rather than the subject of her own narrative, she cannot be the novel's arbiter of meaning. Her eventual drift into matrimony is the reabsorption of her silence by a wartime patriarchy that demands obedience to its law.

Significantly, when Stella does break out of passivity and takes the action of warning Robert, the results are exactly as Harrison said they would be, suggesting that his access to knowledge, and by extension power, is infinitely greater than Stella's. That Harrison disappears after Robert's death is ironically a final show of this power. Stella *wants* to see him, he has the answer (1948/1962: 318–19) and through his absence he withholds the symbolic power of knowledge. In this refusal to answer, Bowen certainly undermines the conventions of the thriller genre. Deprived of the expected and desired answers and reassurance, the reader has to be content with the fact of survival; and of an always already compromised continuance.

Despite the drama of its events, *The Heat of the Day* concludes with a negation of tragedy. This resistance is implicit in the fact of Stella's rather numbed continuance. Her visit to Roderick the day after Robert's death is a conscious anti-climax. Life goes on, and, in the arena of war, death has lost some of its capacity to shock. Bowen suggests that Robert's death, or the death of any individual, is ultimately meaningless. Individual action can have little impact on the impersonal forces of war or history.

The novel concludes with a reinforcement of this arbitrary and unthinking continuity. Alongside Louie's pregnancy there is the establishment of Stella in a new story. Situated in a different (but remarkably similar) flat she encounters Harrison for a final time. Harrison, however, has the air of being left over from the previous narrative, and cannot adjust to the new set: 'A dull little gun-metal ash tray caught his eye – 'Funny, you know,' he confessed, 'how I still seem to be seeing that other place. That other place where you were' (Bowen, 1948/1962: 318). Stella is now to marry a brigadier. We are left in suspense as to the rest of the story, but there seems little doubt that it will be a more conventional tale. The heady disruptions of the Blitz are over, the infant patriarchy is growing stronger, and Stella's transgressive liaison must be superseded by conformity. Stella's continuance has considerable implications. It is at once a rejection of closure, a reminder of artifice and a metaphor of repetition. The actress has a new role, but the story is an old one. *The Heat of the Day* might have offered hope in its chronicle of disruption, but it concludes with a confirmation of the patriarchal myth – marriage, conformity, marginality – a replay of the same old story for women.

Bowen seems to defend the past and to advocate a return to tradition; but the subtext of female marginality, madness and isolation that accompanies the restoration of the symbolic at Mount Morris, acts as a pertinent reminder of the fallibility of the past. In a return to the past, there lies the threat identified by Luce Irigaray in *This Sex Which Is Not One*: 'If we keep on speaking the same language together, we're going to reproduce the same history. Begin the same old stories all over again' (Irigaray, 1985: 205). The difficulty is how to break out of this pattern, and *The Heat of the Day* emphasises that war is not the answer. War may destroy the patriarchy, but ultimately it is patriarchy's game. Its apparent dissolution is more effectively a dispersal, in which the seeds of a new, more powerful manifestation of the old order are scattered to await the spring of peace.

NOTES

1. When writing of her own experiences Bowen is more positive. In 'London 1940' the capital becomes a 'city of villages' and the spirit of community predominates – 'We all have new friends: our neighbours' (Bowen, 1950: 219).
2. Much of Brecht's commentary on the art of his theatre is singularly appropriate to the techniques of Bowen's writing: 'I aim at an extremely classical, cold, highly intellectual style of performance. I'm not writing for the scum who want to have the cockles of their hearts warmed' (Brecht, 1926: 14).
3. Sean O'Faolain, a particular admirer of Bowen's writing, suggests that her detachment was not simply an artistic strategy, but rather a symptom of her inability to undertake emotional engagement. Victoria Glendinning, Bowen's biographer, comments on O'Faolain's criticism: 'It is precisely this tension in her – the fact that she could not howl – that gives her writing its peculiar pent-up intensity. One cannot write baldly of despair and loneliness, but one can instead describe the falling of the petals of a rose on to an escritoire. This is not symbolism: it is a sort of displacement activity' (Glendinning, 1977: 110).
4. 'Lack of choice' might be a phrase more appropriate to Stella's constricted position. Lassner (1990a: 124–5) attempts to read Stella's immobility as an empowering strategy in which it is she who makes sense of the novel's male plots. This is an interesting but problematic idea.
5. Victoria Glendinning's desire to see Bowen as the 'missing link' in the evolution of women's writing, the transition from Virginia Woolf to Iris Murdoch and Muriel Spark, has some grounding in the character of Harrison. His position as a devil's advocate or actual devil figure who destroys the moral and social façades of those around him, represents a design that would be used by Spark in *The Ballad of Peckham Rye* (1960) and by Murdoch in *A Fairly Honourable Defeat* (1970).
6. The comedy of male interchangeability is further emphasised by Louie's discovery, in the course of the promiscuous encounters that are a product of her search for identity, that men are on the whole, indistinguishable: 'To this spot, to which Tom had been so much attached, a sort of piety

made her bring any other man: she had thus the sense of living their Sundays for him' (Bowen, 1948/1962: 18).

7. 'The symbolic order – the order of verbal communication, the paternal order of genealogy – is a temporal order' (Kristeva, 1974: 152).

8. It is significant that Robert's instability in part lies in his rejection of the past. On hearing of Roderick's inheritance he reveals his perception of the past as a burden rather than a resource: 'To unload the past on a boy like that – fantastic!' (1948/1962: 160).

9. Connie also becomes a safely distant surrogate father, organising the discreet and efficient delivery of the baby. Across the boundaries of class, Connie bears considerable resemblance to Robert's sister Ernestine, who has also taken on attributes of the father's role, but without ever escaping from her mother, the dictator in the home.

10. The extent to which Louie's story parallels or even parodies Stella's is emphasised again by this fictionalisation of the father.

10

Conclusion

Never has a cataclysm been so apocalyptically exorbitant. Never has its representation been relegated to such inadequate symbolic modes.

Julia Kristeva, 'The pain of sorrow in the modern world:
the works of Marguerite Duras'

Gillian Beer's claim that the 'alternation between "I" and "We" is the living quarrel of Virginia Woolf's art' (Beer, 1987: 85) is a crucial observation. The tension that Beer uncovers in Woolf's work is perhaps the fundamental tension present in the work of all five writers with whom this book is concerned. In the work of Dorothy L. Sayers, Stevie Smith, Naomi Mitchison, Elizabeth Bowen and Virginia Woolf, a conflict arises between the desired unity of the individual subject and the double-edged fascination of the group ethic that is both the founding strength of Fascism and the necessary prerequisite of its resistance. The result of this conflict is a reassessment of what is understood by the idea of a group. A distinction is created between a group in which the individual is lost or subsumed – what might be termed a 'mass' – and a group of individuals.

Yet the difficulties of this already somewhat arbitrary distinction are compounded by a growing sense of the unreliability of the very individual whose value is so cherished. The textual fascination with a multiplicity of selves and personae forms a challenge to the idea of a single unified subject, and the dominance of this fragmented and unstable subject makes a coherent moral outlook unfeasible. This anxiety receives its most extreme articulation in the novels of Stevie Smith, who suggests that the individual is not only divided but fundamentally corrupt, but to a lesser or greater extent it is present in the work of all five women. Consequently, the use of the individual as the substance and emblem of a last stand against Fascism represents an always already compromised fantasy. Individualism can never be more than a dream of integrity perpetually undermined by the doubts and contradictions of a post-First World War consciousness.

Within Part Two I have utilised the ideas of Julia Kristeva. It has not been my intention to provide a comprehensive 'Kristevan' reading of war, but none the less I believe that her theorisation of the semiotic and the symbolic provide an ideal framework for an understanding of war that recognises the specificity of female experience. Within the context of war, the woman writer is subject to difficulties that stem directly from her complex and constrained relationship to the symbolic order. Her fiction therefore manifests a contradictory need to escape from the very order to which she must cling in order to constitute her subjectivity. Before the chaos of war was unleashed, women writers would seem to have felt secure enough to challenge the insanity of the patriarchal death drive. Once war has begun, dissent becomes a luxury few can afford.

The interaction between the individual and the group, between 'I' and 'We', is also the end point of Kristeva's essay, 'Women's time'. She concludes that the duty of 'aesthetic practices' is:

> to demystify the identity of the symbolic bond itself, to demystify, therefore, the *community* of language as a universal and unifying tool, one which totalizes and equalizes. In order to bring out – along with the *singularity* of each person and, even more, along with the multiplicity of every person's possible identifications . . . the *relativity of his/her symbolic as well as biological existence*, according to the variation in his/her specific symbolic capacities. And in order to emphasize the *responsibility* which all will immediately face of putting this fluidity into play against the threats of death which are unavoidable whenever an inside and an outside, a self and an other, one group and another, are constituted. (Kristeva, 1979: 210; ellipsis mine, Kristeva's italics)

When women writers engage with this paradoxical conception of co-existent states, and reject a totalising homogeneity for fluid community, they are no longer creating strategies for survival but a revolutionary strategy for change. That Kristeva's predecessors were reluctant to explore the implications of their fantasies is not surprising. In time of war, such treasonable thoughts were safer encoded in fiction.

To a certain extent my analysis of writers' strategies for surviving war has been a pessimistic one. Yet it is not my intention to belittle the creative achievement of women writers by suggesting that some or all of their strategies were destined for failure. For the average individual, excluded from access to power, war *is* a no-win situation. Women writers were no exception, and thus their achievement lies less in the success or failure of their projects than in the projects themselves. Elizabeth Bowen encapsulates this distinction when she asks 'I wonder whether in a sense all wartime writing is not resistance writing?' (Bowen, 1950: 50). The act of writing itself is crucial, and by attempting to subvert the 'inadequate symbolic modes' of patriarchal discourse, women's literature of escape constitutes a fitting testimony to the ultimately unrepresentable horror of war.

Bibliography

SELECTED WORKS OF ELIZABETH BOWEN, NAOMI MITCHISON, DOROTHY L. SAYERS, STEVIE SMITH AND VIRGINIA WOOLF

Bowen, Elizabeth (1938/1962) *The Death of the Heart*, Harmondsworth: Penguin.

Bowen, Elizabeth (1941) *Look at All Those Roses*, London: Gollancz.

Bowen, Elizabeth (1942) *Bowen's Court*, London: Longmans, Green & Co.

Bowen, Elizabeth (1943) *Seven Winters*, Dublin: The Cuala Press.

Bowen, Elizabeth (1945) *The Demon Lover and Other Stories*, London: Cape.

Bowen, Elizabeth (1948/1962) *The Heat of the Day*, Harmondsworth: Penguin.

Bowen, Elizabeth (1950) *Collected Impressions*, London: Longmans, Green & Co.

Bowen, Elizabeth (1983) *Collected Stories*, Harmondsworth: Penguin.

Mitchison, Naomi (1935) *We have been Warned*, London: Constable.

Mitchison, Naomi (1938) *The Moral Basis of Politics*, London: Constable.

Mitchison, Naomi (1939a) *The Kingdom of Heaven*, London: Heinemann.

Mitchison, Naomi (1939b/1988) *The Blood of the Martyrs*, Edinburgh: Canongate.

Mitchison, Naomi (1947) *The Bull Calves*, London: Cape.

Mitchison, Naomi (1986a) *Among You Taking Notes . . . The Wartime Diary of Naomi Mitchison*, ed. Dorothy Sheridan, Oxford: Oxford University Press.

Mitchison, Naomi (1979/1986) *You May Well Ask*, London: Flamingo.

Mitchison, Naomi (1986b) *Beyond This Limit: Selected Shorter Fiction of Naomi Mitchison*, ed. Isobel Murray, Edinburgh: Scottish Academic Press.

Sayers, Dorothy L. (1923/1989) *Whose Body*, London: Coronet Crime.

Sayers, Dorothy L. (1926/1988) *Clouds of Witness*, London: Coronet Crime.

Sayers, Dorothy L. (1927/1989) *Unnatural Death*, London: Coronet Crime.

Sayers, Dorothy L. (1928a/1989) *Lord Peter Views the Body*, London: Coronet Crime.

Sayers, Dorothy L. (1928b/1989) *The Unpleasantness at the Bellona Club*, London: Coronet Crime.

Sayers, Dorothy L. (1930/1989) *Strong Poison*, London: Coronet Crime.

Sayers, Dorothy L. (1931/1989) *Five Red Herrings*, London: Coronet Crime.

Sayers, Dorothy L. (1932/1989) *Have his Carcase*, London: Coronet Crime.

Sayers, Dorothy L. (1933a/1989) *Hangman's Holiday,* London: Coronet Crime.

Sayers, Dorothy L. (1933b/1989) *Murder must Advertise*, London: Coronet Crime.

Sayers, Dorothy L. (1934/1989) *The Nine Tailors*, London: Coronet Crime.

Sayers, Dorothy L. (1935/1990) *Gaudy Night*, London: Coronet Crime.

Sayers, Dorothy L. (1937a) 'Gaudy Night', in Howard Haycraft (ed.), *The Art of the Mystery Story,* New York: Grosset & Dunlap, 1961.

Sayers, Dorothy L. (1937b/1988) *Busman's Honeymoon*, London: Coronet Crime.

Sayers, Dorothy L. (1938) 'Are women human?', in Dorothy L. Sayers, *Unpopular Opinions,* London: Gollancz, 1946.

Sayers, Dorothy L. (1939) *In the Teeth of the Evidence,* London: Gollancz.

Sayers, Dorothy L. (1939–40) 'Wimsey papers', *The Spectator.*

Sayers, Dorothy L. (1940) *Begin Here: A War-Time Essay*, London: Gollancz.

Sayers, Dorothy L. (1943) *The Man Born to Be King: A Play Cycle on the Life of Our Lord and Saviour Jesus Christ*, London: Gollancz.

Sayers, Dorothy L. (1946) *Unpopular Opinions*, London: Gollancz.

Sayers, Dorothy L. (1972/1988) *Striding Folly*, London: Coronet Crime.

Smith, Stevie (1936/1980) *Novel on Yellow Paper*, London: Virago.

Smith, Stevie (1937) *A Good Time Was Had by All*, London: Cape.

Smith, Stevie (1938/1980) *Over the Frontier*, London: Virago.

Smith, Stevie (1942) *Mother, What is Man?*, London: Cape.

Smith, Stevie (1949/1979) *The Holiday*, London: Virago.

Smith, Stevie (1981) *Me Again: Uncollected Writings of Stevie Smith*, ed. Jack Barbera and Wiliam McBrien, London: Virago.

Woolf, Virginia (1906) '[The journal of Mistress Joan Martyn]', in *The Complete Shorter Fiction of Virginia Woolf*, ed. Susan Dick, rev. edn, London: Hogarth, 1989.

Woolf, Virginia (1925a) 'The Pastons and Chaucer', in Virginia Woolf, *The Common Reader 2*, London: Hogarth, 1962.

Woolf, Virginia (1925b/1976) *Mrs Dalloway*, London: Grafton.

Woolf, Virginia (1927/1977) *To the Lighthouse*, London: Grafton.

Woolf, Virginia (1928/1977) *Orlando*, London: Grafton.

Woolf, Virginia (1929/1977) *A Room of One's Own*, London: Grafton.

Woolf, Virginia (1931/1977) *The Waves*, London: Grafton.

Woolf, Virginia (1937/1977) *The Years*, London: Grafton.

Woolf, Virginia (1938/1986) *Three Guineas*, London: Hogarth.

Woolf, Virginia (1941/1978) *Between the Acts*, London: Grafton.

Woolf, Virginia (1942a) *The Death of the Moth*, London: Hogarth.

Woolf, Virginia (1942b) 'Thoughts on peace in an air raid', in Virginia Woolf, *The Death of the Moth*, London: Hogarth, 1942.

Woolf, Virginia (1967) *Collected Essays III*, London: Hogarth.

Woolf, Virginia (1977–84) *The Diary of Virginia Woolf*, Vol. IV, 1931–35; Vol. V, 1936–41, ed. Anne Olivier Bell and Andrew McNeillie, London: Hogarth.

Woolf, Virginia (1978) *The Pargiters*, ed. Mitchell A. Leaska, London: Hogarth.

OTHER CONTEMPORARY SOURCES AND POSTWAR CRITICISM

Aldgate, Anthony and Jeffrey Richards (1986) *Britain can Take It: The British Cinema and the Second World War*, Oxford: Blackwell.

Allingham, Margery (1938) *The Fashion in Shrouds*, London: Heinemann.

Allingham, Margery (1941a) *The Oaken Heart*, London: Michael Joseph.

Allingham, Margery (1941b) *Traitor's Purse,* London: Heinemann.

Allingham, Margery (1945/1987) *Coroner's Pidgin,* London: J. M. Dent & Sons.

Barbera, Jack and William McBrien, *Stevie: A Biography of Stevie Smith,* London: Heinemann.

Barrie, J. M. (1902/1914) *The Admirable Crichton,* London: Hodder & Stoughton.

Bax, Clifford and Meum Stewart (eds) (1949) *The Distaff Muse,* London: Hollis & Carter.

Beer, Gillian (1987) 'The body of the people in Virginia Woolf', in Sue Roe (ed.), *Women Reading Women's Writing,* Brighton: Harvester, 1987.

Beer, Gillian (1989) *Arguing with the Past,* London: Routledge.

Beer, Gillian (1992) 'Introduction' to Virginia Woolf, *Between the Acts* (1941), London: Penguin.

Bell, Anne Olivier and Andrew McNeillie (eds) (1977–84) *The Diary of Virginia Woolf,* London: Hogarth.

Benton, Jill (1990) *Naomi Mitchison: A Century of Experiment in Life and Letters,* London: Pandora.

Bergonzi, Bernard (1978) *Reading the Thirties,* Basingstoke: Macmillan.

Bevan, David (ed.) (1990) *University Fiction,* Atlanta: Rodopi.

Blake, Nicholas (1939) *The Smiler with the Knife,* London: Collins.

Boston, Anne (ed.) (1989) *Wave Me Goodbye: Stories of the Second World War,* Harmondsworth: Penguin.

Bowlby, Rachel (1988) *Virginia Woolf, Feminist Destinations,* Oxford: Blackwell.

Brabazon, James (1981) *Dorothy L. Sayers,* New York: Scribner.

Braybon, Gail and Penny Summerfield (1987) *Out of the Cage: Women's Experiences in Two World Wars,* London: Pandora Press.

Brecht, Bertold (1926) 'Conversation with Bert Brecht', in John Willett (ed.), *Brecht on Theatre,* London: Methuen, 1964.

Brittain, Vera (1933) *Testament of Youth,* London: Gollancz.

Brittain, Vera (1934) *Poems of the War and After,* London: Gollancz.

Brittain, Vera (1941) *England's Hour,* London: Macmillan.

Brittain, Vera (1945) *Account Rendered,* London: Macmillan.

Brittain, Vera (1948) *Born 1925, A Novel of Youth,* London: Macmillan.

Burgin, Victor, James Donald and Cora Kaplan (eds) (1986) *Formations of Fantasy,* London: Methuen.

Cadogan, Mary and Patricia Craig (1978) *Women and Children First,* London: Gollancz.

Calder, Angus (1969) *The People's War: Britain 1939–45,* London: Cape.

Calder, Angus (1991) *The Myth of the Blitz,* London: Cape.

Cannadine, David (1981) 'War and death, grief and mourning in modern Britain', in Joachim Whaley (ed.), *Mirrors of Mortality: Studies in the Social History of Death,* London: Europa, 1981.

Cawalti, John G. (1976) *Adventure, Mystery and Romance: Formula Stories as Art and Popular Culture,* Chicago: University of Chicago Press.

Ceadel, Martin (1980) 'Popular fiction and the next war, 1918–1939', in Frank Gloversmith (ed.), *Class, Culture and Social Change: A New View of the 1930s,* Brighton: Harvester, 1980.

Christie, Agatha (1938) *Appointment with Death,* London: Collins.

Christie, Agatha (1941/1962) *N or M?,* London: Fontana.

Cixous, Hélène, (1980) 'The laugh of the Medusa', in Elaine Marks and Isabelle de Courtivron (eds), *New French Feminisms,* Brighton, Harvester, 1980.

Cixous, Hélène, (1991) *Coming to Writing and Other Essays*, Cambridge, Mass.: Harvard University Press.

Cixous, Hélène, (1994) *The Hélène Cixous Reader*, ed. Susan Sellers, London: Routledge.

Cixous, Hélène and Catherine Clement (1986) *The Newly Born Woman*, Manchester: Manchester University Press.

Cixous, Hélène and Catherine Clement (1991) 'The newly born woman', in Mary Eagleton (ed.), *Feminist Literary Criticism*, London: Longman, 1991.

Cobley, Evelyn (1990) 'History and ideology in autobiographical literature of the First World War', *Mosaic*, 23 (3): 37–54.

Cockett, Richard (1989) 'Saluting Hitler', *Guardian*, 17 March 1989.

Cooper, Helen M., Adrienne Auslander and Susan Merrill Squier (1989) *Arms and the Woman: War, Gender and Literary Representation*, Chapel Hill, NC: University of North Carolina Press.

Craig, Patricia (1986) *Elizabeth Bowen*, Harmondsworth: Penguin.

Cramer, Patricia (1991) '"Loving in the war years"': the war of images in *The Years*', in Mark Hussey (ed.), *Virginia Woolf and War: Fiction, Reality and Myth*, New York: Syracuse University Press, 1991.

Croft, Andy (1990) *Red Letter Days: British Fiction in the 1930s*, London: Lawrence & Wishart.

Cudlipp, Hugh (1989) 'The shiver sisters who sought to appease Hitler', *The Independent*, 15 May 1989.

Cunningham, Valentine (1980) 'Neutral?: 1930s writers and taking sides', in Frank Gloversmith (ed.), *Class, Culture and Social Change: A New View of the 1930s*, Brighton: Harvester, 1980.

De Lauretis, Teresa (1989) *Technologies of Gender*, Basingstoke: Macmillan.

Dickson, Beth (1987) 'From personal to global: the fiction of Naomi Mitchison', *Chapman*, 10 (1/2): 34–40.

Douglas, Keith (1979) *Complete Poems*, ed. Desmond Graham, Oxford: Oxford University Press.

Dowson, Jane (1995) *Women's Poetry of the 1930s*. London: Routledge.

Du Maurier, Daphne (1938) *Rebecca*, London: Gollancz.

Du Maurier, Daphne (1941/1976) *Frenchman's Creek*, London: Pan.

Du Plessis, Rachel Blau (1985) *Writing Beyond the Ending*, Bloomington, Ind.: Indiana University Press.

Eagleton, Mary (ed.) (1991) *Feminist Literary Criticism*, London: Longman.

Ferrer, Daniel (1990) *Virginia Woolf and the Madness of Language*, London: Routledge.

Freud, Sigmund (1915) 'Thoughts for the times on war and death', in Sigmund Freud, *The Standard Edition of the Complete Psychological Works of Sigmund Freud*, ed. James Strachey, Vol. XIV, London: Hogarth, 1978.

Freud, Sigmund (1917) 'Mourning and melancholia', in Sigmund Freud, *The Standard Edition of the Complete Psychological Works of Sigmund Freud*, ed. James Strachey, Vol. XIV, London: Hogarth, 1978.

Freud, Sigmund (1978) *The Standard Edition of the Complete Psychological Works of Sigmund Freud*, ed. James Strachey, Vol. XIV, London: Hogarth.

Fussell, Paul (1975) *The Great War and Modern Memory*, New York: Oxford University Press.

Fussell, Paul (1989) *Wartime: Understanding and Behaviour in the Second World War*, New York: Oxford University Press.

Gardner, Brian (ed.) (1966) *The Terrible Rain: The War Poets 1939–45*, London: Methuen.

Garner, Shirley Nelson, Clare Kahane and Madelon Sprengnether (eds) (1985) *The (M)other Tongue: Essays in Feminist Psychoanalytic Interpretation*, Ithaca, NY: Cornell University Press.

Gifford, Douglas (1990) 'Forgiving the past: Naomi Mitchison's *The Bull Calves*', in Joachim Schwend and Horst W. Drescher (eds), *Studies in Scottish Fiction: Twentieth Century*, Frankfurt: Peter Lang, 1990.

Gilbert, Sandra M. (1987) 'Soldier's heart: literary men, literary women and the Great War', in Margaret Randolph Higonnet, Jane Jenson, Sonya Michel and Margaret Collins Weitz (eds), *Behind the Lines: Gender and the Two World Wars*, New Haven: Yale University Press, 1987.

Gilbert, Sandra M. and Susan Gubar (1988) *No Man's Land: The Place of the Woman Writer in the Twentieth Century*, vol. 1 *The War of the Words*, New Haven: Yale University Press.

Ginsburg, Elaine K. and Laura Moss Gottlieb (eds) (1983) *Virginia Woolf: Centennial Essays*, New York: Whitston Publishing Company.

Glendinning, Victoria (1977) *Elizabeth Bowen: Portrait of a Writer*, London: Weidenfeld & Nicolson.

Gloversmith, Frank (ed.) (1980) *Class, Culture and Social Change: A New View of the 1930s*, Brighton: Harvester.

Gottlieb, Laura Moss (1983) '*The Years*: a feminist novel', in Elaine K. Ginsberg and Laura Moss Gottlieb (eds), *Virginia Woolf: Centennial Essays*, New York: Whitson Publishing Company, 1983.

Grosz, Elizabeth (1990) *Jacques Lacan: A Feminist Introduction,* London: Routledge.

Gubar, Susan (1987) 'This is my rifle, this is my gun': World War II and the blitz on women', in Margaret Randolph Higonnet, Jane Jenson, Sonya Michel and Margaret Collins Weitz (eds), *Behind the Lines: Gender and the Two World Wars*, New Haven: Yale University Press, 1987.

Hall, Radclyffe (1928) *The Well of Loneliness*, London: Cape.

Hannay, Margaret P. (ed.) (1979a) *As Her Wimsey Took Her*, Kent, Ohio: Kent State University Press.

Hannay, Margaret P. (1979b) 'Harriet's influence on the characterisation of Lord Peter Wimsey', in Margaret P. Hannay (ed.), *As Her Wimsey Took Her*, Kent, Ohio: Kent State University Press, 1979.

Harper, Sue (1982) 'History with frills: "costume" fiction in World War II', *Red Letters*, 14: 14–23.

Harrisson, Tom (1982) 'Films and the home front – the evaluation of their effectiveness by "Mass-Observation"', in Nicholas Pronay and D. W. Spring (eds), *Propaganda, Politics and Film, 1918–45*, London: Macmillan, 1982.

Harrisson, Tom (1976) *Living Through the Blitz*, London: Collins.

Hartley, Jenny (ed.) (1994) *Hearts Undefeated: Women's Writing of the Second World War*, London: Virago.

Haycraft, Howard (ed.) (1961) *The Art of the Mystery Story*, New York: Grosset & Dunlap.

H. D. (1956/1971) *Tribute to Freud*, London: Carcanet.

H. D. (1960/1984) *Bid Me To Live*, London: Virago.

Heath, Stephen (1986) 'Joan Riviere and the masquerade', in Victor Burgin, James Donald and Cora Kaplan (eds), *Formations of Fantasy*, London: Methuen, 1986.

Heilbrun, Carolyn (1989) *Writing a Woman's Life*, London: Women's Press.

Heilbrun, Carolyn (1991) *Hamlet's Mother and Other Women: Feminist Essays on Literature*, London: Women's Press.

Higonnet, Margaret Randolph and Patrice L.-R. Higonnet (1987) 'The double helix', in Margaret Randolph Higonnet, Jane Jenson, Sonya Michel and Margaret Collins Weitz (eds), *Behind the Lines: Gender and the Two World Wars*, New Haven: Yale University Press, 1987.

Higonnet, Margaret Randolph, Jane Jenson, Sonya Michel and Margaret Collins Weitz (eds) (1987) *Behind the Lines: Gender and the Two World Wars*, New Haven: Yale University Press.

Holden, Inez (1941) *Night Shift*, London: John Lane.

Holden, Inez (1943) *It was Different at the Time*, London: John Lane.

Holtby, Winifred (1936) *South Riding*, London: Collins.

Homans, Peter, (1979) *Jung in Context*, Chicago: University of Chicago Press.

Hone, Ralph E. (1979) *Dorothy L. Sayers: A Literary Biography*, Kent, Ohio: Kent State University Press.

Honey, Maureen (1984) *Creating Rosie the Riveter: Class, Gender, and Propaganda during World War II*, Amherst, Mass.: University of Massachusetts Press.

Humm, Maggie (1991) *Border Traffic: Strategies of Contemporary Women Writers*, Manchester: Manchester University Press.

Hunter, Dianne S. (1985) 'Hysteria, psychoanalysis and feminism: the case of Anna O.', in Shirley Nelson Garner, Clare Kahan and Madelon Sprengnether (eds), *The (M)other Tongue: Essays in Feminist Psychoanalytic Interpretation*, Ithaca, NY: Cornell University Press, 1985.

Hussey, Mark (ed.) (1991) *Virginia Woolf and War: Fiction, Reality and Myth*, New York: Syracuse University Press.

Hynes, Samuel (1976) *The Auden Generation: Literature and Politics in England in the 1930s*, London: Faber & Faber.

Irigaray, Luce (1985) *This Sex Which Is Not One*, Ithaca, NY: Cornell University Press.

Irigaray, Luce (1991) 'Women-mothers, the silent substratum of the social order', in Margaret Whitford (ed.), *The Irigaray Reader*, Oxford: Blackwell.

Jacob, Naomi (1941) *Me – In War-Time*, London: Hutchinson & Co.

Jameson, Storm (1934) *Company Parade*, London: Cassell & Co.

Jameson, Storm (1935) *Love in Winter*, London: Cassell & Co.

Jameson, Storm (1936a) *None Turn Back*, London: Cassell & Co.

Jameson, Storm (1936b) *In the Second Year*, London: Cassell & Co.

Jameson, Storm (1939) *Civil Journey*, London: Cassell & Co.

Jameson, Storm (1969/1984) *Journey from the North*, Vol. 1, London: Virago.

Jardine, Alice and Paul Smith (eds) (1987) *Men in Feminism*, London: Methuen.

Johnston, Judith L. (1987) 'The remediable flaw: revisioning cultural history in *Between the Acts*', in Jane Marcus (ed.), *Woolf and Bloomsbury*, Basingstoke: Macmillan, 1987.

Jung, Carl Gustav (1940), *The Integration of the Personality*, trans. Stanley M. Dell, London: Kegan Paul & Co.

Khan, Nosheen (1989) *Women's Poetry of the First World War*, Brighton: Harvester.

Knowles, Sebastian D. G. (1990) *A Purgatorial Flame: Seven British Writers in the Second World War*, Bristol: The Bristol Press.

Kristeva, Julia (1974) 'About Chinese women', in Toril Moi (ed.), *The Kristeva Reader*. Oxford: Blackwell, 1986.

Kristeva, Julia (1979) 'Women's time', in Toril Moi (ed.), *The Kristeva Reader*, Oxford: Blackwell, 1986.

Kristeva, Julia (1982) *Powers of Horror: An Essay on Abjection*, New York: Columbia University Press.

Kristeva, Julia (1987) 'The pain of sorrow in the modern world: the works of Marguerite Duras', *Publications of the Modern Language Association of America*, 102(2): 138–52.

Lassner, Phyllis (1990a) *Elizabeth Bowen*, London: Macmillan.

Lassner, Phyllis (1990b) 'The quiet revolution: World War II and the English domestic novel', *Mosaic*, 23(3), 87–100.

Laurence, Patricia (1991) 'The facts and fugue of war: from *Three Guineas* to *Between the Acts*', in Mark Hussey (ed.), *Virginia Woolf and War: Fiction, Reality and Myth*, New York: Syracuse University Press, 1991.

Lee, Hermione (1981) *Elizabeth Bowen: An Estimation*, London: Vision Press.

Lee, Hermione (1992) 'Introduction' to Virginia Woolf, *The Years* (1937), Oxford: Oxford University Press.

Lehmann, John (1940) *New Writing in Europe*, Harmondsworth: Penguin.

Lehmann, Rosamond (1936) *The Weather in the Streets*, London: Collins.

Leonardi, Susan J. *Dangerous by Degrees: Women at Oxford and the Somerville College Novelists*, New Brunswick: Rutgers University Press.

Liddington, Jill (1989) *The Long Road to Greenham: Feminism and Anti-Militarism in Britain since 1820*, London: Virago.

Light, Alison (1991) *Forever England: Femininity, Literature and Conservatism Between the Wars*, London: Routledge.

Lukács, Georg (1962) *The Historical Novel*, London: Merlin Press.

McCooey, Chris (ed.) (1989) *Dispatches from the Home Front: The War Diaries of Joan Strange 1939–1945*, Eastbourne: Monarch Publications.

McInnes, Helen (1942) *Assignment in Brittany*, London: Harrap & Co.

MacNeice, Louis (1979) *Collected Poems 1925–40*, London: Faber.

Majumdar, Robin and Allen McLaurin (eds) (1975) *Virginia Woolf: The Critical Heritage*, London: Routledge & Kegan Paul.

Marcus, Jane (ed.) (1981) *New Feminist Essays on Virginia Woolf*, Basingstoke: Macmillan.

Marcus, Jane (ed.) (1987) *Woolf and Bloomsbury*, Basingstoke: Macmillan.

Marks, Elise (1990) 'The alienation of "I": Christa Wolf and militarism', *Mosaic*, 23(3): 73–85.

Marks, Elaine and Isabelle de Courtivron (eds) (1980) *New French Feminisms*, Brighton: Harvester.

Marsh, Ngaio (1937) *Vintage Murder*, London: Geoffrey Bles.

Marsh, Ngaio (1938a) *Artists in Crime*, London: Collins.

Marsh, Ngaio (1938b) *Death in a White Tie*, London: Geoffrey Bles.

Miller, Betty (1945) *On the Side of the Angels*, London: Robert Hale.

Miller, Nancy (1988) *Subject to Change: Reading Feminist Writing*, New York: Columbia University Press.

Minow-Pinkney, Makiko (1987) *Virginia Woolf and the Problem of the Subject*, Brighton: Harvester.

Mitford, Nancy (1940/1961) *Pigeon Pie*, Harmondsworth: Penguin.

Moi, Toril (1985) *Sexual/Textual Politics*, London: Methuen.

Moi, Toril (ed.) (1986) *The Kristeva Reader*, Oxford: Blackwell.

Montieth, Moira (ed.) (1986) *Women's Writing: A Challenge to Theory*, Brighton: Harvester.

Moore, Reginald and Woodrow Wyatt (eds) (1945) *Stories of the Forties, Volume I*, London: Nicholson & Watson.

Morgan, David and Mary Evans (1993) *The Battle for Britain: Citizenship and Ideology in the Second World War*, London: Routledge.

Nicholson, Nigel (ed.) (1980) *The Letters of Virginia Woolf*, Vol. VI, London: Hogarth.

Oldfield, Sybil (1989) *Women Against the Iron Fist*, Oxford: Blackwell.

Orwell, George (1936/1989) *Keep the Aspidistra Flying*, Harmondsworth: Penguin.

Orwell, George (1941/1970) 'The lion and the unicorn', in *Collected Letters, Journalism and Letters of George Orwell*, ed. Sonia Orwell and Ian Angus, 4 vols, Harmondsworth: Penguin, vol. 2.

Orwell, George (1945/1970) 'Antisemitism in Britain', in *Collected Letters, Journalism and Letters of George Orwell*, ed. George Orwell and Ian Angus, 4 vols, Harmondsworth: Penguin, vol. 3.

Orwell, George (1970) *Collected Letters, Journalism and Letters of George Orwell*, ed. Sonia Orwell and Ian Angus, 4 vols, Harmondsworth: Penguin.

Panter-Downes, Mollie (1972) *London War Notes 1939–1945*, ed. William Shawn, London: Longman.

Plain, Gill (1995) 'Great expectations: rehabitating the recalcitrant war poets', *Feminist Review*, 51: 41–65.

Pronay, Nicholas and D. W. Spring (eds) (1982) *Propaganda, Politics and Film, 1918–45*, London: Macmillan.

Pumphrey, Martin (1986) 'Play, fantasy and strange laughter: Stevie Smith's uncomfortable poetry', *Critical Quarterly*, 28(3): 85–96.

Radin, Grace (1981) *Virginia Woolf's The Years: The Evolution of a Novel*, Knoxville, Tenn.: University of Tennessee Press.

Reid, Su (1991) 'Discourses of war and madness in Virginia Woolf', paper presented at the conference 'Other as Self: Women's Writing in the Modernist Period', Nene College, Northampton, November 1991.

Reilly, Catherine (1981) *Scars Upon My Heart: Women's Poetry and Verse of the First World War*, London: Virago.

Reilly, Catherine (1984) *Chaos of the Night: Women's Poetry and Verse of the Second World War*, London: Virago.

Reynolds, Barbara (1993) *Dorothy L. Sayers, Her Life and Soul*, London: Hodder & Stoughton.

Richards, Jeffrey (1988) 'National identity in British wartime films', in Philip M. Taylor (ed.), *Britain and Cinema in the Second World War*, Basingstoke: Macmillan, 1988.

Richards, Jeffrey and Dorothy Sheridan (1987) *Mass Observation at the Movies*, London: Routledge & Kegan Paul.

Riviere, Joan (1929) 'Womanliness as masquerade', in Victor Burgin, James Donald and Cora Kaplan (eds), *Formations of Fantasy*, London: Methuen, 1986.

Roe, Sue (ed.) (1987) *Women Reading Women's Writing*, Brighton: Harvester.

Rose, Jacqueline (1993) *Why War?*, Oxford: Blackwell.

Rossen, Janice (1990) 'Oxford *in loco parentis*: the college as mother in Dorothy Sayers's *Gaudy Night*', in David Bevan (ed.), *University Fiction*, Atlanta: Rodopi, 1990.

Ruddick, Sara (1981) 'Private brother, public world', in Jane Marcus (ed.), *New Feminist Essays on Virginia Woolf*, Basingstoke: Macmillan, 1981.

Sassoon, Siegfried (1983) *Siegfried Sassoon Diaries 1915–1918*, ed. Rupert Hart-Davis, London: Faber & Faber.

Schor, Naomi (1987) 'Dreaming dissymmetry: Barthes, Foucault, and sexual difference', in Alice Jardine and Paul Smith (eds), *Men in Feminism*, London: Methuen, 1987.

Schwend, Joachim and Horst W. Drescher (eds) (1990) *Studies in Scottish Fiction: Twentieth Century,* Frankfurt: Peter Lang.

Segal, Naomi (1990) 'Patrilinear and matrilinear', in Helen Wilcox, Keith McWatters, Ann Thompson and Linda R. Williams (eds), *The Body and the Text: Hélène Cixous, Reading and Teaching*, Hemel Hempstead: Harvester, 1990.

Shaw, Marion (1986) 'Feminism and fiction between the wars: Winifred Holtby and *Virginia Woolf*', in Moira Montieth (ed.), *Women's Writing: A Challenge to Theory*, Brighton: Harvester, 1986.

Sheridan, Dorothy (ed.) (1991) *Wartime Women: An Anthology of Women's Wartime Writing For Mass-Observation 1937–45,* London: Mandarin.

Shires, Linda M. (1985) *British Poetry of the Second World War*, London: Macmillan.

Showalter, Elaine (1987a) 'Rivers and Sassoon: the inscription of male gender anxieties', in Margaret Randolph Higonnet, Jane Jenson, Sonya Michel and Margaret Collins Weitz (eds), *Behind the Lines: Gender and the Two World Wars*, New Haven: Yale University Press, 1987.

Showalter, Elaine (1987b) *The Female Malady: Women, Madness and English Culture, 1830–1980*, London: Virago.

Skelton, Robin (1964) *Poetry of the Thirties*, Harmondsworth: Penguin.

Smith, Helen Zenna (1930) *Not So Quiet . . . Stepdaughters of War*, London: A. E. Marriott.

Spalding, Frances (1988) *Stevie Smith: A Critical Biography*, London: Faber & Faber.

Spivak, Gayatri Chakravorty (1981) 'French feminism in an international context', in Mary Eagleton (ed.), *Feminist Literary Criticism*, London: Longman, 1991.

Stacey, Jackie (1994) *Star Gazing: Hollywood Cinema and Female Spectatorship*, London: Routledge.

Stein, Gertrude (1945/1984) *Wars I Have Seen*, London: Brilliance Books.

Stock, R. L. and Barbara Stock (1979) 'The agents of evil and justice in the novels of Dorothy L. Sayers', in Margaret P. Hannay (ed.), *As Her Wimsey Took Her*, Kent, Ohio: Kent State University Press, 1979.

Struther, Jan (1939/1989) *Mrs Miniver*, London: Virago.

Taylor, A. J. P. (1965/1992) *English History 1914–1945*, Oxford: Oxford University Press.

Taylor, Philip M. (ed.) (1988) *Britain and the Cinema in the Second World War*, Basingstoke: Macmillan.

Thorogood, Julia (1991) *Margery Allingham*, London: Heinemann.

Tröger, Annemarie (1987) 'German women's memories of World War II', in Margaret Randolph Higonnet, Jane Jenson, Sonya Michel and Margaret Collins Weitz (eds), *Behind the Lines: Gender and the Two World Wars*, New Haven: Yale University Press, 1987.

Tylee, Claire M. (1990) *The Great War and Women's Consciousness: Images of Militarism and Womanhood in Women's Writings, 1914–64*, Basingstoke: Macmillan.

Waller, Jane and Michael Vaughan-Rees (1987) *Women in Wartime: The Role of Women's Magazines 1939–1945*, London: Macdonald Optima.

West, Rebecca (1918) *The Return of the Soldier*, London: Nisbet.

Whaley, Joachim (ed.) (1981) *Mirrors of Mortality: Studies in the Social History of Death*, London: Europa.

Whitford, Margaret (ed.) (1991) *The Irigaray Reader*, Oxford: Blackwell.

Wilcox, Helen, Keith McWatters, Ann Thompson and Linda R. Williams (eds) (1990) *The Body and the Text: Hélène Cixous, Reading and Teaching*, Hemel Hempstead: Harvester.

Willet, John (ed.) (1964) *Brecht on Theatre*, London: Methuen.

Wright, Elizabeth (1989) *Postmodern Brecht: A Representation*, London: Routledge.

Wyatt, Woodrow (ed.) (1989) *The Way We Lived Then: The English Story in the 1940s*, London: Collins.

Zwerdling, Alex (1986) *Virginia Woolf and the Real World*, Berkeley and Los Angeles: University of California Press.

Index

Note: Comments on specific works of fiction or poetry are indexed under the title of the work with a cross-reference from the author. Major fictional characters and all points from non-fiction works are indexed directly under their authors.